James Agee//Kutlug Atar
Walter Benjamin//Ursula
Broomberg//Judith Butle
Chudakov//Georges Didi- /
Omer Fast//Joan Fontcub /
David Goldblatt//John G
Griffiths//Craigie Horsfield//
Jacir//Emily Jacir//Lisa F. Jackson//An-My Lê//David Levi Strauss//Elizabeth McCausland//Renzo Martens//Boris Mikhailov//Daido Moriyama//Carl Plantinga//Walid Raad//Jacques Rancière//Martha Rosler//Jean-Paul Sartre//Allan Sekula//W. Eugene Smith//Sean Snyder//Susan Sontag//Hito Steyerl//Trinh T. Minh-ha//Marta Zarzycka

Documentary

Whitechapel Gallery
London
The MIT Press
Cambridge, Massachusetts

Edited by Julian Stallabrass

DOC UME NTA RY

Documents of Contemporary Art

Co-published by Whitechapel Gallery
and The MIT Press

First published 2013

Whitechapel Gallery is the imprint of Whitechapel Gallery Ventures Limited

ISBN 978-0-85488-207-6 (Whitechapel Gallery)
ISBN 978-0-262-51829-1 (The MIT Press)

A catalogue record for this book is available from the British Library

Library of Congress Cataloging-in-Publication Data

Documentary / edited by Julian Stallabrass.
p. cm – (Whitechapel: documents of contemporary art)
Includes bibliographical references and index.
ISBN 978-0-262-51829-1 (pbk. : alk. paper)
1. Documentary mass media and the arts. 2. Arts, Modern–20th century. 3. Arts, Modern–21st century. I. Stallabrass, Julian, editor of compilation.
NX180.D63D63 2013
709.05'1–dc23

2012026831

10 9 8 7 6 5 4 3 2 1

Series Editor: Iwona Blazwick
Commissioning Editor: Ian Farr
Project Editor: Sarah Auld
Design by SMITH
Justine Schuster, Maria Juelisch
Printed and bound in China

Cover, The Atlas Group/Walid Raad, *We Decided To Let Them Say 'We Are Convinced' Twice. It Was More Convincing This Way, Beirut '82, Onlookers* (2005). Digital print, framed, 110 x 171 cm; edition of 5. Courtesy of the artist and Sfeir-Semler Gallery, Beirut/Hamburg.

Whitechapel Gallery Ventures Limited
77–82 Whitechapel High Street
London E1 7QX
whitechapelgallery.org
To order (UK and Europe) call +44 (0)207 522 7888
or email MailOrder@whitechapelgallery.org
Distributed to the book trade (UK and Europe only) by Central Books
www.centralbooks.com

The MIT Press
55 Hayward Street
Cambridge, MA 02142
MIT Press books may be purchased at special quantity discounts for business or sales promotional use. For information, please email special_sales@mitpress.mit.edu or write to Special Sales Department, The MIT Press, 55 Hayward Street, Cambridge, MA 02142

Whitechapel Gallery

Documents of Contemporary Art

In recent decades artists have progressively expanded the boundaries of art as they have sought to engage with an increasingly pluralistic environment. Teaching, curating and understanding of art and visual culture are likewise no longer grounded in traditional aesthetics but centred on significant ideas, topics and themes ranging from the everyday to the uncanny, the psychoanalytical to the political.

The Documents of Contemporary Art series emerges from this context. Each volume focuses on a specific subject or body of writing that has been of key influence in contemporary art internationally. Edited and introduced by a scholar, artist, critic or curator, each of these source books provides access to a plurality of voices and perspectives defining a significant theme or tendency.

For over a century the Whitechapel Gallery has offered a public platform for art and ideas. In the same spirit, each guest editor represents a distinct yet diverse approach – rather than one institutional position or school of thought – and has conceived each volume to address not only a professional audience but all interested readers.

The immediate instruments are two:
the motionless camera and the printed word.
The governing instrument – which is also one of the centres of the subject –
is individual, anti-authoritative human consciousness.

James Agee, with Walker Evans, *Let Us Now Praise Famous Men*, 1941

Again and again similar images are repeated, with only the actors and settings changing.

... Grieving mothers,
... charred human remains,
... sunsets,
... women giving birth,
... children playing with toy guns,
... cock fights,
... bull fights,
... Havana street scenes,
... reflections in puddles,
... reflections in windows,
... football posts in unlikely locations,
... swaddled babies,
... portraits taken through mosquito nets,
... needles in junkies' arms,
... derelict toilets,
... Palestinian boys throwing stones,
... contorted Chinese gymnasts,
... Karl Lagerfeld,
... models preparing for fashion shows backstage,
... painted faces,
... bodies covered in mud,
... monks smoking cigarettes,
... pigeons silhouetted against the sky,
... Indian Sardus,
... children leaping into rivers,
... pigs being slaughtered

Adam Broomberg and Oliver Chanarin, 'Unconcerned But Not Indifferent', 2008

Julian Stallabrass
Introduction//Contentious Relations: Art and Documentary

If in the early 1990s you had predicted that documentary work would come to make up a large and influential strand of contemporary art, the idea would have seemed absurd. It would have been said that documentary had surely had its day, perishing with the liberal politics that had nourished it; and along with it, naïve ideas about humanitarian reform and the ability of visual representation to capture reality. Yet in the early twenty-first century the art world is increasingly fractured between a commercial world of investment and spectacular display, catering to the global elite, and the circulation of art on the biennial scene, dominated by documentary work, particularly in photography and video. This work is documentary in form and political in content, though both exhibit a fair bit of variety. There are three linked reasons behind this striking change: economic, technological and political. Economically, the growth of the biennial scene is part of the general globalization of contemporary art. As artists from nations outside of the US and Western Europe came to prominence, they often brought with them distinct political positions and perspectives that were quite alien from those of the old art world centres. They were also often obliged to perform their nationality through reference to politics (so Chinese artists regularly refer to censorship, Indian artists to sectarian violence, and Russian artists to the communist past). Technologically, it has become much easier and cheaper to make high-quality photography and video, and the media landscape has been changed beyond recognition by mass participation through social media. Politically, given the events of 11 September 2001 and the conflicts that followed, politics and its representation were pushed violently to the fore.

From the moment when 'documentary' was formulated as a category in the 1930s, its relations with the art world were troubled and contentious. In film, it was John Grierson who tried systematically to lay out the character of the new mode, claiming that there need be no tension between documentary and art, and that the 'fact of the matter' could be a path to modern beauty. Relations between art and documentary were tied to the latter's role in industry – via photography, in the illustrated magazines, which were immensely powerful and popular from the 1930s through to the 1960s; and film, through reflections on social relations, often state-sponsored, which provided ways of having a nation see and think about itself. As Grierson points out, documentary was also needed by the state as a tool of social knowledge – and, by implication, control. As a servant of commerce and government, documentary was unsurprisingly looked on with scepticism and mistrust by many in the art world.

If the relations between art and documentary have been highly variable since the 1930s, this is because both realms changed hugely, sometimes in response to one another. The expressive mutations of documentary photography made by Diane Arbus, Robert Frank, Lee Friedlander and Garry Winogrand were promoted by the Museum of Modern Art, New York, as an antidote to the humanist photojournalism of *Life* and *Look*.[1] The decline of the illustrated magazines in the face of competition from television brought forth the most systematic art-world critique of their operations – from Martha Rosler and Allan Sekula, among others. There were, of course, artists who continued to engage intelligently with the documentary tradition – one need only think of Gillian Wearing – but they remained a small minority.

The basis of the tension with art came about to the extent that documentary was thought of as transparent reflection of the world, in which subjectivity, creativity and expression were necessarily suppressed. This idea was linked to a general association of documentary with 'lower' classes of producers – with 'primitives', workers, women and socialists. Elizabeth McCausland, who was prominent in the US Photo League, committed to putting documentary to the service of radical politics, makes this explicit: documentary will be made by workers, not artists, and they will not try to prettify life but will present it 'unretouched', arriving at unadorned truth. It was a minority position, and we shall see that many early documentarians made artistic claims for their work. Yet if such a view now seems strange, it was partly because the Photo League was effectively suppressed in the Cold War era by FBI harassment and media blackout, along with an entire leftist culture.[2]

In the late 1920s, Walter Benjamin – a constructor of elaborate collages of textual documents – wrote of the prejudices against the document, picking them out with extreme clarity so as to delineate their absurdity. His list of ideological prejudices has proved remarkably persistent, and is still heard among art world 'snobs' (in his terms) today. In the face of them, and from the beginning, artists' documentary had to elaborate a meta-critique of the category of documentary, which sometimes took on what now seems a remarkably postmodern hue. James Agee, for instance, made a book in collaboration with Walker Evans, *Let Us Now Praise Famous Men*, about the living conditions of tenant farmers in the 1930s. In Agee's long and involuted text for the book, writer and photographer are often highlighted as actors on (as well as mere recorders of) a scene, readers' and viewers' expectations about how tenant farmers should be depicted are held up for examination, and their motives for wanting to be exposed to such a subject are sceptically judged. Evans' photographs were equally self-conscious exemplars of 'documentary style' carried to a formal extreme. Despite the vicissitudes of documentary in the art world, such traits have remained remarkably constant – especially an emphasis on artifice, which appears to owe a lot to Brecht: an education in political ideology through images.

But, in any case, what is documentary? This turns out to be a very difficult question, and its difficulty persists across a number of ways of arriving at an answer. From the tradition of analytical philosophy, Carl Plantinga reviews two models of definition (one based on a relation to a real subject, the other on the maker merely saying that what he or she has made is 'documentary'), and settles on a definition that is close to documentary by fiat: its status is largely asserted by the maker, and the conventions by which documentary asserts its character as documentary are highly variable historically. For the filmmaker Trinh T. Minh-ha, the category is a fiction. For documentary to function traditionally, its conventions have to remain invisible to the viewer, so that they remain in the accepted realm of framing or common sense, letting the subject seem to speak directly to the viewer. By making these conventions visible in her own films, documentary is demolished. Jacques Rancière makes a distinction between 'ostensive', naked images – mere documents – and the 'metaphoric' ones that artists use to destabilize and critique images. The implication of his schema for documentary is that it may dissolve in a wider image culture in which some form of 'document', linked to presence and testimony, is dominant – from artistic engagements with documentary to advertisements and, we may add, reality TV. Rancière draws on Serge Daney's writings about TV, which were influential on the conception of Documenta X, curated by Catherine David in 1997, one of the first prominent reassertions of the documentary tradition in contemporary art.

So, if it is very difficult to come up with satisfactory definitions, viewers fall back on documentary conventions to assure themselves that what they are seeing has a basis in reality and is not complete fiction. Of these, for a long time, one of the most prominent in photography and film was the use of black and white. In photojournalism, it ran into conflict with industry as advertisers and proprietors increasingly wanted colour stories to run in magazines alongside colour adverts. Philip Jones Griffiths worked in Vietnam during the American war, making many images in colour in the hope of selling them to magazines but printing them in black and white when they appeared in his signal photographic analysis of the war, *Vietnam Inc.*[3] Griffiths writes of the 'curse' of colour in its disruption of documentary meaning, and of the particular technical problems posed for a documentary photographer by colour film, recommending the artifice of black and white as an expressive medium. An-My Lê, from the very different perspective of an artist examining the military, and in her return to Vietnam after many years' absence, also reflects on the choice of black and white in going beyond mere documentary fact to suggest broader schema by making large-scale museum photographs that dwell on a landscape formed by war, and a military sublime. David Goldblatt, who first became known for very fine black-and-white work about social issues in apartheid South Africa, argues that monochrome suited that situation; but he has also made accomplished colour work for the gallery, documenting a rapidly changing social and urban landscape in which the colour of things is often important.

So conventions assure the viewer of documentary status, but this opens the question of what exposure to those conventions does to the viewer. Views of this were long dominated by Susan Sontag's rhetorically brilliant writing in *On Photography*: she argued that the photographic industry and its consumers demanded novelty, so that for example even the most accomplished pictures of famine (by Don McCullin) would dull the viewer by repetition, and corrupt the conscience; and further, that documentary photography yields no knowledge, merely sentimental feeling, and that it is part of an image culture that makes of its habitual users 'image junkies'. For decades, Sontag was ritually invoked on such matters as an ineluctable authority. Some of her arguments were reinforced and developed by Martha Rosler in her striking and influential critique of documentary as a creature of liberal politics. It may show poverty and oppression but cannot account for them other than as natural features of the social landscape, to which the only response is charity. Even on occasions when documentary does establish blame (and here Rosler refers to W. Eugene and Aileen Mioko Smith's celebrated work on the Minamata poisoning), its reception in bourgeois society elevates the messenger above the message.[4] In a clear and conscious case of the owl of Minerva flying at dusk, Rosler encapsulates this system at the moment of its eclipse, at the beginning of the neoliberal moment of Reagan, Thatcher and Pinochet, and at the point when Rupert Murdoch was expelling McCullin and serious photojournalism from the *Sunday Times*, demanding that photographs of starving babies be replaced by those of successful businessmen around their weekend barbecues.[5] At the same time, Allan Sekula holds up documentary photography to severe examination, particularly in an analysis of the famous 'Family of Man' exhibition, staged by the Museum of Modern Art in 1955, which he sees as propagandizing for a universal language of sentiment bent to Cold War purposes. Rosler and Sekula may be contrasted with Jean-Paul Sartre's writing about Henri Cartier-Bresson's photographs of China at the moment of the revolution's success: Sartre, writing from war-devastated Europe in which the memory of starvation was still fresh, sketches out the power of humanist photography at the moment at which he hopes that History will end the 'universal' conditions of oppression on which it feeds.

The reawakening of documentary has been a product of the over-reach of neoliberal power, particularly in the revival of imperialism in the long and continuing 'war on terror'. The launching of controversial wars, starkly dividing the globe into allies and enemies, and violating democratic principles, thrust photojournalism and documentary into renewed prominence in the news media and beyond. This produced, of necessity, a substantial wave of theoretical re-evaluation of documentary for its new roles and its new social and political situation – by Ariella Azoulay, Judith Butler, T.J. Demos, Susie Linfield, Jacques Rancière and many others.[6] Azoulay made the most specific frontal assault on Sontag's views. In her analysis of the citizenship of photography, she writes of the willingness of people to become photographs. While (as Rosler notes) Dorothea Lange's *Migrant Mother* wanted direct help for her plight, and Evans' subjects felt shame at the depiction of their poverty, now photography is seen as an instrument of considerable power. Photography may be used by people to claim rights denied by states – to be considered a citizen, in particular. If Azoulay's arguments seem plausible, it is because the media landscape has changed so much. Azoulay's subjects, unlike Evans' or Lange's, know what it is to be photographed and filmed, see the results soon afterwards, and adjust their behaviour accordingly. Artist and theorist Hito Steyerl also engages with this new scene. She begins her account of documentary with a scenario close to that of Sekula: it is an engine for eliciting standard emotions, especially fear, among an artificially united public. Yet she also points to an emergent sphere that breaks with the broadcast model of documentary, as more people have the means to represent themselves and show their work to others. This development has the potential to produce a documentary 'commons' in which the boundary between makers and subjects is eroded.

For Judith Butler, while the state retains much power over the image, and over influencing whose death is thought worth consideration and mourning, photography has a greater independent power, as the effect of the Abu Ghraib images clearly shows. The prison pictures make the act of taking photographs apparent, and in doing so reveal 'the entire social scene' of production and reception. If in Azoulay our shared condition is one of citizenship, for Butler it is the darker sharing of the perpetrator's burden; and if in Rosler sentiment tends to be reduced to useless wallowing in pity, for Butler it may yield legitimate grieving. Butler also says that Sontag's later writing, exposed to the 9/11 wars, granted documentary greater power than previously, and she echoes Sontag's exhortation: 'let the atrocious images haunt us.'[7]

The reassessment of documentary was accompanied by a revival of interest in photojournalism, for long dismissed, at least by many in the art world, as a simplistic, naïve or compromised practice. This shift may allow us to read the older texts of photojournalism in the light of our new present, and to recognize that few of its major practitioners were quite as simple as they had been made out. W. Eugene Smith, one of the most celebrated documentarians of the illustrated magazines, writes against the idea of objective recording, and celebrates a personal, interpretative expression of a subject, in which the stage management of people and scenes is permitted. Similarly, Daido Moriyama writes of a notorious incident in which Horst Faas and Michel Laurent photographed the torture and murder of men thought to have collaborated with the Pakistani Army at the time of the war in which Bangladesh was created: the controversy centred on how much the presence of their cameras had caused the killings. Moriyama, like Smith, thinks that the photographer's role is to interpret, and not merely to lose oneself in subject matter. Smith's views were partly formed by photographing the US war against Japan in terrible and perilous circumstances; Moriyama's by the long effective occupation of his country by the US following the war, and the slow strangling of its ancient culture – hence his ambition to grasp an outline of the totality of social relations, no matter how ugly.

An indication of the controversy that photojournalism still produces in the art world may be seen in the opposing views offered by David Levi Strauss and the photographic artists Adam Broomberg and Oliver Chanarin. In his essay on Sebastião Salgado, Levi Strauss challenges the widespread assumption that beauty and documentary cannot mix, and that beauty cannot be put into the service of social advancement. This is a defence of a singular figure who has evolved his own distinctive and elegiac style, drawing much from W. Eugene Smith in his celebration of workers, peasants and tribal peoples. In judging the World Press Photo awards, Broomberg and Chanarin were exposed to the regular fare of the industry, and they expose its clichés, its hunt for suffering, doubtful ideologies and complicity with the war machine, which takes its creepiest form in nostalgia for the Vietnam War. Alfredo Jaar, much of whose work has reflected critically on the making and circulation of news photographs, is interviewed about his remarkable installation piece on the life and death of Kevin Carter, who made an infamous Pulitzer Prize-winning picture of a starving Sudanese child stalked by a vulture. Jaar admires photojournalists because through his own practice, which includes work about the Rwandan genocide, he recognizes the insurmountable contradictions which torture them as they depict famine, war and other man-made disasters.

One of the most common critiques of visual documentary has been to do with all that it excludes from view. Jaar made a work about this by displaying every *Life* magazine cover that depicted Africa over sixty years (there are not many and they mostly feature animals). There may be many reasons for such exclusions – pragmatic, commercial, political and ideological. In analysing four of the very few pictures to have emerged from inside Holocaust camps, Georges Didi-Huberman takes the most extreme case: in which the forgetting of the extermination – the attempt to destroy all that documented it – is a part of the extermination. Here, as in Rwanda, we may ask whether the poor and scant images made in the face of that repression of imagery betray their subjects or contribute to understanding. Didi-Huberman's work on the subject caused much controversy in France in a debate with those who believe the Holocaust to be unrepresentable. Harun Farocki examines the partial revelation of the same crime through aerial photography, taken for military purposes and much later re-read as documents of the Holocaust; they are inadequate on their own, Farocki argues, but can be put to work in alliance with other documents and witness statements.

Some wars – especially those conducted by the US and its allies – are staged for the media, and are designed to show off the power of the state to its enemies and its home population. More often, where mass slaughter takes place, cameras are forbidden. Lisa Jackson, who made a film about rape as an act of war in the lengthy, little-reported conflict in the Congo, talks of the difficulties in getting such a subject to public attention. She also talks about the problems of engaging in dialogue with the perpetrators as well as the victims. Struggling against corporate secrecy, another major foe of documentary, Ursula Biemann makes notes on the Black Sea oil industry; here, at least, images can be snatched and access occasionally negotiated. Marta Zarzycka, in paying attention to documentary photography's silence and implied sound, which is now sometimes supplied in multi-media work, explores its use in bringing to life violence against women, in looking at a linked war to Jackson's: rape victims in neighbouring Rwanda.

One logical response to the lack of documents is to invent them. This is a regular tactic in the face of dictatorship and censorship: Joan Fontcuberta, the creator of many fictional photographic 'documents', writes that his suspicion of received information was formed in Spain in the Franco years. Similarly, Kutlug Ataman who makes work in a comparatively young state, Turkey, which still faces fundamental challenges to its foundation, finds the lies that people tell his camera more interesting (and socially motivated) than mere truth. Another clear case here is Walid Raad and his work as The Atlas Group, confecting both plausible and surreal 'documents' of the civil war in Lebanon, which comment on the documentary and archival urges, the paucity of actual documents, and the general inadequacies of visual documents.

The making of such documentary fictions has become one of the most common art-world responses to the rise of documentary, and it is also used by Omer Fast, Sean Snyder and many others. When the fiction is manifest to viewers, the conceit may function like Brecht's use of the chorus to break the narrative flow of theatre, and remind the audience where they are and what they are looking at. Fiction has many advantages in art-world settings: there is no suspicion that the artist has engaged in some naïve reflection of social reality; the artist's handiwork is evident, and with it artistic expression; there is also a built-in commentary on the conventions and rhetoric of the documentary tradition. The price may be paid, of course, in political effect: as with Rosler's account of the treatment of W. Eugene Smith, the focus may switch from subject matter to maker, and if doubt is cast upon the veracity of one element, disbelief may extend to all. Subjects become actors, either formally paid to perform a role, or (as with Ataman) displaying the persona that 'real' people adopt.

Commitment to the subject takes many forms, and may lead documentarians and artists into hardship and danger. In these circumstances, the exposure to risk necessarily becomes a part of the work, as the limits of what may be recorded become apparent, as does the vulnerability of the maker. The exposure to risk is performed, and the action of the maker is clearly seen as an intervention in the scene: in this way, and in tension with the opposition between story-telling and political effect touched on before, it is linked to fiction.

Craigie Horsfield, who is best known for his black-and-white portraits and scenes made in Poland in the 1970s, willingly submitted himself to live under actually existing socialism, and writes here of a faithfulness to radical contingency, to the alien character of a world that exceeds human concerns, recorded through an intense engagement with the surface and a rejection of all pre-existing categories. Boris Mikhailov, who was stuck with the same system, writes of how he made work in the teeth of its many restrictions, including the ban on nakedness in photography. The fall of communism led to the evaporation of the community that had resisted and endured it, and in dramatically changed circumstances, Mikhailov made work that demonstrated the new power relations forged by money.

In the extremely dangerous environment of urban Guatemala, Regina José Galindo makes performances that produce documents of neglected issues, especially about the subjection of women to exploitation and violence. She has lived and had herself photographed as a maid, in a uniform that marks out her lowly status, and makes her a subject to abuse. In a resonant condemnation of her nation's amnesia of its atrocious past, she walked from the Constitutional Court to the National Palace of Guatemala, leaving a trail of bloody footsteps. The performance and resulting video was a conductor for discussion about the presidential candidacy of Efraín Ríos Montt, since arrested for genocide and other crimes against humanity.

While Jackson and Jaar made work in central Africa to highlight issues that barely registered in the Western mass media, Renzo Martens went to the Congo to play an eccentric role as a provocateur, encouraging locals to document (and thus profit) from their own poverty, cutting out Western professionals. In a social scene in which charity is part of the problem and political change apparently remote, Martens' film provides a bleak vision of Western exploitation – in which every consumer is complicit – that refuses any comfort to the viewer. There is an alignment with Rosler here, as documentary is forced painfully to perform its own powerlessness.

Under the US National Defense Authorization Act, 'citizens' (following Azoulay, we may use the term with caution) may be seized and held indefinitely without charge or any right to see the evidence held against them. Artist and academic Hasan Elahi, finding himself on the terrorist watch list and subject to secret surveillance, responded by constantly documenting his actions and whereabouts. His work dramatizes the surveillance to which we are all subject by state and commercial agencies, and also bears upon the extent to which many people document themselves, and offer themselves up for surveillance through social networking. In what has become another front in the 'war on terror', the artist Emily Jacir and her sister, the filmmaker Annemarie Jacir, are exposed to extreme danger. Both have made work that documents the plight of Palestinians living under Israeli occupation, and here they pay the commonplace price for their presence there, coming under fire from the Israel Defense Forces.

The book, unlike the database form, imposes a single form of organization on its contents. I have tried to give substantial extracts of longer texts, and the complete texts of some shorter ones, to allow each element to breathe freely within that constraint. Many texts do more than one thing, and could serve in more than one section: Trinh in conventions, for example, or Sekula in spectators, or Jaar and Goldblatt in commitment. Readers can, of course, make their own combinations. Referring to the database is a way to point to the remarkable mutual transformation of documentary and art: documentary film and the documentary photograph or photographic sequence were once more like books and pages: singular items forced to unfurl in a particular and fixed sequence. Now, usually in digital form, laden with metadata, subject to multiple searches and forms of indexing, and copied with abandon, they become part of a remarkable digital environment – and perhaps, at least ideally, a commons – of which art is increasingly a part. This may, as Rancière suggests, mean an end to documentary as a distinct entity and tradition, but it is also an end to its long marginalization and condemnation as a simplistic and lower mode of representation.

1 See, for example, *New Documents* (New York: The Museum of Modern Art, 1967), curated by John Szarkowski.

2 See Anne Tucker, 'The Photo League', in Liz Heron and Val Williams, eds, *Illuminations: Women Writing on Photography from the 1850s to the Present* (Durham, North Carolina: Duke University Press, 1996) 165–9.

3 Philip Jones Griffiths, *Vietnam Inc.* (New York: Collier Books, 1971).

4 W. Eugene Smith and Aileen M. Smith, *Minamata* (Tucson: Center for Creative Photography, 1981).

5 See Don McCullin with Lewis Chester, *Unreasonable Behaviour: An Autobiography* (New York: Alfred A. Knopf, 1992) 269–70.

6 Aside from the texts included in this collection, see Ariella Azoulay, *Death's Showcase – The Power of Image in Contemporary Democracy* (Cambridge, Massachusetts: The MIT Press, 2001); Robert Hariman and John Louis Lucaites, *No Caption Needed: Iconic Photographs, Public Culture and Liberal Democracy* (Chicago: University of Chicago Press, 2007); Susie Linfield, *The Cruel Radiance: Photography and Political Violence* (Chicago: University of Chicago Press, 2010); Jacques Rancière, *The Emancipated Spectator* (2008); trans. Gregory Elliott (London and New York: Verso, 2009).

7 The '9/11 wars' is the useful shorthand coined by Jason Burke: *The 9/11 Wars* (London: Allen Lane, 2011); Susan Sontag, *Regarding the Pain of Others* (New York: Picador/Farrar, Straus & Giroux/London: Hamish Hamilton 2003).

IT IS A BASIC TENET OF DOCUMENTARY THEORY THAT THE PRIMARY SEARCH IS NOT FOR

BEAUTY,

BUT FOR THE FACT OF THE MATTER,

AND THAT IN THE FACT OF THE MATTER IS THE ONLY PATH TO

THAT WILL NOT SOON WEAR DOWN

John Grierson, 'Postwar Patterns', 1946

ORIGINS AND DEFINITIONS

Walter Benjamin
Thirteen Theses Against Snobs//1928

(Snob in the private office of art criticism. On the left, a child's drawing; on the right, a fetish. Snob: 'Picasso might as well pack it in!')

I. The artist makes a work.	The primitive man expresses himself in documents.
II. The artwork is only incidentally a document.	No document is, as such, a work of art.
III. The artwork is a masterpiece.	The document serves to instruct.
IV. With artworks, artists learn their craft.	With documents, a public is educated.
V. Artworks are remote from one another in their perfection.	All documents communicate through their subject matter.
VI. In the artwork, content and form are one: meaning [*Gehalt*].	In documents the subject matter is wholly dominant.
VII. Meaning is the outcome of experience.	Subject matter is the outcome of dreams.
VIII. In the artwork, subject matter is ballast jettisoned by contemplation.	The more one loses oneself in a document, the denser the subject matter grows.
IX. In the artwork, the formal law is central.	Forms are merely dispersed in documents.
X. The artwork is synthetic: an energy-centre.	The fertility of the document demands analysis.
XI. The artwork intensifies itself under the repeated gaze.	A document overpowers only through surprise.

XII. The masculinity of works lies in assault.

The document's innocence gives it cover.

XIII. The artist sets out to conquer meanings.

The primitive man barricades himself behind subject matter.

Walter Benjamin, 'Thirteen Theses Against Snobs' (1928); trans. Edmund Jephcott and Howard Eiland, in *Walter Benjamin: Selected Writings. Volume 1. 1913–1926*, ed. Marcus Bullock and Michael W. Jennings (Cambridge, Massachusetts: The Belknap Press of Harvard University Press, 1996) 459.

Elizabeth McCausland
Documentary Photography//1939

[...] The rise of documentary photography does not spring from fashion. Rather its rapid growth represents strong organic forces at work, strong creative impulses seeking an outlet suitable to the serious and tense spirit of our age. The proof that documentary photography is not a fad or a vogue lies in the history of other movements in photography. Before the documentary, the technical *capricci* of Moholy-Nagy and Man Ray; before the 'photogram' and the 'rayograph', the Photo-Secession; before that, the pictorialists. What came of these? From the abstract and surrealist tendencies, Cecil Beaton. From the Photo-Secession a few fine workers like Paul Strand, Edward Weston and Charles Sheeler, the best of their mature energies being best employed when they turn to newer and more objective purposes. From the pictorial school, the Oval Table [society of photographers].

Against this pattern of sterility, of ideas which could not reproduce themselves, we have the new function (and evolving from it the new aesthetic) of documentary photography, an application of photography that is direct and realistic, dedicated to the profound and sober chronicling of the external world. To Lewis Hine, who thirty-five years ago was making photographs of child labour in sweat shops and textile mills, the vague tenets of pictorialism, or the even less useful purposes of the 'photogram' or 'rayograph', must be incomprehensible. To the hard-working photographers of the Farm Security Administration, the somewhat remote and abstruse manner of the spiritual heirs of the Photo-Secession may seem too refined. To such a photographer as Berenice Abbott, setting down the tangible visage of New York in precise detail and lineament, the sentimental fantasies of a Fassbender[1] must be well nigh incredible.

The above is not intended as an *ad hominem* argument. The instances are noted merely to indicate different directions and purposes in photography. The reason that the difference may so clearly be illustrated is that the difference in ideas of the new photography and all the old styles is like the difference between two continents: it is a 'passage to India' to travel from the old to the new. We have all had a surfeit of 'pretty' pictures, of romantic views of hilltop, seaside, rolling fields, skyscrapers seen askew, picturesque bits of life torn out of their sordid context. It is life that is exciting and important, and life whole and *unretouched*.

By virtue of this new spirit of realism, photography looks now at the external world with new eyes, the eyes of scientific, uncompromising honesty. 'The camera eye cannot lie' is lightly said. On the contrary, the camera eye usually does nothing but lie, rationalizing the wrinkles of an ageing face, obligingly overlooking peeling paint and rotting wood. But the external world is these facts of decay and change, of social retrogression and injustice – as well as the wide miles of America and its vast mountain ranges. The external world, we may add, is the world of human beings; and, whether we see their faces or the works of their hands and the consequences, tragic or otherwise, of their social institutions, we look at the world with a new orientation, more concerned with what is outside than with the inner ebb and flow of consciousness.

For this reason, a Farm Security Administration photograph of an old woman's knotted and gnarled hands is a human and social document of great moment and moving quality. In the erosion of these deformed fingers is to be seen the symbol of social distortion and deformation: waste is to be read here, as it is read in lands washed down to the sea by floods, in dust storms and in drought bowls. The fact is a thousand times more important than the photographer; his personality can be intruded only by the worst taste of exhibitionism; this at last is reality. Yet, also, by the imagination and intelligence he possesses and uses, the photographer controls the new aesthetic, finds the significant truth and gives it significant form.

This is indeed the vanguard of photography today. For the channels of distribution for truth are no more numerous for the photograph than for the printed or spoken word, the theatre, the moving picture, the arts generally. The censorship that in Hollywood has shifted from leg and kiss sequences to social themes operates also with the publications that use photographs – and by their use support the photographer. The opportunities for publishing honest photographs of present-day life in magazines or newspapers are not many; a Hearst [corporation] press is not the only censor of truth.

For this reason, we find the strongest precedent for documentary photography in the work of the Farm Security Administration photographers and in the Federal Art Project *Changing New York* series by Berenice Abbott. As in soil erosion and flood control, highway engineering, agricultural experiment stations and numerous other important technical activities, the best sponsor of knowledge (even if on too limited a scale) has been the government. By nations of circumstances that we shall not call lucky accidents, these pioneer ventures have been gotten underway and have broken ground for younger workers to till. Already the influence of the new spirit may be observed, as a more straightforward quality pervades much of the work published, even in magazines not avowed to the documentary ideal.

What is this ideal, you have a right to ask. A hundred years ago when photography was born, an enthusiast cried, 'From this day painting is dead.' Nevertheless painting has survived till the present. Thus in the course of the past century certain confusions grew up around photography. In the case of David Octavius Hill, there was no question as to why he took portraits; they were notes to be incorporated in a canvas with over two hundred figures. Julia Margaret Cameron was an elderly woman who pursued a hobby, incidentally turning out masterpieces of portraiture. Eugène Atget had no nonsense about him when he made 'documents pour artistes'; and certainly there was no false aestheticism involved when Mathew Brady went to the Civil War.

But at the turn of the century art got mixed with photography. Some inner insecurity of photographers (seduced, perhaps, by commercial appeals and selling talks) led them to precipitate the battle: 'Is photography Art?' Today progressive photographers are not especially interested in the point; it seems an empty issue. There is the whole wide world before the lens, and reality waiting to be set down imperishably.

Without prejudicing the case, we may say at once that photography is not art in the old sense. It is not a romantic, impressionistic medium dependent on subjective factors and ignoring the objective. It is bound to realism in as complex a way as buildings are bound to the earth by the pull of gravitation, unless we build aerial cities, cantilevering or suspending them in mid-air.

But this is certain from history – that forms and values change under the impact of new energies. The arts alter their modes of expression and emphasis on subject matter, their ideology and iconography, as society changes. Today we do not want emotion from art; we want a solid and substantial food on which to bite, something strong and hearty to get our teeth into, sustenance for the arduous struggle that existence is in eras of crisis. We want the truth, not rationalization, not idealizations, not romanticizations. That truth we get from reading a financial page, a foreign cable, an unemployment survey report. That truth we receive, visually, from photographs recording the undeniable facts of life today, old wooden slums canting on their foundations, an isolated farmer's shack, poor cotton fields, dirty city streets, the chronicles written in the faces of men and women and children.

Yet this truth is not an abstract statement, made in a desert with none to hear.

The new spirit in art (if, after all the talk, we agree that photography is an art) represents a drastic reversal position from the attitudes of the twenties. One cannot imagine a Joyce or a Proust producing documentary photographs, if photography were their medium. On the contrary, one can think of a Thomas Mann finding documentary photography much to his liking, congenial as it is to the careful factual implementation of *The Magic Mountain*.

Instead, for prototypes we turn back to the ages of realism, to Balzac, to Fielding, to Dickens, to a painter like Géricault who painted humble scenes of farm life as well as grandiose mythological scenes. A work of art, on this basis, must have meaning, it must have content, it must communicate, it must speak to an audience. The cult of non-intelligibility and non-communication is no longer fashionable; only a fringe of survivors makes a virtue of a phrase which is a dead issue.

For communication, the photograph has qualities equalled by no other pictorial medium. If one wishes to present the interior of a slum dwelling where eight people live in one room, the camera will reveal the riddled floors, the dirty bedding, the dishes stacked unwashed on a table, the thousand and one details that total up to squalour and human degradation. To paint each item completely would take a dozen Hoochs and Chardins many months. Here with the instantaneous blink of the camera eye, we have reality captured, set down for as long as negative and print will endure.

Actually there is no limit to the world of external reality the photographer may record. Every subject is significant, considered in its context and viewed in the light of historical forces. It is the spirit of his approach which determines the value of the photographer's endeavour; that plus his technical ability to say what he wants to say. First of all, there is no room for exhibitionism or opportunism or exploitation in the equipment of the documentary photographer. His purpose must be clear and unified, and his mood simple and modest. Montage of his personality over his subject will only defeat the serious aims of documentary photography. For the greatest objective of such work is to widen the world we live in, to acquaint us with the range and variety of human existence, to inform us (as it were forcibly) of unnecessary social horrors such as war, to make us aware of the civilization in which we live and hope to function as creative workers. This is a useful work, and as such beyond claims of mere personality or clique.

1 [Adolf Fassbender, photographer and teacher (1884–1980), who published his highly aestheticized photogravures in *Pictorial Artistry: The Dramatization of the Beautiful* (1937)]

Elizabeth McCausland, extract from 'Documentary Photography', *Photo Notes* (January 1939); reprinted in Liz Heron and Val Williams, eds, *Illuminations: Women Writing on Photography from the 1850s to the Present* (London: I.B. Tauris, 1996) 170–73.

James Agee, with Walker Evans
Let Us Now Praise Famous Men//1941

[...] The nominal subject is North American cotton tenantry as examined in the daily living of three representative white tenant families.

Actually, the effort is to recognize the stature of a portion of unimagined existence, and to contrive techniques proper to its recording, communication, analysis and defence. More essentially, this is an independent inquiry into certain normal predicaments of human divinity.

The immediate instruments are two: the motionless camera and the printed word. The governing instrument – which is also one of the centres of the subject – is individual, anti-authoritative human consciousness.

Ultimately, it is intended that this record and analysis be exhaustive, with no detail, however trivial it may seem, left untouched, no relevancy avoided, which lies within the power of remembrance to maintain, of the intelligence to perceive, and of the spirit to persist in.

Of this ultimate intention the present volume is merely portent and fragment, experiment, dissonant prologue. Since it is intended, among other things, as a swindle, an insult and a corrective, the reader will be wise to bear the nominal subject, and his expectation of its proper treatment, steadily in mind. For that is the subject with which the authors are dealing throughout. If complications arise, that is because they are trying to deal with it not as journalists, sociologists, politicians, entertainers, humanitarians, priests or artists, but seriously.

The photographs are not illustrative. They, and the text, are co-equal, mutually independent and fully collaborative. By their fewness, and by the impotence of the reader's eye, this will be misunderstood by most of that minority which does not wholly ignore it. In the interests, however, of the history and future of photography, that risk seems irrelevant, and this flat statement necessary.

The text was written with reading aloud in mind. That cannot be recommended; but it is suggested that the reader attend with his ear to what he takes off the page: for variations of tone, pace, shape and dynamics are here particularly unavailable to the eye alone, and with their loss, a good deal of meaning escapes.

It was intended also that the text be read continuously, as music is listened to or a film watched, with brief pauses only where they are self-evident.

Of any attempt on the part of the publishers, or others, to disguise or in any other way to ingratiate this volume, the authors must express their regret, their intense disapproval and, as observers awaiting new contributions to their subject, their complaisance.

This is a *book* only by necessity. More seriously, it is an effort in human actuality, in which the reader is no less centrally involved than the authors and those of whom they tell. Those who wish actively to participate in the subject, in whatever degree of understanding, friendship or hostility, are invited to address the authors in care of the publishers. In material that is used, privately or publicly, names will be withheld on request.

James Agee, with the photographer Walker Evans, extract from *Let Us Now Praise Famous Men* (Boston: Houghton Mifflin, 1941) ; reprinted edition (London: Violette Editions, 2001) 24–6; 27.

John Grierson
Postwar Patterns//1946

[...] The documentary is the branch of film production which goes to the actual, and photographs it and edits it and shapes it. It attempts to give form and pattern to the complex of direct observation. Intimacy with the fact of the matter is therefore the distinguishing mark of the documentary, and it is not greatly important how this is achieved. Although *Grapes of Wrath* was a studio picture, some of us would not object to its being called a documentary picture, because in the re-enactment little of Steinbeck's original and direct observation was lost. The studios did not, as they so often do, erect a barrier between the spectator and the actual. This time, their filter was permissive rather than preventive of reality.

In contrast, one might say that many films shot on location and face to face with the actual are much less documentary in the true sense than *Grapes of Wrath*. For we can come directly at life and miss its significance and its reality by a mile. On a building at the Paris Exposition there was an inscription that said, in effect, 'If you come with empty hands we can give you nothing, but if you come with gifts we will enrich you greatly.' It is like that with documentary films. The presence of the actual does not make a documentary film, because what one does with the actual can be as meretricious and synthetic and phoney as Hollywood at its worst. One has only to bring a silly eye to the actual and pick the wrong things to shoot. One has only to ask the wrong questions to photograph the wrong answers.

'Vision without understanding is empty', said Kant, and understanding without vision is blind. One may well take this as a special guide for one's approach to the documentary film. No branch of art has ever more deliberately tried to combine research with interpretation, or laid so much emphasis on the intellectual background of art. I represent, I suppose, the very strongest view in this regard. Certainly, so far as my own operations are concerned, I am convinced that the surest way to apprenticeship in documentary is a good degree in political science or economics. I have often been taken to task for this. I have been told that artists do not come out of libraries, and that, all too often, academic abilities are analytical, and exclusive of the aesthetic or creative powers. I answer that if you do not know what you are looking for you will not find it. It is true that there is no exercise of the imagination unless there is eagerness of heart, and no art unless there is affection. But I would say that eagerness of heart and warmth of affection will, by themselves, be only the poorest guides to the vast and difficult complex of realities in which we live today; that if they are not supported by understanding, they must inevitably break down in sentimentalism, pessimism, cynicism and at last in nihilism, and that, in fact, we are seeing this self-destruction in every school of art that does not face up to the hard aesthetic law of Plato and later of Bergson: that it is only when the work has been analysed and thought about and greatly laboured over that the flame shoots up and the light kindles.

How warmth and affection and beauty may come to inhabit the edifices of truth, I hope I shall be able to indicate. I shall be content for the moment to assert that it is a basic tenet of documentary theory that the primary search is not for beauty, but for the fact of the matter, and that in the fact of the matter is the only path to beauty that will not soon wear down. I can best illustrate this distinction with all its many consequences in art and education by telling you about Robert Flaherty. The history of the documentary film so far as I personally have been concerned with it has derived in part from my own theoretical deviation from Flaherty; but I ought also to add that we have been the closest of friends for twenty years and that no difference of opinion has affected our complete dependence on each other. In the profoundest kind of way we live and prosper, each of us, by denouncing the other.

Flaherty's approach to documentary in *Nanook* and *Moana* in the early 1920s was a naturalist's approach. He was in revolt against the synthetic dramas of Hollywood. He believed that the film camera was denying its destiny in shutting itself up inside the studios; that its destiny was to get about on the earth, and be the means of opening the end wall of the theatre on the whole wide world. He added that we would find the truest film drama – that is to say, the drama truest to the film medium – not by imposing synthetic stories on fake or even real backgrounds, but by drawing real drama from real backgrounds. Thus his tale of the fight for food among Eskimos, and his tale of the tattoo as a test of manhood in the South Sea Islands. He added that the film was at its best when fronting the phenomena of nature; that there were no movements so fine in front of the camera as the movements and expressions that were spontaneous, or had been formed in affection for a craft, or worn smooth by tradition and ceremony. All this, of course, was very sensible and exercised an enormous influence on those of us who were thinking our way to the film of reality.

The influence of Flaherty's outlook was the greater because of the highly refined personal talent he brought to his observation. No eye was clearer, nor, for that matter, more innocent. He was by nature a poet in the manner of W.H. Davies. He could see things with great simplicity, and everything he touched found added grace at his hands. So far so good. In any estimate, Flaherty has been one of the greatest film teachers of our day, and not one of us but has been enriched by his example – and I shall add, but has been even more greatly enriched by failing to follow it.

I have said that Flaherty was innocent. He was all too innocent. His revolt was not just against the synthetics of Hollywood; there was at the same time a revolt more dangerous: against the very terms of our actual and present civilization. Flaherty's choice of themes was significant. It was primitive man in Labrador or primitive man in Samoa or primitive man in the Aran Islands, or primitive man in industry, or primitive man, in the significant person of romantic youth, taming elephants in India. Flaherty would be shocked all over again to hear me say so, for he would maintain, with his usual great distinction, that the beauties they enact are age-old beauties and therefore classical. I merely make the point that his people and his themes are noticeably distant from those which preoccupy the minds of mankind today, and that if they were not so notably distant Flaherty would make them so.

But there is a problem of the Eskimo that is all too close to our own problems, as our technological civilization marches northward in Asia and America and takes him in. His hunting grounds today are scientifically observed, and his economy is progressively planned. He is subjected to the white man's religion and the white man's justice and the white man's misunderstanding of polygamy. His clothes and his blankets most often come from Manchester, supplied by a department store in Winnipeg, which, incidentally, has the public health of the Eskimo on its conscience. Some hunt by motor boats, and some travel by air. They listen to fur prices over the radio, and are subjected to the fast operations of commercial opportunists flying in from New York. They operate tractors and bulldozers, and increasingly the northern lands, and with them the Eskimos who inhabit them, become part of our global concern.

Our contrary approach to documentary has been so different as to appear sometimes all too practical and all too materialistic and, in the sense of plain sailing, all too plain. We have not denied the fine first principles of Flaherty's, though, but rather have given them a different application. We have struck out, against every temptation, and not without a grim measure of self-discipline, against the attraction of both romance and commerce, to the here and now of our own society. We have sought not the residuum of the ancient beauties, but the beginnings of new ones in the somewhat unlikely milieu of the chaotic present. We have believed with persistence that the first and last place to find the drama of reality is in what men today are doing and thinking and planning and fighting for. We have indeed found our field of observation and the rough patterns of our work in the clash of forces inside our own metropolitan community. [...]

It may be that we exaggerate the political and social duty of documentary observation; we are often accused of doing so. There is certainly nothing in our theory to demand an avoidance of the play of natural phenomena: of day and night, of the seasons of the year, of people in their more personal relationships, of every *damnum fatale* which, like fire, storm and flood, cut across even the best-ordered pattern of social thought. If we avoid them, as we tend to do, it is, I am sure, lest weakness set in, and the social and political duty tend to be forgotten. I, for one, regret sometimes the hard disciplines we have set ourselves. On the other hand, documentary would not have been the great and growing force that it is today if we had not imposed them.

Most of us are working with governments. [...] This is not simply as a result of the war, because, in fact, nearly all documentary production in the past fifteen years has been sponsored either by government or by industries. The excursions into freedom from this relationship have been rare indeed, and the reason is simple. Our theory of approach has, from the first, been related to the needs of governments and peoples. On the one hand, we wanted to find the patterns of the social processes; on the other hand, governments wanted these patterns found and described and illumined and presented. So, too, with the national associations and public utilities. They were interested in showing what they did in the world, interested in the fine complex of their technological or economic or social stewardship. In each was an opportunity for the documentary film to see and sort out one pattern or another in the social whole. Never, perhaps, did an aesthetic urge find so logical or ready a sponsorship.

The line of development of the British documentary school will illustrate this as well as any other. It was initiated and encouraged by a British government which wanted to use the film as a means of communication between different parts of the British Commonwealth. It wanted to describe how the various people lived, what they did, what they produced, and how well they produced it. They were soon interested in men's skills, and interested in men's researches and the results of them. We led them, step by step, deeper and deeper, to the subject matter of public import; to the web of trade relationships, to the pattern of labour and organization in the technological society which they governed. There followed consideration of problems of public health, slum clearance and town planning, of the improvement of educational and nutritional standards, of the development of local governments.

At every stage there were films to make – though this is to put it all too simply. Themes like these are not easy to handle, but mean first an understanding of how things work and who works them. At every turn we were concerned with the brave but difficult discovery of our own time. There is no wonder, therefore, that many of our first efforts with the new materials of observation were halting and confused. The surfaces were often apparently ugly and the system of their relationships difficult to discern. On the other hand, we had the assurance that in the film, with all its powers of juxtaposition, we had in our hands the only aesthetic instrument that could bring into relationship and order the complexes of a cooperative world. It was our promise that however difficult the theme might be, it could, through film, be brought to order and significance and therefore to beauty. It might not be the same kind of beauty as is to be found in lyric and idyll and epic, but perhaps another kind of beauty altogether, as different from the aesthetic patterns of the past as the patterns of Braque from those of Bellini. We took the view that we might be creating a visual order as radically different from the old as the mental order now being created by political and economic events. We felt that we might be reflecting the deep alteration in the categories of thought which a progressively cooperative society was establishing. In any case, we went step by step with the need on the part of governments for an explanation and understanding of what was going on in the world, and we found therein the source of both our economy and our aesthetic. [...]

I mentioned at the beginning that documentary could only be understood in its relation to the materials of reality which it brings into focus. Today the materials for its observation are extended enormously and in direct proportion to the increase in man's will to bring society to a state of order. We are facing a period of great changes in society, and a first prerequisite of these changes must be a deeper study of society's nature and society's problems, and a closer relationship and understanding between governments and peoples, peoples and governments. In both these developments the documentary film has the power to play an enormous part.

I hardly think you need worry too much about how the artist will come out in the process. I am constantly being told by sentimentalists and romanticists that art in the public service must inevitably lose its freedom. I have been told this for sixteen years, and can only register the fact that I have now been concerned with many hundreds of films and have never made them in any other way than the way I wanted them made. I am told that I have built up a cooperative approach to art which denies personal expression and therefore art itself, and I am told that where so much expert knowledge is involved there must inevitably be experts and that the artist's soul must stifle in contact with the academician and the bureaucrat. I can only say that no man, the artist least of all, can be free from the reality in which he lives, or avoid the duty of bringing it to such order as is within his power and his talents. Only at his peril will he try to escape from it, for he cannot easily take creative root elsewhere, in the isolation of the distant, or the isolation of the East, or the isolation of his own fancy. [...]

By the very conditions of that reality, we are concerned not with a personal work, but with a public work. We are not concerned with personal expression in the old, private sense: we are concerned, each man, with whatever contribution can be made to a difficult and complex work for which many varieties of talent are needed. It is, of very necessity, cooperative, and no one, technician or creative worker so-called, is more important than his neighbour. I believe that the individual is not less rich in his life and his expression for entering such a cooperative, but vastly richer. [...] They [documentary films] have together and cumulatively set their mark on education; they have inspired the public service and the service of the public; they have put an instrument of progressive understanding and progressive citizenship into the hands of labour and management alike. Few of the films have been great, perhaps, and not all have been notable, but, again, by some inner law of documentary itself, they have almost always been authentic and honest. It would be a wonder if, in the presence of the living forces of our time, and the drama of man's needs, sacrifices, efforts and achievements, they had not sometimes found the materials of beauty. I am sure they have.

John Grierson, extracts from 'Postwar Patterns', *Hollywood Quarterly*, vol. 1, no. 2 (January 1946) 159–65.

Let's assume that all the cassettes of monochrome film Cartier-Bresson ever exposed had somehow been surreptitiously loaded with colour film. I'd venture to say that about two thirds of his pictures would be ruined and the remainder unaffected, neither spoiled nor improved. And perhaps one in a thousand enhanced

CONVENTIONS

Philip Jones Griffiths
The Curse of Colour//2000

I arrived at the refugee camp before dawn. The sounds of hunger came from the makeshift huts, the moaning, the coughing and the cries of starving babies. My cameras were loaded with colour film dictated by the editor of the magazine who'd assigned me. Perhaps this time the soft dawn light would bathe the victims in the monochrome brown of dusty Africa, so that the emotions of suffering, helplessness and the humanity and the grace of an anguished people could be captured on colour film.

Alas, as dawn broke, I was confronted with a kaleidoscope of bright happy colours. Not only were the thorn-bush walls covered with glistening blue plastic sheeting but the ground was littered with gaudy feeding bowls of many colours, all primary.

A few frames to record the traditional Western arrogance that assumes that starving people are somehow cheered up by bright colours might be in order, but the significant reality of the situation was impossible to capture.

I believe that photography owes its status to achieving what no other medium can, capturing the reality of the defining moments of human existence as decisively as possible. It's not easy, for the perceptive eye has to make split-second decisions about what to record and, naturally, compose everything within a geometric whole that adds to the comprehension of the intention. It's difficult but not impossible to achieve this visual orgasm – that confirmation from some inscrutable part of the brain that verifies success. Possible in black and white, rarely achievable in colour.

The evidence shows that, working in those media where control can be exercised, colour can be a vital tool in the repertoire of visual devices. But control is antithetical to real photography – we are there with our cameras to record reality. Once we start modifying that which exists, we are robbing photography of its most valuable attribute. We would be enervating the very core of our medium. For us, colour is the ultimate distraction.

Why colour anyway? In the example of the refugee camp the answer is a trite one: the magazine's advertisements are in colour, therefore it's considered prudent for the editorial content to follow suit. Yet no one can deny the ability of colour to produce a psychological effect on the viewer. Those reproducing reality, rather than capturing it, have a free hand. Peckinpah's film *Pat Garrett and Billy the Kid* took place in a Wild West turned into a blistering hell by the use of a red-enhancing Didymium filter. In 1966 Antonioni took to painting the very streets of London a different colour to convey the sensation he was after in his film *Blow-up*. And painters, unhindered by the strictures of reality, have used colour in a most meaningful way, skewing the palette to enchant us, although not always with profound understanding, as Picasso once revealed: 'Why do two colours, put one next to the other, sing? Can one really explain this? No!'

Obviously, logically, within the visual arts it cannot be denied that colour is an important element that can effectively be used to convey or illustrate passions and feelings. But let's assume that the Polaroid Corporation invented tomorrow a camera that somehow captured smell (and no one could doubt that smell is a perfectly valid and useful addition to the many means of communication) so that by looking closely at the print the viewer could inhale the aroma of the subject photographed. Here would be an exciting new dimension to our medium. However, if the only smell that came from the print was the body odour of the photographer, I'd venture to say the exciting new medium would soon be dropped.

Once the camera is loaded with colour film, the problems begin. A significant moment between two people is ruined because one overpowers the other by wearing a crimson shirt. A voluptuous scene of a breast-feeding mother and baby is rendered a dirty green by fluorescent light. In 'mixed lighting' situations people's faces are either burning red or glacial blue. All these deficiencies can be overcome to some extent. But at a cost that involves the minimizing of that which gives photography its standing as the greatest visual medium the world has ever known.

Colour as an obstacle to great photography can be illustrated as follows: Let's assume that all the cassettes of monochrome film Cartier-Bresson ever exposed had somehow been surreptitiously loaded with colour film. I'd venture to say that about two thirds of his pictures would be ruined and the remainder unaffected, neither spoiled nor improved. And perhaps one in a thousand enhanced. Low odds, indeed.

Obviously most of us know when our cameras are loaded with colour film, and, if intelligent and not suffering from colour blindness, we will recognize the challenge and attempt to rise to it. Wide-angle lenses are used to minimize the size of, and telephoto ones to avoid, unwanted colourful objects within the frame. Coloured flash (an anathema to reality) is used to correct unwanted colour. But beyond these attempts a more subtle shift takes place – we become consumed with colour composition and neglect the message. For it's hard to concentrate on capturing an exquisite moment of tenderness between lovers in a café whilst trying to minimize distracting bottles of ketchup!

When colour photography became popular with the invention of the four-colour printing process that allowed magazines like *National Geographic* to print 'naturalistic' ethnographic scenes of the world, advertisers were the first to take advantage. Colour was promoted with unquestioning gusto, with scant thought being given to its psychological effectiveness. The editorial content followed suit.

This led to various peculiarities: in America new motor car models were photographed in black and white and, using a Kodak process known as Flexichrome, the prints were coloured by hand – red cars for the East coast and blue ones for California. (Market research had shown people's favourite colours were not the same.) Not to be outdone, the French weekly *Paris Match* became addicted to Flexichrome. (Flexichrome was still sold in France long after it was discontinued elsewhere.) Monochrome pictures were regularly colourized and, as if to prove their sense of fairness, colour pictures were just as likely to appear converted into black and white. This questionable practice led to a better-looking magazine by 'taming' the disharmony of colourful reality.

Using colour, we find ourselves looking for hyper-reality. Not in its crudest form, as practised by countless *National Geographic* photographers who carried red sweaters to adorn subjects in scenic views as a way to add depth to a landscape, but those hours spent waiting for that celestial splash of light on an otherwise boring scene. The preoccupation with colour tends to minimize concerns about content – it is the light-show that reigns supreme.

The problems of colour go further: there are technical limitations that stifle its use. It cannot handle contrast, with the result that people are often reduced to silhouettes in the noon-day sun, set against Rothko-like backgrounds of intense brilliance. Or the photographer simply gives up and waits for cloudy weather. One five-month assignment on a drought in the Sahara showed virtually no pictures when the sun was shining – a remarkable achievement! (And a costly one; the photographer spent days in his tent waiting for clouds.)

Then there is the nagging problem of the colour balance of the emulsion. Colour film is like an apple: green when young and red when mature. Because Kodachrome has dyes with a spectral response that tends to exaggerate reds, in the early days irate users would write to the company to complain that their wives looked like Red Indians. So the film was released with a green balance to minimize this effect. (It was this that helped Fuji make inroads into the American market by selling film with a warmer, more natural colour balance.) Green film also has a longer shelf-life that proved useful in the hotter Southern States. So for years it was necessary to test each batch of film to find a neutral emulsion. In Vietnam during the war, all the film on sale was very green, so I built a small oven on the roof of my hotel where I would incubate the film until the green was gone.

Furthermore, the piece of colour film that is in the camera when the shutter is pressed ends up on the editor's desk, and sometimes miraculously survives the printing process. Making a duplicate of the original (and nowadays digital scans) is only partly successful – caring editors still want the original. Certainly photographic agencies such as Magnum would not exist if fifty years ago printers demanded the original black and white negatives to reproduce from. After a few trips to the printer they would be scratched and ink-splattered to oblivion.

Using colour negative film is an option, but the processed film has a limited life (especially when processed in one-hour photo booths). In twenty years there will be no record of the Gulf War as the negatives will have faded away. The conflict was exclusively photographed on negative film because it could be processed locally for censorship by the military. It is to be hoped that someone will have made digital files for posterity. And as for prints made from colour negatives, they are even less permanent. The joke was that Kodak designed their prints to last as long as the average American marriage, 7.2 years! When your mate's face in the wedding photo on the mantelpiece started to turn green, it was time to find a new one.

As I sit writing this in my hotel room in Phnom Penh, the vagaries of the Cambodian electrical system cause the TV to keep jumping between colour and black and white every few minutes. I recall an old observation – the same scene, glitzy in colour, attains a profundity when the set switches to black and white. A resonance occurs that triggers a strange emotional identification within the labyrinths of the mind. An empathy that has its roots deep in the brain's visual cortex – a mechanism that awards an importance to memory in monochrome. The same mechanism, I believe, that causes us to dream in black and white.

Philip Jones Griffiths, 'The Curse of Colour', first published as 'Der Fluch der Farbe', *Du* magazine (July 2000).

An-My Lê
Interview with *Art21*//2007

Art21 Do people often misinterpret your work as documentary photography?

An-My Lê When you photograph the real world, you cannot escape the reality of it. But I think the magic of photography happens when you can escape the facts – the factual aspect of what's being represented. One is always striving to suggest something beyond what is described. It's something I'm very aware of. Someone who doesn't know straight photography would have issues with this, and maybe would see my work as plain documentary. It does describe certain facts. But I think the strength of it comes from what I can suggest that was not in the photograph at first – what was not in what I saw, and not in the situation itself.

Art21 Have you always approached photography in this way?

An-My Lê I feel so much more confident about the kind of photography I do now. It has answered a lot of the questions and the anxiety I had as a graduate student – feeling that I wasn't doing enough as an artist. All I did was push the button and set my frame. I really wanted to have a hand at transforming things and making things. It was very frustrating. So I started making this stylized work where I sampled, lit and rephotographed things that were very contrived and arty. But I think it was necessary for me to do that and then go back to making 'straight' pictures and to realize how powerful they could be. [...]

Art21 Part of your childhood was spent in Vietnam during the war.

An-My Lê We lived in Vietnam through many of the offensives and coups. In 1968 after the Tet offensive the Viet Cong took over part of the city for a while. My mother was distraught, and she thought she should try to get us out and live somewhere a bit more peaceful. She received a fellowship to go to France. She took us – the three children – to Paris, and our father stayed in Vietnam as a guarantor. We came back after the Paris Agreement in 1973 and stayed in Vietnam for another year and a half before the war ended. War was part of life for us. People ask, 'Wasn't it frightening?' We were really too young to know it the way an adult would. As a child, it's just part of your life and you deal with it when it happens.

Art21 How has your background influenced your world view?

An-My Lê I think we're all dealt a card in life, and I used to think that I was dealt a very difficult one. Then I came to realize that it has made my life richer and that it has been a great foil for my work. Without really being conscious of it when doing my work, I've always tried to understand the meaning of war, how it has affected my life, and what it means to live through times of turbulence like that. A lot of those questions fuel my work. You approach different issues at different times of your life. When I first made the pictures in Vietnam, I was not ready to deal with the war. Being able to go back to Vietnam was a way to reconnect with a homeland, or with the idea of what a homeland is and with the idea of going home. As soon as I got to Vietnam, I realized that I was not so interested in the specific psychology of each person. I was much more interested in their activities, and how those activities splayed onto the landscape. It seemed to me that this suggested a lot more about the culture and history of the country. And this was more fitting for me in terms of the way I worked and what I was interested in. There are some people (like Judith Ross) who can photograph one person and somehow suggest a collective history, a collective memory. But it seems that I try to do that with landscape. When you live in exile, things like smells and memories and stories from childhood all take on such importance. So this was an opportunity to reconnect with the real thing, and to be confronted with contemporary Vietnam. It's not the way it was twenty years ago, or the way it's described in folktales my grandmother and mother used to tell me, or even in stories from my mother's own childhood in the North. So I really looked for things that suggested a certain way of life – agrarian life – things that connect you to the land. Unfortunately, pictures don't smell, but if I could do that they would be about smells as well.

Art21 Do you see your work as part of any particular photographic tradition?

An-My Lê I love nineteenth-century landscape photography. O'Sullivan, Fenton, Le Gray, they're all my heroes. I love the Civil War photographers. And more recently, Eugène Atget and Robert Adams. I love looking at their work and seeing the suggestion of history. For example, Atget photographed Paris at a time when it was changing considerably and somehow he managed to capture that. I really respond to that. I think the work is extremely poetic and lyrical all at the same time, being so tied to the moment. Those are qualities I really admire [...]

Art21 Scale seems to play an important role in your photographs.

An-My Lê Scale is important to me because it shows how insignificant we are. Especially with the military, no matter how advanced we are, how hard we work, it's still about transporting all of these tanks across vast landscapes. It's all about strategy. Suddenly a hill is much more than a hill, it's something that you have to surmount. I'm interested in the effort that you have to invest in the landscape to actually get to somewhere.

Art21 How did you first decide upon the Vietnam War as a subject matter for your work (*Viêt Nam*, 1994–98, and *Small Wars*, 1999–2002)?

An-My Lê When I became a photographer one of the first things I learned from speaking to other artists who had more experience was that unless you're a conceptual artist it's best to draw from what you know the most. And what did I know the most? It was how much of a mess my life was, and trying to make sense of it and the questions of war and destruction – how things are still unresolved with the Vietnam War in America. That's something I wanted to touch, as well as the representation of war in movies and, now, the war in Iraq. I was distraught when the war started in March 2003, and I felt my heart going out to the soldiers being sent to Iraq. I wanted to explore that (in *29 Palms*, 2003–4) and to know more about how we were preparing for the war.

Art21 There must be a fine line between making a representation of war and aestheticizing it.

An-My Lê The kind of work that I make is not the standard political work. It's not agitprop. You would think, because I've seen so much devastation and lived through a war, that I should make something that's outwardly anti-war. But I am not categorically against war. I was more interested in drawing people into my work to think about the issues that envelop war – representations of war, landscape and terrain in war. When I'm working with the military, I still think of myself as a landscape photographer. My main goal is to try to photograph landscape in such a way that it suggests a universal history, a personal history, a history of culture. But I also wanted to address issues of preparation (moral and military). It drew me in, but at the same time it was repellent. I'm fascinated by the military structure, by strategy, the idea of a battle, the gear. But at the same time, how do you resolve the impact of it? What it is meant to do is just horrible. But war can be beautiful. I think it's the idea of the sublime – moments that are horrific but at the same time beautiful – moments of communion with the landscape and nature. And it's that beauty that I wanted to embrace in my work. I think that's why the work seems ambiguous. And it's meant to be. War is an inextricable part of the history of high civilization; I think it's here to stay. But I also think we need to try to avoid it as much as possible. I was not so interested in making work that you see on the news page, which has the effect of wanting you to condemn war immediately. I wanted to approach the idea in a more complicated and challenging way.

Art21 But the work is also a kind of protest.

An-My Lê It is somewhat a condemnation of war. I think it was an awful mistake. And I think some of these marines and soldiers feel that it was a mistake. That's something that I've learned about people who join the military, that it is a profession. Some of them have a natural inkling for it and want to join combat services, but for some it's just a profession. Once they sign up, it is a job and they want to do it well. So no matter what happens they give up their own decision-making and follow whatever the government decides. And they are just trying to finish that job. I think many of the marines and soldiers feel that we shouldn't be there. Or maybe that what we were trying to do has not really panned out.

Art21 There's a quiet subtlety to your photographs of the Vietnam War re-enactors in *Small Wars* (1999–2000). Why is that?

An-My Lê The pictures of the re-enactors shy away from some of the more subversive scenes that they performed – whether taking prisoners or their rough handling of the other camp. I didn't find it fruitful to dwell on that or try to replicate some of the horrific moments that happened during the war. I stayed away from that, and obviously that comes from my personal background. But with the help of the re-enactors, this was a way to direct my own movie without having the means and potential to be my own director. I don't have such a great imagination, so seeing certain things that they did inspired me. I was able to make a Vietnam War that was ultimately safe, a game. In that way, I was able to bring in my own experience.

Art21 Why have you chosen black and white versus colour photography for certain projects?

An-My Lê Black and white was always my choice because of my interest in drawings. A black and white photograph is just more pronounced because it's all about lines and the changes are tonal, from greys to darker greys to blacks and to whites. So drawing is conserved in the black and white palette. What's interesting to me is that the fact that colour is removed somehow makes certain things more obvious. One is not distracted by the fact that it's connected to real lives – or perhaps I should say that black and white is a little bit more removed from real life than colour photography is. It is removed from reality – it's its own thing.

People talk about black and white and how it's associated with memory, but that doesn't really work for me. They also talk about it being old-fashioned or obsolete, but I think it is very contemporary. It's so unlike anything else and so removed from reality that if you use the right subject matter it can be very powerful. I thought of using colour for the project on the military and the sea mostly because I was drawn to the way colour would describe a grey on the hull of a ship versus a grey that's more organic – the grey of the ocean at certain times of the day or the grey of the sky on an overcast day. I don't think black and white could distinguish between a cold or metallic grey and something that may have a bit more warmth and that's more organic. That's my only reason for switching to colour, and that's a good instinct. I tend not to like garish things, so I have probably developed my own palette – which is black and white, and colour – perhaps. I'm learning, and over time I think I'll develop my own colour palette.

Art21 What is the impact upon the work of using a large format camera?

An-My Lê It's the same camera I've been using since 1991, and it's a very cumbersome camera. Because it's so cumbersome, it makes me make a particular type of picture. It forces me to resolve certain questions. If you want to photograph something and the camera is not suitable for it, how do you figure it out? How do you solve the problem? These questions came up photographing military exercises. Of course Timothy O'Sullivan did it in the nineteenth century during the Civil War and other photographers like Roger Fenton did it, but it just seems unsuitable. So how do you resolve those issues? I'm interested in what I have to go through to make it work. It forces me to make a particular type of picture and I like what it makes me do. Working against the grain forces me to come up with new ways of resolving something [...] It just forces you to work in a different way.

Art21 Do you think there's a built-in relationship between photography and the sublime?

An-My Lê I think there's always an element of something not quite understood in the sublime, something otherworldly, conflicting – something beautiful that's not always beautiful, and something that's not quite controllable and not within our reach. I don't think that photography is made to capture and describe magic, but there are great magical moments in still photographs. [...]

An-My Lê, extracts from interview with *Art21* online magazine (April 2007); a longer, re-edited version was reprinted in *Art21: Art in the Twenty-First Century*, vol. 4, ed. Marybeth Sollins (New York: Harry N. Abrams, 2007). Interviews by Susan Sollins.

David Goldblatt
Interview with Mark Haworth-Booth//2005

Mark Haworth-Booth You were the first photographer who shocked me by saying – in the early 1990s, I think – that you had used a computer to manipulate a photograph. As I recall, you were photographing a building on assignment and found that a car was parked inconveniently in front of it. Your new colour pictures seem intrinsically connected with digital technology. What is the story of your involvement with digital photography?

David Goldblatt I distinguish sharply between professional and personal work. While in the former I try, strange as it may seem, to respect the integrity of what I photograph. I will, if I have to, manipulate the reality with which I am confronted, or, if that is not possible, the photograph of it that I take. At the end of the day I am responsible for delivering what the client needs. If what he needs is something that I find morally or politically reprehensible then I will not accept the assignment. But if it passes that first critical test then I will do whatever seems appropriate to fulfil the brief. In the case of the offending VW Beetle I would have physically moved the car if it had been possible. But it wasn't. Nor was it feasible for me to return to the scene. So I took the photograph knowing that it would have to be manipulated.

In my personal work that choice would not have arisen. I take as given. Its existence, the given-ness of it, is precisely why I am stirred to photograph it. However I think a lot of humbug surrounds this notion of a reality unsullied by photographic intervention. The fact is that I, together with my cumbersome camera on its tripod, are part of reality, and I can't pretend that quite often my presence does not in some way alter or influence the outcome and that I don't take this as a 'pure' print. Every single choice made by the photographer influences the manner in which the abstraction from reality, which is the final product, will be rendered. Very little of the above has to do with digital technology. In pre-Photoshop days, if the budget had permitted it, I could have had that Beetle removed by an expert colour retoucher. It was always possible for Joseph Stalin to remove Trotsky from a group photograph. Digital technology made it simpler, easier, faster (to quote the advertising punch line of one of our banks).

My involvement with digital technology arose from quite different considerations. While I had used colour photography extensively in professional work for some forty years I had very rarely used it for personal work. There were two principal reasons:

1. During those years colour seemed too sweet a medium to express the anger, disgust and fear that apartheid inspired.

2. Colour photography was quite limited in its possibilities. Colour transparency material had very little latitude. Colour negative materials had more latitude but frequently had a tendency toward colour casts. I did not make my own colour prints and I found it extremely difficult to get satisfying prints from laboratories. I disliked the plastic paper on which colour prints were made. The dye-transfer process offered beautiful prints but they were extremely expensive and virtually unobtainable in South Africa.

During the 1980s and 1990s I had been heavily involved in the production of magazines and, although I never acquired the skills for doing it myself, I became familiar with the potential and methods of applying digital technology to the editing and reproduction of photography. In the late 1990s I began to use a new generation of colour negative emulsions that had considerable latitude and a very even-handed palette. When I felt the sweet breath of the end of apartheid and the wish to become somewhat more expansive in my photography, it was natural to put the two together: the new colour emulsions and photographic printing through digital technology on non-plastic papers that I like.

After the negative has been scanned I sit with a man of remarkable skill and sensitivity, Tony Meintjes, at his computer and we work on the screened image in much the same way as one would in the darkroom – darkening the image here, holding it back there, increasing/decreasing contrast and adjusting colour and its saturation. Yes, the whole armoury of manipulative possibilities is there. We could radically alter the content and effect of a photograph. But we don't. For the same reasons that I never have done: that would defeat the object of taking the picture in the first place. [...]

Aside from the photographer Sam Haskins, who was extremely generous in showing me how photographs can be made to work with each other on the page, and whose strongly graphic sensibility influenced me for a time, my principal South African influences have been literary rather than photographic. The early stories of Nadine Gordimer made vivid for me what I knew of the smell and taste and touch, and the social weight of things here, but which I had never seen or heard expressed. They led me to want to put these understandings into photographs. The succinct, earthy, penetrating yet compassionate irony of Herman Charles Bosman's stories of Afrikaner life helped shape my photography. Bosman's pupil and editor, the writer Lionel Abrahams, gave me much encouragement and the benefit of his wit and profound wisdom. I was excited by correlations between the substance of Athol Fugard's early plays and my photography. And the writer and theatrical director Barney Simon provoked me into developing a photographic 'independence' by his critical appreciation of my work. An extraordinary if eccentric influence was that of the poet Charles Eglington, then editor of the Anglo American Corporation's house magazine, *Optima*. We had an arrangement under which I undertook to provide photographic essays which were to be my 'personal work' rather than designed for magazine consumption. If he liked them he was free to publish; if he didn't he would pay me anyway. Under this benign rule he published my work on Soweto, Transkei and shaftsinking. After his death a new editor disliked my essay on the white community of Boksburg, but honoured the arrangement. [...]

Haworth-Booth Can I press you on the idea of the photographer as a witness? Isn't this fundamental to your work?

Goldblatt In an obvious sense, photographers, by virtue of being there and 'recording' the scene, are witnesses and their work becomes evidence in an almost forensic sense. But if I had to report on my activities to a heavenly labour ministry, I would, under the heading of job description, say that I am a self-appointed observer and critic of the society into which I was born, with a tendency to doing honour or giving recognition to what is often overlooked or unseen.

Haworth-Booth Is there a sense in which the colour materials you have used in this body of work have allowed you to gather different kinds of evidence and represent other forms of the generally overlooked or unseen?

Goldblatt Much of the subject matter of the recent – i.e. the colour – work, is the kind that would engage me whatever the medium in which I was photographing. Obviously colour photography makes it possible to encompass some subjects that I would not otherwise be able satisfactorily to render – e.g. blue asbestos or a pot of brightly painted plastic flowers. But in general I don't think there has been a fundamental shift in my interests. However, in becoming aware of the colour of things as a quality to be explored, I have had to take colour into account in a way that I didn't before and I have become intrigued by trying to bring the rendition of colour in the print into congruence with my sense of colour or the lack of it in 'reality'. This has much to do with the material and the process I am using. They seem peculiarly suited to what I want to do. They enable me to tackle subjects and to render them in ways that would previously have been well nigh impossible in colour.

David Goldblatt and Mark Haworth-Booth, extracts from interview, *South African Intersections* (Munich: Prestel, 2005) 94–8.

THERE IS NO SUCH THING AS DOCUMENTARY –

WHETHER THE TERM DESIGNATES A CATEGORY OF MATERIAL, A GENRE, AN APPROACH OR A SET OF TECHNIQUES. THIS ASSERTION – AS OLD AND AS FUNDAMENTAL AS THE ANTAGONISM BETWEEN NAMES AND REALITY – NEEDS INCESSANTLY TO BE RESTATED,

DESPITE THE VERY VISIBLE EXISTENCE OF A DOCUMENTARY TRADITION

Trinh T. Minh-ha, 'Documentary Is/Not a Name', 1990

DOES DOCUMENTARY EXIST?

Carl Plantinga
What a Documentary Is, After All//2005

The question of how best to define the documentary film and video and to distinguish it from the fiction film continues to fascinate and baffle philosophers and film theorists. It is clear that the special nature of the film medium – and in particular its use of photographic images and sound recordings – has proven particularly difficult to conceptualize in relation to the fiction/non-fiction film distinction. Here I offer a characterization of the documentary that can account for the visual and aural nature of the medium and that furthers our understanding of what we mean when we use the word 'documentary'. I call my theory a characterization rather than a definition, because rather than posit necessary and sufficient conditions, I will be content to identify and describe the central tendencies of the typical, or usual, documentary film.

Terminological confusion often results from various uses of the word 'documentary' and the phrase 'non-fiction film'. In its most expansive sense, a non-fiction film is any film not fictional, for example, instructional films, advertisements, corporate films, or historical or biographical documentaries. The Scottish filmmaker and theorist John Grierson called the documentary the 'creative treatment of actuality', a characterization that simultaneously distinguishes the documentary from the fiction film (not thought to be primarily a treatment of actuality) and the non-fiction film (not thought to be creative or dramatic).[1] Although the distinction between non-fiction film and documentary cannot bear much theoretical weight, it might be useful to think of the documentary as a subset of non-fiction films, characterized by more aesthetic, social, rhetorical and/or political ambition than, say, a corporate or instructional film. [...]

It would be useful to begin by identifying and briefly examining the two best candidates for traditional definitions of the documentary. These are what I call the Documentary as Indexical Record (DIR) and the Documentary as Assertion (DA) accounts. In the next two sections of this essay I give descriptions of the basic claims of these accounts, noting internal problems and proposing a plausible statement of each. In the third section, I show how both accounts fail as traditional definitions of the documentary. In Sections IV and V, I develop an alternative account, in which I argue that the typical or usual documentary is what I call an 'asserted veridical representation'.

I. Documentary as Indexical Record

Documentary as Indexical Record (DIR) accounts, in their most plausible form, characterize documentaries as films comprised predominantly of moving photographic images that are indexical records or traces of the pro-filmic scene(s). Charles Sanders Peirce defines an indexical sign as one that bears a relationship of *causality* or *proximity* to that which it represents. He distinguishes the index from the icon, which *resembles* its referent, and the symbol, which bears an *arbitrary* or purely *conventional* relationship with its referent.[2]

Photographs and sound recordings can (and often do) function as icons, indices and symbols. It is their indexicality, however, that has been most intriguing for filmmakers and theorists. It is a well-known claim that the photograph is in part the product of a series of mechanical cause-and-effect operations performed in and through a machine – the camera. In so far as the photograph is produced by causal processes governed by physical laws (and not by human intentionality), this allows us to impart a veracity to photographs that we do not allow for a painting.[3] The filmmaker often must choose what to shoot and how to shoot it; photography certainly involves intentions and plans on the part of the photographer. Nonetheless, the mechanical nature of the photograph's provenance allows us to attribute to the photograph an evidentiary status that we would not grant to a painting.

DIR theories have often made much of the ability of the documentary photograph to record the world and tend to underestimate the creative, interpretive nature of documentary filmmaking. Some early practitioners of direct cinema or *cinema verité* talked as though their purpose were merely to record reality and leave all interpretation to the spectator. This led some to think of documentaries as mere 're-presentations' of reality, or simple records, rather than creative interpretations, of their subjects. Poststructuralist theorists were quick to note that no documentary can perfectly re-present or reproduce anything, and they declared the very idea of documentary to be suspect.[4] The problem, however, is not with the documentary, but with confused theories of documentary; a solution would be to provide a better conception of what a documentary actually is, as I attempt to do in this essay.

Though the practitioners of direct cinema and various theorists have overstated the degree to which a documentary is a mere recording of its subject (and not an interpretation of it), it is nonetheless undeniable that the documentary has relied on the power of the moving photograph to 'show us the world', and to do so with an authenticity that depends not only on the visual wealth and detail of the photograph, but also on the indexical, causal bond between photograph and pro-filmic scene.

Gregory Currie has recently taken up the DIR banner.[5] To begin to describe Currie's theory, we must first explore his notion of photographic representation. Currie distinguishes between what he calls 'traces' and 'testimonies'. A testimony, for Currie, is a representation that is a record of 'what someone thought the facts the matter were' ('Visible Traces', 287). Testimonies, unlike traces, are thoroughly mediated by the producer's intentions. Moreover, persons are capable of giving testimony about all kinds of things that might never have existed, while only real things can leave traces of themselves. Examples of testimonies include paintings, drawings, histories and journalism.

Photographs, like footprints and death masks, are traces of the world left by the subjects themselves. Photographs are traces in part because *they are independent of belief in a way that paintings are not.*[6] The painter may hallucinate while painting and paint an empty room as though it were full of apparitions. The photographer, similarly hallucinating while photographing the room, will be surprised to find a photograph of an empty room. To some degree, the making of the photograph is independent of belief, and the photograph is a trace.

Moving photographs in fiction films are also traces, however, so the use of photographs as traces cannot by itself define the documentary. Currie argues that the 'ideal' documentary is 'a filmically sustained narrative the constitutive film images of which represent only photographically: they represent only what they are of' ('Visible Traces', 291). A fiction film may use an image of Gregory Peck to represent the fictional character Atticus Finch. An ideal documentary, in contrast, 'may not represent things and events other than the things and events they are traces of'.

Let us leave aside for now Currie's problematic claim that documentaries must be narratives. Currie's account contains a fundamental confusion that is more germane to the present discussion. He sometimes (as above) implies that a documentary is a film that uses photographs to represent what the photographs are traces of, such images being employed to support an 'asserted' narrative. At other times, however, Currie writes that a documentary film *itself* is the trace of that which it represents. He writes, for example, 'to be a documentary the thing in question must be a trace' ('Visible Traces', 289).

These seem to be two quite different notions of documentary. The former defines the documentary as a filmic narrative supported by visible traces used to represent what they are of, while the latter defines a documentary *itself* as a visible trace. But what would it mean to claim that a documentary film is a trace? Were Currie to suggest that documentaries *themselves* are traces in the same sense that individual photographs are, then Currie should want to attribute the same kind of belief-independence to documentaries that he does to discrete photographic images. This cannot be done, however.

Let us grant that individual documentary shots, in addition to their status as interpretations or expressions (through all the creative choices involved in cinematography), are also traces in the sense that Currie claims. Documentary films are also edited, and editing almost invariably further interprets the event and involves intentionality in a way that indexical signs such as traces do not. When one adds music or titles or voice-over narration, additional mediation between documentary and subject is added. A documentary itself might be considered a trace only under conditions that very few, if any, documentaries ever meet. The surveillance film would seem to be the best example of such a documentary.

Currie recognizes this problem and attempts to resolve it by claiming that most documentary films have parts that are not documentary (such as bits of voice-over narration, non-diegetic music, animated maps, and so forth). Yet this attempted resolution, rather than clearing up the issue, foregrounds the basic mistake in Currie's formulation. Like many before him, Currie confuses a document with a documentary. A photographic document can be a physical trace, and documentaries often make use of such traces. There are very few documentaries, however, that can legitimately be said to function as traces.

For the purposes of this paper, then, we will formulate the DIR account to be claiming the following: *a documentary is a sustained discourse of narrative, categorical, rhetorical, or other form that makes use of moving or still photographic images predominantly as traces to represent what the photographic images are of.*

II. Documentary as Assertion

Documentary as Assertion (DA) accounts have been formulated in various ways, but their similarities legitimate taking them as a single category of definition .[...]

In a conceptual analysis of the word 'documentary', Noël Carroll introduced the idea of the 'film of presumptive assertion', which he also terms the film of 'putative fact' and 'presumptive fact'.[7] This essay is characteristically clear and insightful, even if his idea of presumptive assertion is faulty in one regard. Carroll invokes what he calls an intention-response model of communication, which presupposes that the artist or maker communicates with an audience in part by indicating that the audience is meant to respond in a certain way.

In the film of presumptive assertion, 'the filmmaker intends that the audience entertain the propositional content of his film in thought as asserted'.[8] Carroll calls documentaries films of *presumptive* assertion (rather than simply 'films of assertion') in part because the audience *presumes* that it is to entertain the propositions as asserted; this is the response part of the intention-response model of communication. [...]

It strikes me that in such cases, the producer's *intention*, together with the textual cues and markers that signal such intention, makes the work one that can be said to make assertions, and not the actual presumptions of any particular audience. An intention-response model of a type of film need not rely on the actual response of spectators. To do so would imply a thoroughgoing subjectivism, such that, depending on its audience, a film could be a documentary for some and not for others.

It makes more sense to leave the actual spectator response out of the definition, since what is most important about such a relational definition is that a filmmaker intends that the text be received in a certain way, and that he or she design the text according to that expected reception. It is quite plausible, then, for Carroll to say that documentaries are films for which the relevant propositional content therein is meant to be taken as asserted, but the qualifier 'presumptive' in 'presumptive assertion' ought to be dropped. Why not call it, simply, 'the film of assertion'? [...]

These DA accounts, then, share much in common. They go beyond the formal elements of films to distinguish between fiction and non-fiction on the basis of the *illocutionary act* performed through or with the work. Moreover, they all implicitly appeal to the intentions of filmmakers. Roughly speaking, DA accounts hold that *documentaries are moving picture texts in or through which filmmakers assert that the states of affairs represented in the work hold in the actual world*. In other words, filmmakers take an assertive stance toward the world of the work. These definitions also take into account the response of the spectator as a factor that enters into the filmmaker's plans in making the film. At the receiving end, the spectator of a documentary is meant to form or continue to hold an attitude of belief toward the state of affairs so represented.

III. The Failure of DIR and DA definitions

The question I ask here is whether the DIR and DA definitions, when plausibly stated, capture what we mean when we use the word 'documentary'. To begin to answer this question, we need to explore the usage of the word 'documentary' a bit further. What kind of moving image non-fictions do we have in mind when we use the term 'documentary'?

Films that are considered to be documentaries come in many varieties. If we survey the territory, we see journalistic documentaries such as those found on the public television series *Frontline*, associational and poetic documentaries such as *Anima Mundi* (1992) and *Koyanisqaatsi* (1983), propaganda films such as *Why We Fight* (1942–45) and *Triumph of the Will* (1935), the films of the direct cinema or *cinema verité* movements, films that make heavy use of re-enactments such as the documentaries of John Grierson, Robert Flaherty and Humphrey Jennings, and documentaries in the making of which the filmmaker becomes a kind of provocateur (*Chronicle of a Summer* [1960], *Sherman's March* [1985]).

There exist many ways to carve out this diverse body of films, but perhaps the most influential has been Bill Nichols' description of six documentary modes: the poetic, expository, observational, participatory, reflexive and performative.[9] For my purposes, it will be sufficient to describe just two of the six modes – the expository and the observational – to show inadequacies in the DIR and DA accounts.

Expository. Typically, a voice-over narrator provides an explanatory conceptual framework, and images and sounds are used to illustrate or provide (loose) evidence for what is stated by the voice-over narrator. Expository documentaries tend to be heavily scripted and many make an overt argument for a position or for a particular interpretation of history. Examples include the *Why We Fight* series, *The Sky Above, the Earth Below* (1962), and most journalistic television documentaries, such as CBS Reports' *Harvest of Shame* (1962) and most of the current films of the PBS Frontline series.

Observational. Eschews voice-over narration and many other traditional techniques in favour of the observation of the pro-filmic event and a more open-ended and ambiguous treatment of its subject. Often thought to allow greater freedom of interpretation on the part of the viewer than the expository mode. Associated with American direct cinema and, to a lesser extent, with *cinema verité*. Examples include any of the documentaries of Frederick Wiseman such as *High School* (1968), *Hospital* (1980) and *Racetrack* (1985) and the Maysles brothers' *Salesman* (1969) and *Grey Gardens* (1975). More recent examples are *The War Room* (1993) and *Startup.com* (2001).

Equipped with this new terminology, let us return once again to the DIR and DA accounts, with a view toward assessing whether either, taken as a traditional definition, seems to fit both of these rather central modes of documentary. The DIR account, which I will consider first, has little trouble with observational films. The observational documentary, of course, is directly rooted in the ability of the moving image and sound recording to provide a kind of indexical record, or trace, of the pro-filmic event.

It is the expository documentary, in many of its historical manifestations, that DIR accounts describe poorly. This is obviously true in the case of historical documentaries about subjects that existed before the invention of photography. In these cases there can be no photographic trace of such subjects. Currie admits that his version of DIR would preclude documentaries about Napoleon, for example.

DIR accounts would also have trouble with the first sixty-five or so years of documentary history. The films produced under the aegis of John Grierson, the man who did so much to fix the meaning of the word 'documentary,' commonly used recreations and stagings of events, as did other pioneers of the documentary form such as Robert Flaherty and Humphrey Jennings. Shots of re-enacted events clearly do not represent what they are photographs of and are thus problematic for DIR accounts. The kind of cinematography favoured by DIR accounts, in fact, did not become strongly associated with the documentary until after the direct cinema and *cinema verité* movements of the 1960s.

This issue aside, DIR accounts, it seems to me, do not capture the most important features of expository documentaries. Currie writes that under his definition, documentary films are those in which 'meaning passes from image to narrative, while in nondocumentary meaning goes the other way.'[10] Although Currie admits that this passage is put 'loosely' (and thus I may be misinterpreting it), I take Currie to be saying that whatever meaning documentaries might have originates in or stems from the photographic traces that make up the documentaries, and not from some prior argument, previously researched historical account, political analysis, scientific explanation, and so forth. This claim, however, is implausible for a wide range of documentaries. Well-known documentaries such as *The Life and Times of Rosie the Riveter* (1980), *The Thin Blue Line* (1987), and *Roger and Me* (1989) are carefully crafted films organized around an argument, broadly conceived. It is quite obvious that the images support a scripted argument or narrative, the meaning of which does not necessarily arise from the images used.

Neither would it be right to find the essence of these films, qua documentary, to lie in the particular use of motion picture photographs as traces. In these cases, it seems to me, the use of cinematography is harnessed to the broader argumentative strategy of the filmmakers, which, I believe, DA accounts can account for. DIR accounts, then, fail as traditional definitions in part because they are too narrow. They would not only rule out many paradigm examples of the documentary, but they do not fit one central mode of the documentary – the expository documentary.

DA accounts, in my view, are far more plausible, but nonetheless must contend with conceptual problems. With their emphasis on truth claims, the assertion of propositional content, and/or cueing spectators to take a stance of belief toward what is presented, DA accounts are well able to distinguish prose fiction from prose non-fiction, since the assertion of propositions and/or the assertive stance are well suited to linguistic discourse. DA accounts do less well in characterizing the documentary, however, in part due to the peculiar nature of the photographic and sonic, as opposed to linguistic, discourse. [...]

[A] series of images, without voice-over narration, should be taken to assert a series of propositions about its subject, stated in linguistic terms. This claim is problematic, however. If photographs are traces, as Currie claims, then we should say that they have a communicative life that in part escapes the intentions of the filmmaker(s). The filmmakers cannot have in mind, when making the film, all the propositions that might plausibly be gleaned from the film's images. Wiseman and the makers of *Trance and Dance in Bali* need not be committed to any particular propositional account of what occurs in each moving image. Why is this? It is because the moving photograph and the sound recording are to some degree belief-independent. Their communicative richness extends beyond the intentions of the filmmakers and leaves something for interpretation and discovery by audiences.

In addition, it may be that certain images and sounds, or sequences thereof, are meant to approximate some element of the phenomenological experience of the event, such as how it looked or sounded from a particular vantage point, or how it was full of energetic good cheer or a strong sense of foreboding. Thus the film may be taken to assert that the relevant scenes give a sense of how the filmmakers were 'appeared to' aurally and/or visually. This is still a case of assertion in some sense because the filmmakers might be taken to be asserting that a scene shows what the pro-filmic event looked like, or approximates how the filmmakers 'were appeared to'. The apprehension conditions of such scenes, however, cannot be linguistic in nature. That is, we can grasp those phenomenological qualities the scene embodies only by viewing the scene.

We might get at this by drawing a distinction between *saying* and *showing*. *Saying*, in the context of a documentary, characteristically involves the assertion of specific propositional content. It is something like making an assertion or assertions about the representee, saying that it is thus and so. *Showing*, on the other hand, is something like standing in for the representee and may not involve the assertion of specific propositional content. For example, showing a person a series of snapshots taken of an event need not commit the shower to an assertion of the propositional content of the photographs. The shower is simply presenting the photographs as veridical representations of the event and allowing the viewer to learn and perhaps form beliefs about the event on the basis of those photographs.

Most documentaries, it seems to me, are representations that combine saying and showing and do so in different proportions depending on the type of documentary. [...]

In a documentary, what the filmmaker asserts, in the first instance, is that the images, sounds, and other materials presented are what I will call *veridical representations* of whatever the documentary takes as its subject. As I describe below, documentary representation commits the filmmaker to assert the reliability or functionality of whatever materials are used to show the spectator how something is, was, or might be in the actual world. [...]

IV. Asserted Veridical Representation

My argument is that central to our idea of the typical or usual documentary, and prior to any notion of the photograph as a trace, is the implicit directorial assertion of *veridical representation*, representation that is, in the case of implicitly or directly asserted propositions, truthful; and in the case of images, sounds, or combinations thereof, a reliable guide to relevant elements of the pro-filmic scene or scenes. When a filmmaker presents a film as a documentary, he or she not only intends that the audience come to form certain beliefs, but also implicitly asserts something about the use of the medium itself – that the use of motion pictures and recorded sounds offer an audiovisual array that communicates some phenomenological aspect of the subject, from which the spectator might reasonably be expected to form a sense of that phenomenological aspect and/or form true beliefs about that subject.

I have introduced the notion of AVR in an attempt to account for what people often mean when they use the word 'documentary'. In claiming that AVR is expected of documentary films, I am not claiming that audiences, critics and filmmakers share a well-defined conception of what constitutes AVR. Far from it. Audiences need not have a philosophically precise idea of what constitutes AVR for the concept, vague though it is, to play a central role in thinking about the typical or usual documentary. People *do* expect of the documentary that it is intended to offer a reliable record, account of, argument about, or analysis of some element of the actual world, that is, they expect an assertedly veridical representation.

What counts as AVR, however, differs in various contexts. For example, what is accepted as a veridical representation depends in part on the *mode* of documentary in question. In expositional documentaries, the assertion of propositions or truth claims becomes central. The implicit rules for veridical representation through images are relaxed somewhat, allowing for animated maps, occasional re-enactments, the relatively loose use of archival footage, and so forth, as long as such images and sounds are not fundamentally misleading.

Typical observational documentaries have stricter conventions for the use of motion picture photography. Within the context of the observational film, AVR requires that the filmmaker refrain from overt manipulation and staging in the making of recorded images and sounds. In any documentary, however, when photographic images and sound recordings are used as documents, that is, as evidence that the pro-filmic event occurred in a certain way, the requirements of veridical photographic representation are quite strict.

Conventions of veridical representation also change with history. A quick look at the history of documentary shows that the staging and re-enactment of scenes was routine and commonly accepted as legitimate documentary practice for the first sixty-five years of documentary history. The films of Robert Flaherty, John Grierson and Humphrey Jennings, arguably the most important documentary filmmakers of the first half of the twentieth century, commonly make use of staged and re-enacted scenes.

The development of lightweight cameras and sound-recording equipment in the late 1950s contributed to the rise of a new ethos of authenticity, fully developed in the direct cinema and *cinema verité* movements of the 1960s. The project of the documentary film, some *cinema verité* filmmakers claimed, was to record and represent reality, and not to make interpretations. The documentary filmmaker became, then, not an artist or teacher so much as a facilitator, one who self-effacingly records the pro-filmic event in order to represent it, as is, to the spectator. The sense that the filmmaker's duty was to record and not interpret led to conventional practices of documentary film production. Voice-over narration was rejected as manipulative and patronizing; the spectator should be allowed to interpret the film himself or herself. The filmmaker refrained, as much as possible, from manipulating or influencing the pro-filmic event, and attempted to become a proverbial fly on the wall. *Cinema verité* filmmakers used images and recorded sounds predominantly as traces, in Currie's sense. Some rejected the use of programme music because it did not originate from the pro-filmic scene.[11] [...]

In some cases, differences between documentary practices of asserted veridical representation and fictional practices might be subtle and complex. In almost no case, for example, would we accept actors playing purely fictional characters as asserted veridical representation, yet we might accept actors playing historical figures if we were convinced that quality research had figured into the historical accuracy of what the actors wore, said and did. Some fiction films intend the audience to take a stance of belief toward portions of their propositional content, but we rarely accept as asserted veridical representation the offering of fictional characters, imaginary worlds and made-up stories. [...]

V. What a Documentary Is

Now I am prepared to say what a documentary is, after all.

I propose that the typical or usual documentary film be conceived of as an asserted veridical representation, that is, as an extended treatment of a subject in one of the moving-image media, most often in narrative, rhetorical, categorical or associative form, in which the film's makers openly signal their intention that the audience (1) take an attitude of belief toward relevant propositional content (the 'saying' part); (2) take the images, sounds, and combinations thereof as reliable sources for the formation of beliefs about the film's subject and, in some cases; (3) take relevant shots, recorded sounds and/or scenes as phenomenological approximations of the look, sound, and/or some other sense or feel of the pro-filmic event (the 'showing' part). [...]

The interesting task now would be to explore the conventions of asserted veridical representation in various documentary modes or exemplars, in the docudrama or what some call 'non-fiction movies',[12] and in various documentary techniques and practices. Veridical representation is widely assumed, but poorly understood, and much work remains to be done. Yet the notion of asserted veridical representation is clearly needed to account for what people typically mean when they use the word 'documentary'.

1 Grierson quoted in the editor Forsyth Hardy's introduction to *Grierson on Documentary* (Berkeley and Los Angeles: University of California Press, 1966) 13.

2 [footnote 4 in source] C.S. Peirce, 'The Icon, Index and Symbol', in *Collected Papers*, 8 vols., ed. C. Hartshorne and P. Weiss (Cambridge, Massachusetts: Harvard University Press, 1931–58) vol. II.

3 [5] See my *Rhetoric and Representation in Nonfiction Film* (Cambridge: Cambridge University Press, 1997) 59.

4 [7] For a critique of postmodernist and poststructuralist theories of the documentary, see Noël Carroll, 'Non-fiction Film and Postmodernist Scepticism' in *Post-Theory: Reconstructing Film Studies*, ed. David Bordwell and Noël Carroll (Madison: University of Wisconsin Press, 1996) 283–306; see also my essay, 'Moving Pictures and the Rhetoric of Non-fiction Film: Two Approaches' in the same volume, 307–24.

5 [8] Gregory Currie, 'Visible Traces: Documentary and the Contents of Photographs', *The Journal of Aesthetics and Art Criticism*, no. 57 (1999) 285–97.

6 [9] Here Currie refers to Kendall Walton's 'Transparent Pictures: On the Nature of Photographic Realism', *Critical Inquiry*, no. 11 (1984) 246–77.

7 [16] Carroll, 'Fiction, Non-Fiction, and the Film of Presumptive Assertion: A Conceptual Analysis' in *Film Theory and Philosophy*, ed. Richard Allen and Murray Smith (Oxford: Clarendon Press, 1997) 173–202.

8 [17] Ibid., 186.

9 [2] Bill Nichols, *Introduction to Documentary* (Indianapolis: Indiana University Press, 2001) 99–138.

10 [26] Currie, 'Visible Traces', op. cit., 296.

11 [29] For a discussion of the philosophical implications of *cinema verité*, see Carroll's 'From Real to Reel', *Philosophic Exchange*, no. 14 (1983) 5–46.

12 [36] This is the term used by filmmaker Carl Byker for his historical films, for example, *Woodrow Wilson* and *The Saga of the Israelites*, which make heavy use of historical re-enactments.

Carl Plantinga, extracts from 'What a Documentary Is, After All', *The Journal of Aesthetics and Art Criticism*, vol. 63, no. 2 (Spring 2005) 105–17 [footnotes abbreviated].

Jacques Rancière
Naked Image, Ostensive Image, Metamorphic Image//2003

The images exhibited by our museums and galleries today can in fact be classified into three major categories. First of all, there is what might be called the naked image: the image that does not constitute art, because what it shows us excludes the prestige of dissemblance and the rhetoric of exegeses. Thus a recent exhibition entitled 'Mémoires des camps' devoted one of its sections to photographs taken during the discovery of the Nazi camps. The photographs were often signed by famous names – Lee Miller, Margaret Bourke-White, and so on – but the idea that brought them together was the trace of history, of testimony to a reality that is generally accepted not to tolerate any other form of presentation.

Different from the naked image is what I shall call the ostensive image. This image likewise asserts its power as that of sheer presence, without signification. But it claims it in the name of art. It posits this presence as the peculiarity of art faced with the media circulation of imagery, but also with the powers of meaning that alter this presence: the discourses that present and comment on it, the institutions that display it, the forms of knowledge that historicize it. This position can be encapsulated in the title of an exhibition recently organized at the Brussels Palais des Beaux-Arts by Thierry de Duve to exhibit 'one hundred years of contemporary art': 'Voici'. The affect of the *that was* is here apparently referred to the identity without residue of a presence of which 'contemporaneity' is the very essence. The obtuse presence that interrupts histories and discourses becomes the luminous power of a face-to-face: *facingness*, as the organizer puts it, obviously contrasting this notion with Clement Greenberg's *flatness*. But the very contrast conveys the meaning of the operation. Presence opens out into presentation of presence. Facing the spectator, the obtuse power of the image as being-there-without-reason becomes the radiance of a face, conceived on the model of the icon, as the gaze of divine transcendence. The works of the artists – painters, sculptors, video-makers, installers – are isolated in their sheer haecceity. But this haeccity immediately splits in two. The works are so many icons attesting to a singular mode of material presence, removed from the other ways in which ideas and intentions organize the data of sense experience. 'Me voici', 'Nous voici', 'Vous voici' – the three rubrics of the exhibition – make them witness to an original co-presence of people and things, of things between themselves, and of people between themselves. And Duchamp's tireless urinal once again does service, via the pedestal on which Stieglitz photographed it. It becomes a display of presence making it possible to identify the dissemblances of art with the interactions of hyper-resemblance.

Contrasting with the ostensive image is what I shall call the metamorphic image. Its power as art can be summarized in the exact opposite of 'Voici': the 'Voilà' that recently gave its title to an exhibition at the Musée d'art moderne de la Ville de Paris, sub-titled 'Le monde dans la tête'. This title and subtitle involve an idea of the relations between art and image that much more broadly inspires a number of contemporary exhibitions. According to this logic, it is impossible to delimit a specific sphere of presence isolating artistic operations and products from forms of circulation of social and commercial imagery and from operations interpreting this imagery. The images of art possess no peculiar nature of their own that separates them in stable fashion from the negotiation of resemblances and the discursiveness of symptoms. The labour of art thus involves playing on the ambiguity of resemblances and the instability of dissemblances, bringing about a local reorganization, a singular rearrangement of circulating images. In a sense the construction of such devices assigns art the tasks that once fell to the 'critique of images'. Only this critique, left to the artists themselves, is no longer framed by an autonomous history of forms or a history of deeds changing the world. Thus art is led to query the radicalism of its powers, to devote its operations to more modest tasks. It aims to play with the forms and products of imagery, rather than carry out their demystification. This oscillation between two attitudes was evident in a recent exhibition, presented in Minneapolis under the title 'Let's Entertain' and in Paris as 'Au-delà du spectacle'. The American title invited visitors both to play the game of an art freed from critical seriousness and to mark a critical distance from the leisure industry. For its part, the French title played on the theorization of the game as the active opposite of the passive spectacle in the texts of Guy Debord. Spectators thus found themselves called upon to accord Charles Ray's merry-go-round or Maurizio Cattelan's giant table football set their metaphorical value and to take playful semi-distance from the media images, disco sounds or commercial mangas [cartoon imagery] reprocessed by other artists.

The device of the installation can also be transformed into a theatre of memory and make the artist a collector, archivist or window-dresser, placing before the visitor's eyes not so much a critical clash of heterogeneous elements as a set of testimonies about a shared history and world. Thus the exhibition 'Voilà' aimed to recap a century and illustrate the very notion of a century, by bringing together, *inter alia*, Hans-Peter Feldmann's photographs of one hundred people aged 0–100, Christian Boltanski's installation of telephone subscribers, Alighiero Boetti's 720 *Letters from Afghanistan*, or the *Martins* room devoted by Bertrand Lavier to exhibiting 50 canvases linked only by the family name of their authors.

The unifying principle behind these strategies clearly seems to be to bring about, on a material that is not specific to art and often indistinguishable from a collection of utilitarian objects or a projection of forms of imagery, a double metamorphosis, corresponding to the dual nature of the *aesthetic* image: the image as cipher of history and the image as interruption. On the one hand it involves transforming the targeted, intelligent productions of imagery into opaque, stupid images, interrupting the media flow. On the other, it involves reviving dulled utilitarian objects or the indifferent images of media circulation, so as to create the power of the traces of a shared history contained in them. Installation art thus brings into play the metamorphic, unstable nature of images. The latter circulate between the world of art and the world of imagery. They are interrupted, fragmented, reconstituted by a poetics of the witticism that seeks to establish new differences of potentiality between these unstable elements.

Naked image, ostensive image, metaphorical image: three forms of 'imageness', three ways of coupling or uncoupling the power of showing and the power of signifying, the attestation of presence and the testimony of history; three ways, too, of scaling or refusing the relationship between art and image. Yet it is remarkable that none of these three forms thus defined the function within the confines of its own logic. Each of them encounters a point of undecidability in its functioning that compels it to borrow something from the others.

This is already true of the image that seems best able, and most obliged, to guard against it – the 'naked' image intent solely on witnessing. For witnessing always aims beyond what it presents. Images of the camps testify not only to the tortured bodies they do show us, but also to what they do not show: the disappeared bodies, obviously, but above all the very process of annihilation. The shots of the reporters from 1945 thus need to be viewed in two different ways. The first perceives the violence inflicted by invisible human beings on other human beings, whose suffering and exhaustion confront us and suspend any aesthetic appreciation. The second perceives not violence and suffering, but a process of dehumanization, the disappearance of the boundaries between the human, animal and mineral. Now, this second view is itself the product of an aesthetic education, of a certain idea of the image. A photograph by George Rodger, displayed at the 'Mémoires des camps' exhibition, shows us the back of a corpse whose head we cannot see, carried by an SS prisoner whose bowed head shields his face from our eyes. This horrendous assemblage of two truncated bodies presents us with an exemplary image of the common dehumanization of victim and executioner. But it does so only because we see it with eyes that have already contemplated Rembrandt's skinned ox and all the forms of representation which have equated the power of art with obliteration of the boundaries between the human and the inhuman, the living and the dead, the animal and the mineral, all alike merged in the density of the sentence or the thickness of the pictorial paste.

The same dialectic characterizes metamorphic images. These images, it is true, are based on a postulate of indiscernibility. They simply set out to displace the representations of imagery, by changing their medium, by locating them in a different mechanism of vision, by punctuating or recounting them differently. But the question then arises: what exactly is produced as a difference attesting to the specific work of artistic images on the forms of social imagery? This was the question behind the disenchanted thoughts in Serge Daney's last texts: have not all the forms of critique, play and irony that claim to disrupt the ordinary circulation of images been annexed by that circulation? Modern cinema and criticism claimed to interrupt the flow of media and advertising images by suspending the connections between narration and meaning. The freeze-frame that closes Truffaut's *Quatre cent coups* was emblematic of this suspension. But the brand thus stamped on the image ultimately serves the cause of the brand image. The procedures of cutting and humour have themselves become the stock-in-trade of advertising, the means by which it generates both adoration of its icons and the positive attitude towards them created by the very possibility of ironizing it.

No doubt the argument is not decisive. By definition, what is undecidable can be interpreted in two ways. But it is then necessary discreetly to draw on the resources of the opposite logic. For the ambiguous montage to elicit the freedom of the critical or ludic gaze, the encounter must be organized in accordance with the logic of the ostensive face-to-face, representing advertising images, disco sounds, or television sequences in the space of the museum, isolated behind a curtain in small dark booths that give them the aura of the work, damming the flood of communication. Even so, the effect is never guaranteed, because it is often necessary to place a small card on the door of the booth making it clear to viewers that, in the space they are about to enter, they will learn anew how to see and to put the flood of media messages that usually captivates them at a distance. Such exorbitant power attributed to the properties of the device itself corresponds to a rather simplistic view of the poor morons of the society of the spectacle, bathing contentedly in a flood of media images. The interruptions, derivations and reorganizations that alter the circulation of images less pretentiously have no sanctuary. They occur anywhere and at any time.

But it is doubtless the metamorphoses of the ostensive image that best express the contemporary dialectic of images. For here it proves decidedly difficult to furnish the appropriate criteria for discerning the proclaimed face-to-face, for making presence present. Most of the works put on the pedestal of 'Voici' cannot in any way be distinguished from those that contribute to the documentary displays of 'Voilà'. Portraits of stars by Andy Warhol, documents from the mythical section of the *Aigles du Musée* by Marcel Broodthaers, an installation by Joseph Beuys of a batch of commodities from the ex-GDR, Christian Boltanksi's family album, Raymond Hains' stripped posters, or Michelangelo Pistoletto's mirrors – these scarcely seem conducive to extolling the undiluted presence of 'Voici'.

Here too it is then necessary to draw on the opposite logic. The supplement of exegetical discourse proves necessary in order to transform a readymade by Duchamp into a mystical display or a sleek parallelepiped by Donald Judd into a mirror of intersecting relations. Pop images, neo-realist décollages, monochrome paintings or minimalist sculptures must be placed under the common authority of a primal scene, occupied by the putative father of pictorial modernity: Manet. But the father of modern painting must himself be placed under the authority of the Word made flesh. His modernism and that of his descendants are indeed defined by Thierry de Duve on the basis of a painting from his 'Spanish' period – *Christ mort soutenu par les anges* – inspired by a canvas of Ribalta's. Unlike his model, Manet's dead Christ has his eyes open and is facing the spectator. He is thus an allegory for the task of substitution assigned painting by the 'death of God'. The dead Christ comes back to life in the pure immanence of pictorial presence. This pure presence is not that of art, but instead of the redeeming Image. The ostensive image celebrated by the 'Voici' exhibition is the flesh of material presence raised, in its very immediacy, to the rank of absolute Idea. On this basis, readymades and Pop images in sequence, minimalist sculptures or fictional museums, are construed in advance in the tradition of icons and the religious economy of the Resurrection. But the demonstration is obviously double-edged. The Word is only made flesh through a narrative. An additional operation is always required to transform the products of artistic operations and meaning into witnesses of the original Other. The art of 'Voici' must be based on what it refused. It needs to be presented discursively to transform a 'copy', or a complex relationship between the new and the old, into an absolute origin.

Without a doubt Godard's *Histoire(s) du cinéma* affords the most exemplary demonstration of this dialectic. The filmmaker places his imaginary Museum of cinema under the sign of the Image that is to come at the Resurrection. His words counterpose to the deathly power of the Text the living force of the Image, conceived as a cloth of Veronica on which the original face of things is imprinted. To Alfred Hitchcock's obsolete stories they oppose the pure pictorial presence represented by the bottles of Pommard in *Notorious*, the windmill's sails in *Foreign Correspondent*, the bag in *Marnie*, or the glass of milk in *Suspicion*. I have shown elsewhere how these pure icons had themselves to be removed by the artifice of montage, diverted from their arrangement by Hitchcock, so as to be reintegrated into a pure kingdom of images by the fusing power of video superimposition. The visual production of iconic pure presence, claimed by the filmmaker's discourse, is itself only possible by virtue of the work of its opposite: the Schlegelian poetics of the witticism that invents between fragments of films, news strips, photos, reproductions of paintings and other things all the combinations, distances or approximations capable of eliciting new forms and meanings. This assumes the existence of a boundless Store/Library/ Museum where all films, texts, photographs and paintings coexist; and where they can all be broken up into elements each of which is endowed with a triple power: the power of singularity (the *punctum*) of the obtuse image; the educational value (the *studium*) of the document bearing the trace of a history; and the combinatory capacity of the sign, open to being combined with any element from a different sequence to compose new sentence-images *ad infinitum*.

The discourse that would salute 'images' as lost shades, fleetingly summoned from the depths of Hell, therefore seems to stand up only at the price of contradicting itself, transforming itself into an enormous poem establishing unbounded communication between arts and mediums, artworks and illustrations of the world, the silence of images and their eloquence. Behind the appearance of contradiction, we must take a closer look at the interaction of these exchanges.

Jacques Rancière, 'Naked Image, Ostensive Image, Metaphoric Image', from *Le Destin des Images* (Paris: La Fabrique, 2003); trans. Gregory Elliott, *The Future of the Image* (London and New York: Verso, 2007) 22–31 [footnotes not included].

Trinh T. Minh-ha
Documentary Is/Not a Name//1990

Nothing is poorer than a truth expressed as it was thought.
– Walter Benjamin

There is no such thing as *documentary* – whether the term designates a category of material, a genre, an approach or a set of techniques. This assertion – as old and as fundamental as the antagonism between names and reality – needs incessantly to be restated, despite the very visible existence of a documentary tradition. In film, such a tradition, far from undergoing crisis today, is likely to fortify itself through its very recurrence of declines and rebirths. The narratives that attempt to unify/purify its practices by positing evolution and continuity from one period to the next are numerous indeed, relying heavily on traditional historicist concepts of periodization. [...]

Documentary is said to have come about as a need to inform the people (Dziga

Vertov's *Kino-Pravda* or Camera-Truth), and subsequently to have affirmed itself as a reaction against the monopoly of the movie as entertainment came to have on the uses of film. Cinema was redefined as an ideal medium for social indoctrination and comment, the virtues of which lay in its capacity for 'observing and selecting from life itself', for 'opening up the screen on the real world', for photographing 'the living scene and the living story' for giving cinema 'power over a million and one images', as well as for achieving 'an intimacy of knowledge and effect impossible to the shimsham mechanics of the studio and the lily-fingered interpretation of the metropolitan actor'.[1] Asserting its independence from the studio and the star system, documentary has its *raison d'être* in a strategic distinction. It puts the social function of film *on the market*. It takes real people and real problems from the real world and *deals with them*. It *sets a value* on intimate observation and *assesses its worth* according to how well it succeeds in capturing reality on the run, 'without material interference, without intermediary'. Powerful living stories, infinite authentic situations. There are no retakes. The stage is thus no more and no less than life itself. *With the documentary approach the film gets back to its fundamentals ... By selection, elimination and coordination of natural elements, a film form evolves which is original and not bound by theatrical or literary tradition ... The documentary film is an original art form. It has come to grips with facts – on its own original level. It covers the rational side of our lives, from the scientific experiment to the poetic landscape-study, but never moves away from the factual.*[2]

The real world: so real that the Real becomes the one basic referent – pure, concrete, fixed, visible, all-too-visible. The result is the advent of a whole aesthetic of objectivity and the development of comprehensive technologies of truth capable of promoting what is right and what is wrong in the world and, by extension, what is 'honest' and what is 'manipulative' in documentary. This involves an extensive and relentless pursuit of naturalism across all the elements of cinematic technology. Indispensable to this cinema of the authentic image and spoken word are, for example, the directional microphone (localizing and restricting in its process of selecting sound for purposes of decipherability) and the Nagra portable tape-recorder (unrivalled for its maximally faithful ability to document). Lip-synchronous sound is validated as the norm; it is a 'must' – not so much in replicating reality (this much has been acknowledged among the fact-makers) as in 'showing real people in reallocations at real tasks.' (Even non-synchronized sounds recorded in context are considered 'less authentic' because the technique of sound synchronization and its institutionalized use have become 'nature' within film culture.) Real time is thought to be more 'truthful' than filmic time, hence the long-take (that is, a take lasting the length of the 400-foot roll of commercially available film stock) and minimal or no editing (change at the cutting stage is 'trickery', as if montage did not happen at the stages of conception and shooting) are declared to be more appropriate if one is to avoid distortions in structuring the material. The camera is the switch onto life. Accordingly, the close-up is condemned for its partiality, while the wide angle is claimed as more objective because it includes more in the frame; hence it can mirror the event-in-context more faithfully. (The more, the larger, the truer – as if wider framing is less a framing than tighter shots.) The lightweight, hand-held camera, with its independence from the tripod – the fixed observation post – is extolled for its ability 'to go unnoticed', since it must be at once mobile and invisible, integrated into the milieu so as to change as little as possible, but also able to put its intrusion to use to provoke people into uttering the 'truth' they would not otherwise unveil in ordinary situations.

Thousands of bunglers have made the word [documentary] come to mean a deadly, routine form of filmmaking, the kind an alienated consumer society might appear to deserve – the art of talking a great deal during a film, with a commentary imposed from the outside, in order to say nothing, and to show nothing.[3] The perfectly objective social observer may no longer stand as the cherished model among documentary makers today, but with every broadcast the viewer, Everyman, continues to be taught that he or she is first and foremost a Spectator. Either one is not responsible for what one sees (because only the event presented counts) or the only way one can have some influence on things is by sending in (monetary) donations. Thus, though the filmmaker's perception may readily be admitted as unavoidably personal, the objectiveness of the reality of what is seen and represented remains unchallenged. [*Cinéma-vérité*:] *it would be better to call it cinema-sincerity ... That is, that you ask the audience to have confidence in the evidence, to say to the audience, 'This is what I saw. I didn't fake it, this is what happened ... I look at what happened with my subjective eye and this is what I believe took place ... It's a question of honesty.'*[4]

What is presented as evidence remains evidence, whether the observing eye qualifies itself as being subjective or objective. At the core of such a rationale dwells, untouched, the Cartesian division between subject and object that perpetuates a dualistic inside-versus-outside, mind-against-matter view of the world. Again, the emphasis is laid on the power of film to capture reality 'out there' for us 'in here'. The moment of appropriation and of consumption is either simply ignored or carefully rendered invisible according to the rules of good and bad documentary. The art of talking-to-say-nothing goes hand-in-hand with the will to say, and to say only to confine something in a meaning. Truth has to be made vivid, interesting; it has to be 'dramatized' if it is to convince the audience of the evidence, whose 'confidence' in it a lows truth to take shape. *Documentary – the presentation of actual facts in a way that makes them credible and telling to people at the time.*[5]

The real? Or the repetitive, artificial resurrection of the real, an operation whose overpowering success in substituting the visual and verbal signs of the real for the real itself ultimately helps challenge the real, thereby intensifying the uncertain ties engendered by any clear-cut division between the two. In the scale of what is more and what is less real, subject matter is of prime importance ('It is very difficult if not impossible', says a film festival administrator, 'to ask jurors of a panel in the documentary film category not to identify the quality of a film with the subject it treats'). The focus is undeniably on common experience, by which the 'social' is defined: an experience that features, as a famed documentary-maker (Pierre Perrault) put it (paternalistically): 'man, simple man, who has never expressed himself'.[6]

The socially oriented filmmaker is thus the almighty voice-giver (here, in a vocalizing context that is all-male), whose position of authority in the production of meaning continues to go unchallenged, skilfully masked as it is by its righteous mission. The relationship between mediator and medium, or the mediating activity, is either ignored – that is, assumed to be transparent, as value-free and as insentient as an instrument of reproduction ought to be – or else, it is treated most conveniently: by humanizing the gathering of evidence so as to further the status quo ('Of course, like all human beings I am subjective, but nonetheless, I have confidence in the evidence!'). Good documentaries are those whose subject matter is 'correct' and whose point of view the viewer agrees with. What is involved may be a question of honesty (vis-à-vis the material), but it is often also a question of (ideological) adherence, hence of legitimization.

Films made about the common people are, furthermore, naturally promoted as films made for the same people, and only for them. In the desire to service the needs of the un-expressed, there is, commonly enough, the urge to define them and their needs. More often than not, for example, when filmmakers find themselves in debates in which a film is criticized for its simplistic and reductive treatment of a subject, resulting in a maintenance of the very status quo it sets out to challenge, their tendency is to dismiss the criticism by arguing that the film is not made for 'sophisticated viewers like ourselves, but for a general audience', thereby situating themselves above and apart from the real audience, those 'out there', the simple-minded folks who need everything they see explained to them. Despite the shift of emphasis – from the world of the upwardly mobile and the very affluent that dominates the media to that of 'their poor' – what is maintained intact is the age-old opposition between the creative, intelligent supplier and the mediocre, unenlightened consumer. The pretext for perpetuating such division is the belief that social relations are determinate, hence endowed with objectivity. *By 'impossibility of the social' I understand … the assertion of the ultimate impossibility of all 'objectivity' … society presents itself, to a great degree, not as an objective, harmonic order, but as an ensemble of divergent forces which do not seem to obey any unified or unifying logic. How can this experience of the failure of objectivity be made compatible with the affirmation of an ultimate objectivity of the real?*[7]

The silent common people – those who 'have never expressed themselves' unless they are given the opportunity to voice their thoughts by the one who comes to redeem them – are constantly summoned to signify the real world. They are the fundamental referent of the social, hence it suffices to point the camera at them, to show their (industrialized) poverty, or to contextualize and package their unfamiliar lifestyles for the ever-buying and donating general audience 'back here', in order to enter the sanctified realm of the morally right, or the social. In other words, when the so-called 'social' reigns, how these people (/we) come to visibility in the media, how meaning is given to their (/our) lives, how their (/our) truth is construed or how truth is laid down for them (/us) and despite them (/us), how representation relates to or is ideology, how media hegemony continues its relentless course, is simply not at issue.

There isn't any cinéma-vérité. *It's necessarily a lie, from the moment the director intervenes – or it isn't cinema at all.* (Georges Franju)

When the social is hypostatized and enshrined as an ideal of transparency, when it itself becomes commodified in a form of sheer administration (better service, better control), the interval between the real and the image/d or between the real and the rational shrinks to the point of unreality. Thus, to address the question of production relations, as raised earlier, is endlessly to reopen the question: how is the real (or the social ideal of good representation) produced? Rather than catering to it, striving to capture and discover its truth as a concealed or lost object, it is therefore important also to keep asking: how is truth being ruled? *The penalty of realism is that it is about reality and has to bother forever not about being 'beautiful' but about being right.*[8]

The fathers of documentary initially insisted that documentary is not News, but Art (a 'new and vital art form,' as Grierson once proclaimed): that its essence is not information (as with 'the hundreds of tweedledum "industrials" or worker-education films'); not reportage; not newsreels; but something close to 'a creative treatment of actuality' (Grierson's renowned definition).

Documentary may be anti-aesthetic, as some still affirm in the line of the British forerunner, but it is claimed to be no less an art, albeit an art within the limits of factuality. When, in a world of reification, truth is widely equated with fact, any explicit use of the magic, poetic or irrational qualities specific to the film medium itself would have to be excluded a priori as non-factual. The question is not so much one of sorting out – illusory as this may be – what is inherently factual from what is not in a body of *pre-existing* filmic techniques, as it is one of abiding by the laws of naturalism in film. In the reality of formula-films, only validated techniques are *right*, others are de facto wrong. All, however, depend on their degree of invisibility in producing meaning. Thus, shooting at any speed other than the standard 24-frames-per-second (the speed necessitated for lip-sync sound) is, for example, often condemned as a form of manipulation, implying thereby that manipulativeness has to be discreet – that is, acceptable only when not easily perceptible to the 'real audience.' Although the whole of filmmaking *is* a question of manipulation – whether 'creative' or not – those endorsing the law unhesitatingly decree which technique is manipulative and which, supposedly, is not; and this judgement is made according to the degree of visibility of each. *A documentary film is shot with three cameras: 1) the camera in the technical sense; 2) the filmmaker's mind; and 3) the generic patterns of the documentary film, which are founded on the expectations of the audience that patronizes it. For this reason one cannot simply say that the documentary film portrays facts. It photographs isolated facts and assembles from them a coherent set of facts according to three divergent schemata. All remaining possible facts and factual contexts are excluded. The naïve treatment of documentation therefore provides a unique opportunity to concoct fables. In and of itself, the documentary is no more realistic than the feature film.*[9]

Reality is more fabulous, more maddening, more strangely manipulative than fiction. To understand this is to recognize the naïveté of a development of cinematic technology that promotes increasingly unmediated access to reality. It is to see through the poverty of what Benjamin deplored as 'a truth expressed as it was thought' and to understand why progressive fiction films are attracted by and constantly pay tribute to documentary techniques. These films put the 'documentary effect' to advantage, playing on the viewer's expectations in order to 'concoct fables'. The documentary can easily thus become a 'style': it no longer constitutes a mode of production or an attitude toward life, but proves to be only an element of aesthetics (or anti-aesthetics), which at best, and without acknowledging it, it tends to be in any case when, within its own factual limits, it reduces itself to a mere category, or a set of persuasive techniques. Many of these techniques have become so 'natural' to the language of broadcast television that they 'go unnoticed'. These are, for example, the 'personal testimony' technique (a star appears on screen to advertise his or her use of a certain product) ; the 'plain folks' technique (a politician arranges to eat hot dogs in public); the 'band wagon' technique (the use of which conveys the message that 'everybody is doing it, why not you?') ; or the 'card stacking' technique (in which pre-arrangements for a 'survey' show that a certain brand of product is more popular than any other to the inhabitants of a given area).[10]

You must re-create reality because reality runs away; reality denies reality. You must first interpret it, or re-create it ... When I make a documentary, I try to give the realism an artificial aspect ... I find that the aesthetic of a document comes from the artificial aspect of the document … it has to be more beautiful than realism, and therefore it has to be composed … to give it another sense.[11] A documentary aware of its own artifice is one that remains sensitive to the flow between fact and fiction. It does not work to conceal or exclude what is normalized as 'non-factual', for it understands the mutual dependence of realism and 'artificiality' in the process of filmmaking. It recognizes the necessity of composing (on) life in living it or making it. Documentary reduced to a mere vehicle of facts may be used to advocate a cause, but it does not constitute one in itself; hence the perpetuation of the bipartite system of division in the content-versus-form rationale. To compose is not always synonymous with ordering-so-as-to-persuade, and to give the filmed document another sense, another meaning, is not necessarily to distort it. If life's paradoxes and complexities are not to be suppressed, the question of degree and nuance is incessantly crucial. Meaning can therefore be political only when it does not let itself be easily stabilized, and when it does not rely on any single source of authority, but, rather, empties or decentralizes it. Thus, even when this source is referred to, it stands as one among many others, at once plural and utterly singular. In its demand to mean at any rate, the 'documentary' often forgets how it comes about and how aesthetics and politics remain inseparable in its constitution. For, when not equated with mere techniques of beautifying, aesthetics allows one to experience life differently, or as some would say, to give it 'another sense', remaining in tune with its drifts and shifts. […]

Reality runs away, reality denies reality. Filmmaking is after all a question of 'framing' reality in its course. However, it can also be the very place where the referential function of the film image/sound is not simply negated, but reflected upon in its own operative principles and questioned in its authoritative identification with the phenomenal world. In attempts to suppress the mediation of the cinematic apparatus and the fact that language 'communicates itself in itself', there always lurks a bourgeois conception of language. *Any revolutionary strategy must challenge the depiction of reality … so that a break between ideology and text is effected.*[12]

To deny the *reality* of film in claiming (to capture) *reality* is to stay 'in Ideology' – that is, to indulge in the (deliberate or not) confusion of filmic with phenomenal reality. By condemning self-reflexivity as pure formalism instead of challenging its diverse realizations, this ideology can 'go on unnoticed', keeping its operations invisible and serving the goal of universal expansionism. Such aversion against reflexivity goes hand in hand with its widespread appropriation as a progressive, formalistic device in cinema, since both work to reduce its function to a harmlessly decorative one. (For example, it has become commonplace to hear such remarks as 'a film is a film' or 'this is a film about a film'. Film-on-film statements are increasingly challenging to work with because they can easily fall prey to their own formulae and techniques.) Furthermore, reflexivity, at times equated with a personal perspective, is at other times endorsed as scientific rigour. [...]

As an aesthetic closure or an old relativizing gambit in the process nonetheless of absolutizing meaning, reflexivity proves critically insignificant when it merely serves to refine and to further the accumulation of knowledge. No going beyond, no elsewhere-within-here seems possible if the reflection on oneself is not at one and the same time the analysis of established forms of the social that define one's limits. Thus to drive the self into an abyss is neither a moralistic stricture against oneself nor a task of critique that humanizes the decoding self but never challenges the very notion of self and decoder. Left intact in its positionality and its fundamental urge to decree meaning, the self conceived both as key and as transparent mediator, is more often than not likely to turn responsibility into licence. The licence to name, as though meaning presented itself to be deciphered without any ideological mediation. As though specifying a context can only result in the finalizing of what is shown and said. As though naming can stop the process of naming: that very abyss of the relation of self to self.

The bringing of the self into play necessarily exceeds the concern for human errors, for it cannot but involve as well the problem inherent in representation and communication. Radically plural in its scope, reflexivity is thus not a mere question of *rect*ifying and *just*ifying (*subject*ivizing). What is set in motion in its praxis are the self-generating links between different forms of reflexivity. Thus, a subject who points to him or herself as subject-in-process, a work that displays its own formal properties or its own constitution as work, is bound to upset one's sense of identity – the familiar distinction between the Same and the Other since the latter is no longer kept in a recognizable relation of dependence, derivation, or appropriation. The process of self-constitution is also that in which the self vacillates and loses its assurance. The paradox of such a process lies in its fundamental instability; an instability that brings forth the disorder inherent in every order. The 'core' of representation is the reflexive interval. It is the place in which the play within the textual frame is a play on this very frame, hence on the borderlines of the textual and extra-textual, where a positioning within constantly incurs the risk of de-positioning, and where the work, never freed from historical and socio-political contexts nor entirely subjected to them, can only be itself by constantly risking being no-thing.

A work that reflects back on itself offers itself infinitely as nothing else but work ... and void. Its gaze is at once an impulse that causes the work to fall apart (to return to the initial no-work-ness) and an ultimate gift to its constitution. A gift, by which the work is freed from the tyranny of meaning as well as from the omnipresence of a subject of meaning. To let go of the hold at the very moment when it is at its most effective is to allow the work to live, and to live on independently of the intended links, communicating itself in itself, like Benjamin's 'the self is a text' – no more and no less 'a project to be built'.[13] *Orpheus' gaze ... is the impulse of desire which shatters the song's destiny and concern, and in that inspired and unconcerned decision reaches the origin, consecrates the song.*[14]

Meaning can neither be imposed nor denied. Although every film is in itself a form of ordering and closing, each closure can defy its own closure, opening on to other closures, thereby emphasizing the interval between apertures and creating a space in which meaning remains fascinated by what escapes and exceeds it. The necessity to let go of the notion of intentionality that dominates the question of the 'social' as well as that of creativity cannot therefore be confused with the ideal of non-intervention, an ideal in relation to which the filmmaker, trying to become as invisible as possible in the process of producing meaning, promotes empathic subjectivity at the expense of critical inquiry even when the intention is to show and to condemn oppression. *It is idealist mystification to believe that 'truth' can be captured by the camera or that the conditions of a film's production (e.g. a film made collectively by women) can of itself reflect the conditions of its production. This is mere utopianism: new meaning has to be manufactured within the text of the film ... What the camera, in fact grasps is the 'natural' world of the dominant ideology.*[15]

In the quest for totalized meaning and for knowledge-for-knowledge's sake, the worst meaning is meaninglessness. A Caucasian missionary nun based in a remote village of Africa qualifies her task in these simple, confident terms: 'We are here to help people give meaning to their lives.' Ownership is monotonously circular in its give-and-take demands. It is a monolithic view of the world the irrationality of which expresses itself in the imperative of both giving and meaning, and the irreality of which manifests itself in the need to require that visual and verbal constructs yield meaning down to their last detail. *The West moistens everything with meaning, like an authoritarian religion which imposes baptism on entire people.*[16] Yet such illusion is real; it has its own reality, one in which the subject of Knowledge, the subject of Vision, or the subject of Meaning continues to deploy established power relations, assuming Himself to be the basic reserve of reference in the totalizing quest for the referent, the true referent that lies out there in nature, in the dark, waiting patiently to be unveiled and deciphered correctly. To be redeemed. Perhaps then, an imagination that goes toward the texture of reality is one capable of working upon the illusion in question and the power it exerts. The production of one irreality upon the other and the play of non-sense (which is not mere meaninglessness) upon meaning may therefore help to relieve the basic referent of its occupation, for the present situation of critical inquiry seems much less one of attacking the illusion of reality as one of displacing and emptying out the establishment of totality.

1 [footnote 3 in source] John Grierson, in Forsyth Hardy, ed., *Grierson On Documentary* (New York: Praeger, 1971) 146–7.

2 [4] Hans Richter, 'Film as an Original Art Form', in R. Dyer MacCann, ed., *Film: A Montage of Theories* (New York: Dutton, 1966) 183.

3 [5] Louis Morcorelles, *Living Cinema: New Directions in Contemporary Filmmaking*, trans. I. Quigly (New York: Praeger, 1973) 37.

4 [6] Jean Rouch, as quoted in G.R. Levin, *Documentary Explorations: Fifteen Interviews with Filmmakers* (Garden City, New York: Doubleday, 1971) 135.

5 [7] William Stott, *Documentary Expression and Thirties America* (New York: Oxford University Press, 1976) 73.

6 [8] Quoted in *Living Cinema*, op. cit., 26.

7 [9] Ernesto Laclau, as quoted in 'Building a New Left: An Interview with Ernest Laclau', *Strategies*, no. 1 (Fall 1988) 15.

8 [10] Grierson, *Grierson on Documentary*, op. cit., 249.

9 [11] Alexander Kluge, as quoted in *Alexander Kluge: A Retrospective* (New York: The Goethe Institutes of North America, 1988) 4.

10 [12] John Mercer, *An Introduction to Cinematography* (Champaign, Illinois: Stipes Publishing Co., 1968) 159.

11 [13] Georges Franju, as quoted in *Documentary Explorations*, op. cit., 121, 128.

12 [16] Claire Johnston, 'Women's Cinema as Counter-Cinema', in *Movies and Methods*, vol. 1 (1976) 215.

13 [23] Walter Benjamin, *One Way Street* (1928) (London: Verso, 1979) 14.

14 [24] Maurice Blanchot, trans. L. Davis, in P. Adams Sitney, ed., *The Gaze of Orpheus and Other Literary Essays* (Tarrytown, New York: Station Hill Press, 1981) 104.

15 [25] Johnston, 'Women's Cinema as Counter-Cinema', op. cit., 211.

16 [26] Roland Barthes, *L'Empire des signes* (1970); trans. Richard Howard, *Empire of Signs* (New York: Hill & Wang, 1982) 70.

Trinh T. Minh-ha, extracts from ' Documentary Is/Not a Name', *October*, vol. 52 (Spring 1990) 76; 78–89; 90; 95–7.

A close textual reading of

The Family of Man

would indicate that it moves from the celebration of patriarchal authority – which finds its highest embodiment in the United Nations – to the final construction of an imaginary utopia that resembles nothing so much as a protracted state of infantile, pre-Oedipal bliss

Allan Sekula, 'The Traffic in Photographs', 1981

PHOTOJOURNALISM AND DOCUMENTARY: FOR, AGAINST AND BEYOND

W. Eugene Smith
Photographic Journalism//1948

Photography is a potent medium of expression. Properly used it is a great power for betterment and understanding; misused, it can kindle many troublesome fires. Photographic journalism, because of the tremendous audience reached by publications using it, has more influence on public thinking and opinion than any other branch of photography. For these reasons, it is important that the photographer-journalist have (beside the essential mastery of his tools) a strong sense of integrity and the intelligence to understand and present his subject matter accordingly.

Those who believe that photographic reportage is 'selective and objective, but cannot interpret the photographed subject matter', show a complete lack of understanding of the problems and the proper workings of this profession. The journalistic photographer can have no other than a personal approach; and it is impossible for him to be completely objective. Honest – yes. Objective – no.

Working with different techniques, all of which are common to others in the field, photographers Lisette Model, Cartier-Bresson, Gjon Mili, rise far above mere technical proficiency. Yet each of the three, were they to handle the same subject matter, would be capable of giving the world fine and individual interpretations. Cartier-Bresson and Leonard McCombe are two photographers who work almost exclusively with 35mm cameras and natural light. Here again, it could almost be guaranteed that their interpretations of the same subject would be quite different. Which is the objective truth? Perhaps all of these photographers are telling the truth — truth being 'many things to many people'.

Up to and including the instant of exposure, the photographer is working in an undeniably subjective way. By his choice of technical approach (which is a tool of emotional control), by his selection of the subject matter to be held within the confines of his negative area, and by his decision as to the exact, climactic instant of exposure, he is blending the variables of interpretation into an emotional whole which will be a basis for the formation of opinions by the viewing public.

It is the responsibility of the photographer-journalist to take his assignment and examine it – to search with intelligence for the frequently intangible truth; and then very carefully (and sometimes very rapidly) work to bring his insight, as well as the physical characteristics of the subject, to his finished pictures.

It is important that the inspiration for the interpretation should come from a study of the people or places to be photographed. The mind should remain as open and free from prejudice as possible, and the photographer should never try to force the subject matter into his or the editor's preconceived idea. Too often, an assignment is given, the photographer reads the instructions and the suggestions, and then follows them without much more thought – except to photograph as closely as possible to what he believes are the desires of the editors. All too frequently, due to faulty research, to inadequate knowledge or to the preconceived notions just mentioned, the directional theme of the assignment is a misconception of the living actuality. But because he does not wish to offend the editors who pay him his bread money, the photographer frequently tries to make his story conform to someone else's shortsighted or warped judgment.

The photographer must bear the responsibility for his work and its effect. By so much as his work is a distortion (this is sometimes intangible, at other times shockingly obvious), in such proportion is it a crime against humanity. Even on rather 'unimportant' stories, this attitude must be taken – for photographs (and the little words underneath) are moulders of opinion. A little misinformation plus a little more misinformation is the kindling from which destructive misunderstandings flare.

The majority of photographic stories require a certain amount of setting up, rearranging and stage direction, to bring pictorial and editorial coherency to the pictures. Here, the photojournalist can be his most completely creative self. Whenever this is done for the purpose of a better translation of the spirit of the actuality, then it is completely ethical. If the changes become a perversion of the actuality for the sole purpose of making a 'more dramatic' or 'saleable' picture, the photographer has indulged in 'artistic licence' that should not be. This is a very common type of distortion. If the photographer has distorted for some unethical reasons, it obviously becomes a matter of the utmost gravity.

A personal belief of mine is that all the events in the world which cause great emotional upheavals, such as wars, riots, mine disasters, fires, the death of leaders (such as the reaction to the death of Gandhi) – these and similar happenings which tend to release human emotions from control should be photographed in a completely interpretational manner. Under no circumstances should an attempt be made to recreate the moods and happenings of these moments.

I prefer this unposed interpretive approach in the doing of all stories – that is, wherever possible. Regardless of the 'how' of interpretations, the journalistic field must find men of integrity, open-minded and sincere in purpose, with the intelligence and insight to penetrate to the vital core of human relationships – and with the very rare ability to give the full measure of their unbiased findings to the world. [...]

W. Eugene Smith, extract from 'Photographic Journalism', *Photo Notes* (June 1948) 4–5.

Daido Moriyama
The Decision to Shoot//1972

For some years now, I've been thinking about the potential of photography. What is it capable of? Of course, this question is inextricably linked to a more fundamental question: what is human existence itself? To seek an easy answer to either of these questions is to enter a boundless, unknowable labyrinth.

Furthermore, knowing the horror of the connection between our forcibly resigned, befuddled selves and the oppressive cruelty of world events, unfolding inexorably before our eyes into an indeterminate future, we become lost in the powerlessness of the self. Having said this, to propose that photography is capable of nothing (as if to say *one must die if one cannot find a reason for living*) compounds the cruelty, just as the Subject suffers the ravages of time.

Until a few years ago, I was able to stave off an awareness that there is not an ounce of beauty in the world, and that humanity is a thing of extreme hideousness. So I could shoot and believe in something. But there came a point where rationalization and belief became impossible – a sensibility that continued until quite recently.

This lasted for more than ten years, during which time – with camera in hand – I passed intuitively and corporeally through an intricate weave of dramas, with countless individuals in various spheres, to find myself possessed, at one point, by thought, as though my very body had been wrapped in that woven tapestry. In other words, I came to focus solely on the darkest, coldest regions at the heart of human existence. I was tortured by an incomprehensible feeling of unease, an indescribable sense of powerlessness. Until recently, I have been plagued by the feeling that I was missing something entirely. It's only now that I've finally come to feel myself being steadily released from such plagues.

For almost two years, outside of a few very rare assignments, I almost never carried a camera – but lately I've begun to put my heart back into the effort. I now take my camera with me every day, and have started again to make photographs incessantly. Just as I used to do, I now photograph *everything*, as if possessed. But, disliking photographs as static, strictly decorative visual art pieces, and being distrustful of the fanatical emphasis on realism in photojournalism, I am now striving to go beyond established styles and widen the boundaries of photographic expression. Unlike in the past, however, when my zeal was informed by rote repetition, an almost overbearingly methodical approach, my photographs now contain a certain *decisiveness*. Of course, the word 'decisive' may sound overbearing in itself, but it's actually an extremely simple concept. It just means that I have no choice but to photograph within the context of this life, rather than searching for a hidden ideal beyond it.

No matter how bleak the times – or the situation in which I find myself – may seem, no matter how ugly the relationships of human society may be, I must not allow myself to be marginalized by them, or all will be lost. There is no way that a single person can have a truly comprehensive view of the world, but it is possible for him to conceive of an outline of its totality. It is therefore from the gap between his perceptions of cruel reality and his *Weltanschauung* – in other words, from the interplay between the extremes of the real and the ideal, as they are juxtaposed in his shutter – that meaning arises.

It is without question precisely in this juxtaposition that one can find the potential relevance of photography to history, culture and politics most closely approaching the realm of probability. One may never be able to discover anything so enigmatic as 'the truth' in a photograph, but if one were to settle for something close to it, it may be that it consists of neither an absolute affirmation nor an absolute denial of anything, but something between the two. For example, if one were to photograph a single tree as an *absolute instance* of a tree, and at the same time doubt the established concept of 'tree-ness' itself, and see it as a physical entity that is something other than a tree, then one would begin to realize the necessity of having multiple vantage points.

I recently saw a multi-page photo spread titled 'The Bangladesh Atrocities' in a certain weekly men's magazine. The spread, shot by two Associated Press cameramen,[1] had won the 1972 Pulitzer Prize for journalism. True to its title, the piece depicted, with a realism that verged on cruelty, the massacre of suspected collaborators by their Bengali compatriots that occurred throughout Dacca after the Pakistani army initiated its withdrawal from the capital in December 1971. The extent to which those photographs portrayed human suffering was shocking. But I was only somewhat emotionally moved by them. I tried to form a mental picture of how the rays of sunlight must have looked on that day, the sounds that might have occurred at the scene and even the final sights that those dead people's eyes might have looked upon. It was all certainly gruesome, but there was nothing for me beyond those imaginings. Naturally, I thought to myself: 'Why is this?' Why do Robert Capa's photographs of war, or William Klein's candid street scenes feel so *real* that they weigh upon me even to this day, yet these other, utterly shocking photographs don't take me anywhere beyond the scenes they depict?

Perhaps it's this: perhaps the cameramen *lost themselves* in the Bangladesh photographs and became an intrinsic part of the recording device, so that the only effect that the photographs could have was as illustrations of the misery of war. Photographs such as those by Capa and Klein, on the other hand, contain the living pulse of the human being behind the camera. The former is nothing more than a journalistic photograph of an atrocity, while the latter is a framed *portion of the world* that bears a poignant relationship to the world as a whole.

I have two favourite passages by Albert Camus, to the effect of: 'Even if you could trace the course of the entire world with your finger, you wouldn't understand the world any better', and 'The graceful green hill, that hand thrust toward my uneasy heart, have more to teach me about this world than anything else.' I want to perceive the world from this vantage point, and I ask to do it with camera in hand. If, in the actuality of the world that engulfs me, and occasionally even in its reverie – if, in the very midst of its most ordinary, mundane scenes 'love', say, or 'fate' lies dormant under the surface, and if those *noumena* are at some point connected to the world at large, then there is nothing left for me to do but continue releasing the shutter.

1 The journalists were Horst Faas and Michel Laurent. [See the introduction to this volume, 18.]

Daido Moriyama, extract from 'The Decision to Shoot', *Yomiuri Shimbun* (Tokyo, 1 August 1972); reprinted in Ivan Vartanian, et al., eds, *Setting Sun: Writings by Japanese Photographers* (New York: Aperture, 2006) 34–6.

Jean-Paul Sartre
From One China to Another//1954

The picturesque has its origins in war and a refusal to understand the enemy: our enlightenment about Asia actually came to us first from irritated missionaries and from soldiers. Later came travellers – traders and tourists – who are soldiers that have cooled off. Pillaging is called shopping, and rape is practised onerously in specialized shops. But the basic attitude has not changed: the natives are killed less frequently but they are scorned collectively, which is the civilized form of massacre; the aristocratic pleasure of counting the *differences* is savoured. 'I cut my hair, he plaits his; I use a fork, he uses chopsticks; I write with a goose quill, he draws characters with a paintbrush; I have ideas which are straight, and his are bent: have you noticed that he is horrified by movement in a straight line, that he is only happy if everything goes sideways?' This is called the game of anomalies: if you find another one, if you discover another reason for not understanding, you will be given a prize for sensitivity in your own country. You must not be surprised if those who in this way reconstruct those who resemble them, like a mosaic of irreducible differences, then wonder how anyone can be Chinese. [...]

There are photographers who encourage war because they produce literature. They seek out a Chinese who looks more Chinese than the others; in the end they find one. They make him adopt a typically Chinese pose and surround him with chinoiseries. What have they captured on film? *One* Chinaman? No ... the Idea of what is Chinese.

Cartier-Bresson's photographs never gossip. They *are not* ideas; they give us ideas. Without doing so deliberately. His Chinese are disconcerting: most of them never look quite Chinese enough. Being a witty individual, the tourist asks himself how they manage to recognize each other. Personally, having looked through the album, I ask myself rather how we could confuse them, and classify them all under the same rubric. The idea of what is Chinese recedes and pales: it is no longer any more than a convenient label. What remain are human beings who resemble each other *in that they are human beings* – living presences of flesh and blood who have not yet been given their *appellation contrôlée*. We must be grateful to Cartier-Bresson for his nominalism. [...]

This peasant is having lunch. He has come to the town to sell the produce of his land. At this moment he is eating rice soup, in the open air, in the midst of the townsfolk who ignore him, with the voracity of country people: famished, weary, solitary, he has brothers, at this very moment, in all the world's large farming towns, from the Greek who drives his sheep along the boulevards of Athens to the *Chleuh*, who has come down from his mountains and is wandering through the streets of Marrakech. Here we have other peasants: hunger has brought them down to Peking and there they have stayed. What can they do in a capital without industry, when craft skills require a long apprenticeship? They will ride bicycle taxis. We have scarcely glanced at them, but these vehicles look familiar to us: we had our own during the Occupation. It is true that they seemed less filthy; that is because we put our filth elsewhere. And poverty is the best-distributed thing in the world: we are not short of wretched people. It is true that we are no longer in the habit of harnessing them to carriages to make them pull the rich. But have they, for all that, ceased to be our beasts of burden? We now harness them to machines. [...]

Images, when they are materialistic, bring men together; that is to say when they begin at the beginning: with bodies, with needs, with work. [...]

Poverty is there, however, unbearable and discreet. On every page it manifests itself, in three elementary actions: carrying, scavenging, pilfering.

In all the capitals of poverty, the poor carry bundles. They always keep them close by. When they sit down, they place them by their side and watch over them. What do they put in them? Everything: wood gathered in a park, hastily, crusts of bread, bits of wire pulled off a fence, scraps of cloth. If the bundle is too heavy, they drag it along, in wheelbarrows or handcarts. Poverty always seems to be doing a moonlight flit. In Peking, Shanghai, Nanking, everyone is pulling or pushing: here men are straining to make their cart go forward; there they are on a bridge; the road climbs; they must struggle twice as hard; there are urchins about, always ready to help for a hand-out. Like the unemployed man in *Deux sous d'espoir* who positions himself halfway up a hill and pulls the carriage horses by the bridle. The tall building in the background is a lighthouse. At the top of the lighthouse is the eye of the West; its revolving gaze sweeps across China. The top three levels have been reserved for foreign press correspondents. How high up they are! Much too high to see what is happening down below. They dance high in the sky with their wives and mistresses. Meanwhile, at ground level, the porters push their carts and Chiang Kai-shek is being defeated by the communist armies. The Americans see neither the little flat dwellings of China nor the armed peasants nor the porters. Yet the porters have only to look up to see the lighthouse of America.

In all the capitals of poverty, people scavenge. They scavenge in the soil and the subsoil; they gather round refuse bins; they slip right into the rubble: 'What others throw away is mine; what is no longer of any use to them is good enough for me.' On waste ground near Peking, the rubbish piles up. This is the refuse of the poor; they have sifted through everything, they have already rummaged through their own rubbish; they have only left, reluctantly, what is uneatable, unusable, unspeakable, revolting. And yet the flock is there. On all fours. They will scavenge all day, every day.

In all the capitals of poverty, there is pilfering. Is it stealing? No, just picking things up. These bales of cotton have just been unloaded. If they stay an hour longer on the dock, they will disappear. No sooner have they been put down than the crowd rushes forward and surrounds them. Everyone attempts to pull off a handful of cotton. Many handfuls of cotton, gathered day after day – that makes an item of clothing. I recognize the look on the women's faces, I have seen it in Marseilles, in Algiers, in London, in the streets of Berlin; it is serious, quick and hounded, anguish mingles with greed. You have to grab before you are grabbed. When the bales have been loaded onto a lorry, the kids will run after it with outstretched hands. Meanwhile, in Nanking, there is shooting in the streets. Alone in the middle of a boulevard, a man is bent over an armchair which is ripped open; he wants to get its stuffing. If he does not get hit right between the eyes by one of the bullets whistling around his ears, he will have gathered enough fuel for one hour of just one winter's day.

Every day the poor people dig, scavenge and gather. Every day the artisans repeat their traditional movements. At every dawn, officers do their exercises in the gardens of the Forbidden City, while ageing ghosts drift through the palaces. Every morning Peking reconstructs its appearance of the previous day, the previous week, the previous millennium. In our country, industry is destroying all the old frameworks; but over there, why should they change? Cartier-Bresson has photographed eternity.

Fragile eternity; it is a tune played over and over again. To stop it, you would have to smash the record. And indeed it is going to be smashed. History is at the city gates; from day to day, in the rice fields, in the mountains, and on the plains, it is being made. One more day and then another one: it will be over; the old record will be smashed to pieces. These timeless snapshots are precisely dated; they fix forever the last moments of the Eternal.

Between the circular time of old China and the irreversible time of new China, there is an intermediate phase, a gelatinous duration equally distant from History and repetition: the time of *waiting*. The city has undone the sheaf of its millions of daily gestures: no longer does anyone file, or carve, or scrape, or trim, or adjust, or burnish. Abandoning their small living spaces, their ceremonies, their neighbours, people go and crowd together, in shapeless masses, in front of stations, on the docks. Houses empty. And the workshops. And the markets. In outlying locations, crowds gather, compact together, coagulate; their fine structures are crushed. Heavy, dense pictures replace the airy photos of old Peking. Waiting. Whenever they do not take control of History, the masses experience great events as periods of endless waiting. The masses of Peking and Shanghai are not making History; they are subjected to it. As are, moreover, the police who watch them, the soldiers who move among them, who return from the front, who never stop returning and who never go, the mandarins who take flight, and the generals who flee. Those who are making History have never seen the great imperial cities; they only know the mountains and the fields; in the fields and in the mountains, the destiny of China has been decided. For the first time, a capital awaits the pleasure of the country. History will appear in the form of a procession of peasants. Townspeople think of the country as an inert space which links the towns and which is crossed and devastated by armies until, in the towns, they have decided to make peace. But suddenly it reveals itself: it is living flesh, muscle; within this muscle, the towns are lodged like grains of urate. Yet the crowds are not afraid. Up there, the eye of America is spinning round in panic. But on the ground they have known for a long time that the communists have won. The rich curse Chiang Kai-shek as much as Mao Tse-tung. The peasants want to go back home: since everything is in the hands of the communists, they might as well go and meet them in the villages as in the towns. The workers and the poor begin to hope; the thousand individual waits of the time of Repetition have come together and fused in a single hope. The rest of the population march in processions and pray for peace: for any peace. It is a way of killing time. Before joining the bonzes and burning paper wands, they make the most of the opportunity to put their personal affairs in order. They go and rub the nose of an idol, for their own benefit; infertile girls press their stomachs against the stomachs of statues; after the ceremony, in the large pharmacy near the temple, people will be buying dried pellets which restore ardour to listless husbands and which warm the feet of wives.

As long as the authorities remain at their post, the crowd stays under pressure. The police surround it and contain it; but, unlike ours, they rarely strike: this policeman is getting impatient because they are hemming him in too tightly. He lifts his leg: is he going to kick out? No, he stamps in a puddle; having been splashed, the people will step back. But the gentlemen of the Kuomintang will not stay in place; they go off. There are a thousand left; a hundred left. Soon there will be none. The gentlemen who cannot leave, yellow men and white men, are pale with fear. During the period of transition, the base instincts of the population will be let loose: there will be pillaging, rape and murder. As a result the bourgeois of Shanghai pray for the communists to come; any kind of order rather than the fury of the people.

This time it is all over. The important people have left, the last policeman has disappeared; the bourgeoisie and the populace alone remain in the city. Will there be pillaging or not? Admirable crowds – when they no longer felt the weight of the burden that was crushing them, they hesitated for a moment and then, little by little, became decompressed; great masses return to a gaseous state. Look at the photographs; everybody has started to run. Where are they going? Pillaging? Not even that; they have entered the fine, abandoned houses and have scavenged, just as, only yesterday, they scavenged in the piles of rubbish. What have they taken? Practically nothing: the floorboards to make a fire. All is calm; let them come now, the peasants from the north: they will find an orderly city.

Remember June 1940, and those funereal giants who raced across a deserted Paris in their lorries and their tanks? Now, that was picturesque: not much voluptuousness, but blood and death, and a lot of pomp. The Germans wanted a ceremonious victory. That is what they had, and the handsome SS officers, standing on camouflaged vehicles, looked like priests, like executioners, like martyrs, like Martians, like anything except men. Now open the album. Children and youths are massed along the path of the victors; they are amused, curious; calm, they cross their arms and watch. Where is the victory? Where is the terror? Here is the first communist soldier seen in Shanghai since the beginning of the civil war. He is a little man with a dark, handsome face, who is carrying his equipment on the end of a stick, like our old soldiers when they came back from the war. This exhausted little man, these young spectators: you might think that you were at the finish of a running race. Turn the page and now look at the soldiers of the Eighth Army from behind, beneath their sunshades, lost on one of Shanghai's main avenues. Have these peasants taken the city, or will the city take them? They sit down. On the road or on the pavement, at the very spot where, only the day before, a seated crowd awaited them. That crowd has stood up and pushed up against them, dominating them with its size and looking at them. Usually, victors hide in order to rest; but it appears that these men are not interested in intimidating. Yet they are the ones who defeated the Kuomintang troops, armed by the Americans, they are the ones who held the Japanese army in check. They seem crushed by the tall buildings which surround them. The war is over; the peace must be won. The photos express wonderfully the solitude and the anguish of these peasants in the heart of a magnificent and rotting city. Behind their blinds, the gentlemen take heart: 'We will lead them by the nose.'

It did not take very long for those gentlemen to change their minds. But that is another story, one that Cartier-Bresson does not tell us. Let us thank him for being able to show us the most human of victories, the only one that we can love without reservation.

Jean-Paul Sartre, extracts from preface, *D'une Chine à l'autre* [photographs by Henri Cartier-Bresson] (Paris: Robert Delpire, 1954); trans. Azzedine Haddour, Steve Brewer, Terry McWilliams, in *Colonialism and Neocolonialism* (London and New York: Routledge, 2001) 17–29.

Allan Sekula
The Traffic in Photographs//1981

[...] August Sander, that rigorously and comprehensively sociologistic portraitist of the German people, delivered a radio talk in 1931 entitled 'Photography as a Universal Language'. The talk, the fifth in a series by Sander, stresses that a liberal, enlightened and even socially critical pedagogy might be achieved by the proper use of photographic means. Thus Sander's emphasis is less on the pictorial archive anticipated by François Arago in 1839 than on a global mode of communication that would hurdle barriers of illiteracy and language difference. But at the same time, Sander echoes the scientistic notions of photographic truth that made their initial authoritative appearance in Arago's report [on the Daguerrotype][1]:

Today with photography we can communicate our thoughts, conceptions and

> realities to all the people on the earth; if we add the date of the year we have the power to fix the history of the world ...
>
> Even the most isolated Bushman could understand a photograph of the heavens – whether it showed the sun or the moon or the constellations. In biology, in the animal and plant world, the photograph as picture language can communicate without the help of sound. But the field in which photography has so great a power of expression that language can never approach it, is physiognomy ...[2]

Perhaps it is understandable that in his enthusiasm for photographic enlightenment Sander led his unseen radio audience to believe that a Copernican cosmology and a mechanically rendered Albertian perspective might constitute trans-historical and trans-cultural discourses: photography could deliver the heliocentric and perspectival truths of the Renaissance to any human viewer.

Further, Sander describes photography as the truth vehicle for an eclectic array of disciplines, not only astronomy but history, biology, zoology, botany and physiognomy (and clearly the list is not meant to be exhaustive). Two paragraphs later, his text seeks to name the source of the encyclopaedic power to convey virtually all the world's knowledges: 'No language on earth speaks as comprehensively as photography, always providing that we follow the chemical and optic and physical path to demonstrable truth, and understand physiognomy. Of course you have to have decided whether you will serve culture or the marketplace.'[3] In opposing photographic truth to commercial values, and in regarding photography as 'a special discipline with special laws and its own special language',[4] Sander is assuming an uncompromisingly modernist stance. This position is not without its contradictions. Thus, on the one hand Sander claims that photography constitutes a 'language' that is born autonomous and universal; on the other, photography is subsumed within the logical order of the natural sciences. The 'laws' that are 'special' to photography turn out to be those of chemistry and optics. From this subordinate position photography functions as the vehicle for a scientific pedagogy. For Arago, photography is a means of aggressively acquiring the world's truth; for Sander, photography benignly disseminates these truths to a global audience. Although the emphasis in the first instance is on acquisition, and in the second on distribution, both projects are fundamentally rooted in a shared epistemology. This epistemology combines a faith in the universality of the natural sciences and a belief in the transparency of representation.

For Sander, physiognomy was perhaps the highest of the human sciences, which are in turn merely extensions of natural scientific method. Physiognomic empiricism serves as the basis for what Alfred Döblin, in his preface to Sander's *Antlitz der Zeit* (Face of Our Time, 1929), described as a project methodologically analogous to medical science, thereby collapsing history and sociology into social-anatomy:

> You have in front of you a kind of cultural history, better, sociology of the last 30 years. How to write sociology without writing, but presenting photographs instead, photographs of faces and not national costumes, this is what the photographer accomplished with his eyes, his mind, his observations, his knowledge and last but not least his considerable photographic ability. Only through studying comparative anatomy can we come to an understanding of nature and the history of the internal organs. In the same way this photographer has practised comparative anatomy and therefore found a scientific point of view beyond the conventional photographer.[5]

The echoes of nineteenth-century positivism and its Enlightenment antecedents are deafening here, as they are in Sander's own implicit hierarchy of knowledge. The grim master-voice is that of Auguste Comte's systematic and profoundly influential effort to invent sociology (or 'social physics', as he initially labelled the new discipline) on the model of the physical sciences, in his *Cours de philosophie positive* of 1830-42.[6] [...]

Of course Sander never proffered so vigorous a mode of physiognomical interpretation for his photographs. He never suggested that each fragment of facial anatomy be isolated through the kind of pictorial surgery sketched by Lavater [the founder of physiognomics] and practised by his myriad disciples. I suspect Sander wanted to envelop his project in the legitimating aura of science without violating the aesthetic coherence and semantic ambiguity of the traditional portrait form. Despite his scientistic rhetoric, his portraits never achieve the 'precision' and 'exactitude' so desired by physiognomists of all stripes. Sander's commitment was, in effect, to a sociologically extended variant of formal portraiture. His scientism is revealed in the ensemble, in the attempt to delineate a social anatomy. More than anything else, physiognomy served as a telling *metaphor* for this project.

The historical trajectories of physiognomy, and of the related practices of phrenology and anthropometrics, are extremely complicated and are consistently interwoven with the history of photographic portraiture. And as was the case with photography, these disciplines gave rise to the same contradictory but connected rationales. These techniques for reading the body's signs seemed to promise both egalitarian and authoritarian results. At the one extreme, the more liberal apologetic promoted the cultivation of a common human understanding of the language of the body: all of humanity was to be both subject and object of this new egalitarian discourse. At the other extreme – and this was certainly the dominant tendency in actual social practice – a specialized way of knowledge was openly harnessed to the new strategies of social channelling and control that characterized the mental asylum, the penitentiary and eventually the factory employment office. Unlike the egalitarian mode, these latter projects drew an unmistakable line between the professional reader of the body's signs – the psychiatrist, physiologist, criminologist or industrial psychologist – and the 'diseased', 'deviant' or 'biologically inferior' object of cure, reform or discipline.

August Sander stood to the liberal side of positivism in his faith in a universal pedagogy. Yet like positivists in general, he was insensitive to the *epistemological* differences between peoples and cultures. Difference would seem to exist only on the surface; all peoples share the same modes of perception and cognition, as well as the same natural bodily codes of expression. For nineteenth-century positivism, anthropological difference became quantitative rather than qualitative. This reduction opened the door to one of the principal justifications of social Darwinism. Inferiority could presumably be measured and located on a continuous calibrated scale. Armed with calipers, scalpel and camera, scientists sought to prove the absence of a governing intellect in criminals, the insane, women, workers and non-white people. Here again, one lineage stretches back beyond positivism and social Darwinism to the benign figure of Lavater, who proclaimed both the 'universality of physiognomic discernments' and defined a 'human nature' fundamentally constituted by a variable mixture of 'animal, moral and intellectual life.'[7]

But Sander, in contrast to his nineteenth-century predecessors, refused to link his belief in physiognomic science to biological determinism. He organized his portraiture in terms of a social, rather than a racial, typology. As Anne Halley has noted in a perceptive essay on the photographer, herein lay the most immediate difference between Sander's physiognomic project and that of Nazi race 'theorists' like Hans F.K. Günther who deployed physiognomic readings of photographic portraits to establish both the biological superiority of the Nordic 'race' and the categorical otherness of the Jews.[8] The very universalism of Sander's argument for photographic and physiognomic truth may well have been an indirect and somewhat naïve attempt to respond to the racial particularism of the Nazis, which 'scientifically' legitimated genocide and imperialism.

The conflict between Sander and Nazi *Rassentheorie*, which culminated in the gestapo's destruction of the plates for *Antlitz der Zeit* in 1934, is well remembered and celebrated by liberal historians of photography. One is tempted to emphasize a contrast between Sander's 'good' physiognomic science and the 'bad' physiognomic science of Günther and his ilk, without challenging the positivist underpinnings of both projects. That is, what is less apparent is that Sander, in his 'scientific' liberalism, shared aspects of the same general positivist outlook that was incorporated into the fascist project of domination. But in this, Sander was little different from other social democrats of his time. The larger questions that loom here concern the continuities between fascist, liberal capitalist, social democratic and bureaucratic socialist governments as modes of administration that subject social life to the authority or an institutionalized scientific expertise.

The politics of social democracy, to which Sander subscribed, demand that government be legitimated on the basis of formal representation. Despite the sense of impending collapse, of crisis-level unemployment and imminent world war conveyed by Sander in his radio speech of 1931, he sustains a curiously inflected faith in the *representativeness* of bourgeois parliamentary government. 'The historical image will become even clearer if we join together pictures typical of the many different groups that make up human society. For instance, we might consider a nation's parliament. If we began with the Right Wing and moved across the individual types to the farthest Left, we would already have a partial physiognomic image of the nation.'[9] Just as a picture stands for its referent, so parliament stands for a nation. In effect, Sander regards parliament as a picture in itself, a synecdochic sample of the national whole. This conflation of the mythologies of pictorial and political representation may well be fundamental to the public discourse of liberalism. Sander, unlike Bertolt Brecht or the left-wing photomontagist John Heartfield, believed that political relations were evident on the surface of things. Political revelation was a matter of careful sampling for Sander, his project shares the logic of the opinion poll. In this, Sander stands in the mainstream of liberal thinking on the nature of journalism and social documentation; he shares both the epistemology and the politics that accompany bourgeois realism. The deceptively clear waters of this mainstream flow from the confluence of two deep ideological currents. One current defends science as the privileged *representation* of the real, as the ultimate source of social truth. The other current defends parliamentary politics as the *representation* of a pluralistic popular desire, as the ultimate source of social good.

Despite Sander's tendency to collapse politics into a physiognomic typology, he never loses sight of the political arena as one of conflict and struggle. And yet, viewed as a whole, Sander's compendium of portraits from the Weimar period and earlier possess a haunting – and ideologically limiting – synchronicity for the contemporary viewer. One witnesses a kind of false stasis, the appearance of a tense structural equilibrium of social forces. Today, Sander's project suggests a neatly arranged chessboard that was about to be dashed to the floor by brown-shirted thugs. But despite Sander's and Döblin's claims to the contrary, this project was not then and is not now an adequate reading of German social history.

What of an even more ambitious photographic project, one that managed not only to freeze social life but also to render it invisible? I'm thinking here of that celebrated event in American postwar culture, the exhibition 'The Family of Man'. Almost thirty years after Sander's radio talk, the photographer Edward Steichen, who was director of the photography department at the Museum of Modern Art, voiced similarly catholic sentiments in an article published in 1960 in *Daedalus*, the journal of the American Academy of Arts and Sciences. Despite the erudite forum, the argument is simplistic, much more so than anything Sander ever claimed. 'Long before the birth of a word language the caveman communicated by visual images. The invention of photography gave visual communication its most simple, direct, universal language.' Steichen went on to tout the success of his Museum of Modern Art exhibition, 'The Family of Man', which by 1960 had been seen by 'some seven million people in the twenty-eight countries'. He continued, introducing a crude tautological psychologism into his view of photographic discourse: 'The audiences not only understand this visual presentation, they also participate in it, and identify themselves with the images, as if in corroboration of the words of a Japanese poet, "When you look into a mirror, you do not see your reflection, your reflection sees you".' Steichen, in this moment of fondness for Zen wisdom, understandably neglected to mention that the Japanese recipients of the exhibition insisted on the inclusion of a large photographic mural depicting the victims of the atomic bombings of Hiroshima and Nagasaki, thus resisting the ahistoricity of the photo essay's argument.

'The Family of Man', first exhibited in 1955, may well be the epitome of American cold war liberalism, with Steichen playing cultural attaché to Adlai Stevenson, the would-be good cop of US foreign policy, promoting a benign view of an American world order stabilized by the rule of international law. 'The Family of Man' universalizes the bourgeois nuclear family, suggesting a globalized, utopian family album, a family romance imposed on every corner of the earth. The family serves as a metaphor also for a system of international discipline and harmony. In the foreign showings of the exhibition, arranged by the United States Information Agency and co-sponsoring corporations like Coca-Cola, the discourse was explicitly that of American multinational capital and government – the new global management team – cloaked in the familiar and musty garb of patriarchy. Nelson Rockefeller, who had served as president of the MoMA board of trustees between 1946 and 1953, delivered a preview address that is revealing in terms of its own father fixation.

Rockefeller began his remarks in an appropriately internationalist vein, suggesting that the exhibition created 'a sense of kinship with all mankind'. He went on to say that 'there is a second message to be read from this profession of Edward Steichen's faith. It demonstrates that the essential unity of human experience, attitude and emotion are perfectly communicable through the medium of pictures, The solicitous eye of the Bantu father, resting upon the son who is learning to throw his primitive spear in search of food, is the eye of every father, whether in Montreal, Paris or in Tokyo.' For Rockefeller, social life begins with fathers teaching sons to survive in a Hobbesian world; all authority can be metaphorically equated with this primary relationship.

A close textual reading of 'The Family of Man' would indicate that it moves from the celebration of patriarchal authority – which finds its highest embodiment in the United Nations – to the final construction of an imaginary utopia that resembles nothing so much as a protracted state of infantile, pre-Oedipal bliss. The best-selling book version of the exhibition ends with the following sequence. First, there appears an array of portraits of elderly couples, mostly peasants or farmers from Sicily, Canada, China, Holland and the United States. The glaring exception in regard to class is a Sander portrait of a wealthy German landowner and his wife. Each picture is captioned with the repeated line from Ovid, 'We two form a multitude'. From these presumably archetypal parent figures we turn the page to find a large photograph of the United Nations General Assembly, accompanied by the opening phrases of the UN Charter. The next page offers a woman's lower body, bedecked in flowers and standing in water. The following five pages contain smaller photographs of children at play throughout the world, ending with W. Eugene Smith's famous photograph of his son and daughter walking from darkness into light in a garden. The final photograph in the book is quite literally a depiction of the oceanic state, a picture by Cedric Wright of churning surf.

A case could also be made for viewing 'The Family of Man' as a more-or-less unintentional popularization of the then dominant school of American sociology, Talcott Parsons's structural functionalism. Parsons' writings on the family celebrate the modern nuclear family as the most advanced and efficient of familiar forms, principally because the nuclear family establishes a clear-cut division of male and female roles. The male function, in this view, is primarily 'instrumental' and oriented towards achievement in the public sphere. The female function is primarily 'expressive' and restricted to the domestic sphere. Although 'The Family of Man' exhibits a great deal of nostalgia for the extended family engaged in self-sufficient agrarian production, the overall flow of the exhibition's loosely knit narrative traces a generalized family biography that adheres to the nuclear model.[10] [...]

My main point here is that 'The Family of Man', more than any other single photographic project, was a massive and ostentatious bureaucratic attempt to universalize photographic discourse. [...]

But this dream rings hollow, especially when we come across the following oxymoronic construction in Carl Sandburg's prologue to the book version of the exhibition: Sandburg describes *The Family of Man* as a 'multiplication table of living breathing human faces.'[11] Suddenly, arithmetic and humanism collide, forced by poetic licence into absurd harmony. Here, yet again, are the twin ghosts that haunt the practice of photography: the voice of a reifying technocratic objectivism and the redemptive voice of a liberal subjectivism. The statistics that seek to legitimate the exhibition, to demonstrate its value, begin to carry a deeper sense: the truth being promoted here is one of enumeration. This is an anaesthetized job of global accounting, a careful Cold War effort to bring about the ideological alignment of the neocolonial peripheries with the imperial centre. American culture of both elite and mass varieties was being promoted as more universal than that of the Soviet Union. [...]

Again, what are we to make of the argument that photography constitutes a universal language? Implicit in this claim is the suggestion that photography acts as a miraculous universal solvent upon the linguistic barriers between peoples. Visual culture, having been pushed to an unprecedented level of technical refinement, loses specificity, cultural difference is cancelled, and a 'common language' prevails on a global scale. Paradoxically, a medium that is seen as subtly responsive to the minutest details of time and place delivers these details through an unacknowledged, naturalized, epistemological grid. As the myth of a universal photographic language would have it, photography is more natural than natural language, touching on a common, underlying system of desire and understanding closely tied to the senses. Photography would seem to be a way of *knowing* the world directly – this is the scientistic aspect of our faith in the powers of the photographic image. But photography would also seem to be a way of *feeling* the world directly, with a kind of pre-linguistic, affective openness of the visual sense – this is the aestheticist aspect of our faith in the medium. As a symbolic practice, then, photography constitutes not a universal language but a paradoxical yoking of a primitivist, Rousseauian dream, the dream of romantic naturalism, with an unbounded faith in a technological imperative. The worldliness of photography is the outcome, not of any immanent universality of meaning, but of a project of global domination. The language of the imperial centres is imposed, both forcefully and seductively, upon the peripheries. [...]

IV. Conclusion

A final anecdote to end this essay, much too long already. Crossing the cavernous main floor of New York's Grand Central Station recently, I looked up to see the latest instalment in a thirty-odd year series of monumental, back-illuminated dye-transfer transparencies; a picture, taken low to the wet earth of rural Ireland, a lush vegetable apparition of landscape and cottage, was suspended above this gloomy urban terminal for human traffic. With this image – seemingly bigger and more illusionistic, even in its stillness, than Cinerama – everything that is absent is made present. Above: stillness, home, hearth, the soil, the remote old country for many travellers, an affordable or unaffordable vacation spot for others, a seductive sight for eyes that must strain hurriedly in the gloom to read timetables. Below: the city, a site for the purposeful flow of bodies. Accompanying this giant photograph, a caption read, as nearly as I can remember: 'PHOTOGRAPHY: THE UNIVERSAL LANGUAGE / EASTMAN KODAK 1880 –1980.'

And what of the universality of this name, Kodak, unknown to any language until coined in 1888 by George Eastman, inventor of roll film, pioneer in horizontal and vertical corporate integration, in the global mass-marketing of consumer goods? Eastman offered this etymological explanation in 1924 in American Photography: 'Philologically, therefore, the word 'kodak' is as meaningless as a child's first "goo". Terse, abrupt to the point of rudeness, literally bitten off by firm unyielding consonants at both ends, it snaps like a camera shutter in your face. What more could one ask?'[12] And so we are introduced to a 'language' that is primitive, infantile, aggressive – the imaginary discourse of the machine. The crucial question remains to be asked: can photography be anything else?

1 [footnote 8 in source] See Helmut and Alison Gernsheim, *L.J.M. Daguerre: The History of the Diorama and the Daguerreotype* (New York, 1968) 88, 99.

2 [12] August Sander, 'Photography as a Universal Language', trans. Anne Halley, *Massachusetts Review*, vol. XIX, no. 4 (1978) 674–5.

3 [13] Ibid., 675.

4 [14] Ibid., 679.

5 [15] Alfred Döblin, 'About Faces, Portraits and Their Reality: Introduction to August Sander, *Antlitz der Zeit*' (1929), in *Germany: The New Photography 1927–33*, ed. David Mellor (London, 1978) 58.

6 [16] Auguste Comte, *Cours de philosophie positive* (1830–42) in *Auguste Comte and Positivism: The Essential Writings*, ed. Gertrud Lenzer (New York, 1975).

7 [19] Johann Caspar Lavater, *Essays on Physiognomy*, trans. Henry Hunter (London, 1792) 13.

8 [20] Anne Halley, 'August Sander', *Massachusetts Review*, vol. XIX, no. 4 (1978) 663–73. See also Robert Kramer, 'Historical Commentary', in *August Sander: Photographs of an Epoch* (Philadelphia, 1980) 11–38, for a discussion of Sander's relation to physiognomic traditions.

9 [22] Sander, 'Photography as a Universal Language', op. cit., 678.

10 [27] See Talcott Parsons et al., *Family, Socialization and Interaction Progress* (New York, 1955) and the critique provided in Mark Poster, *Critical Theory of the Family* (New York, 1978) 78–84.

11 [29] Carl Sandburg, 'Prologue', *The Family of Man* (New York, 1955).

12 [51] George Eastman, quoted in J.M. Eder, *History of Photography*, op. cit., 489.

Allan Sekula, extracts from 'The Traffic in Photographs', *Art Journal*, vol. 41, no. 1 (Spring 1981) 15–16; 17–18; 18–20; 21; 23.

Adam Broomberg and Oliver Chanarin
Unconcerned But Not Indifferent[1]//2008

The most political decision you make is where you direct people's eyes.
– Wim Wenders, *The Act of Seeing*.[2]

The tremendous development of photojournalism has contributed practically nothing to the revelation of the truth about conditions in this world. On the contrary photography, in the hands of the bourgeoisie, has become a terrible weapon against the truth. The vast amount of pictured material that is being disgorged daily by the press and that seems to have the character of truth serves in reality only to obscure the facts. The camera is just as capable of lying as the typewriter.
– Bertolt Brecht, 1931[3]

A recent photograph, taken during the assassination of Benazir Bhutto in December 2007, captures the essence of the photojournalistic image as it was originally conceived by early pioneers like Robert Capa. Taken an instant after the bomb detonated, at a distance of just ten metres from its epicentre, it is not really a photograph at all, but a blur, a piece of smudged evidence that testifies to the fact that our journalist was there, as close as he could possibly be to the lethal action, when the shutter opened and closed.

Photographs hardly ever break the news these days. In Scotland Yard's recent investigation into the series of events that lead to Bhutto's death, videos taken on mobile phones, rather than the work of professional photojournalists (like this one above), were used as evidence. In recent years some of the most striking visual images of major news events, such as 9/11, Abu Ghraib, the Tsunami and Hurricane Katrina, have been captured by ordinary people who just happen to be there with their mobile phones or video cameras. Where does this leave the photojournalist who has been acting as our brave proxy, sending us reports from the front line of life since the Spanish Civil War?

The World Press Photo has been handing out annual awards to professionals for the past 51 years, and has just announced its winners for 2007 (the photograph above won first prize for 'spot news'). We were asked to participate as jury members in awarding the prizes this year; a good opportunity to gauge the vital signs of a photographic genre in crisis.

The impact of the awards on the industry cannot be underestimated. An exhibition of the winning images are seen by over 2 million people in 50 different countries and 45,000 copies of the book circulates in six languages.

Clearly they have a profound effect on the way world events are represented by professional photojournalists.

Flicking through the 81,000 images originally submitted, a sense of *déjà vu* is inevitable. Again and again similar images are repeated, with only the actors and settings changing. Grieving mothers, charred human remains, sunsets, women giving birth, children playing with toy guns, cock fights, bull fights, Havana street scenes, reflections in puddles, reflections in windows, football posts in unlikely locations, swaddled babies, portraits taken through mosquito nets, needles in junkies' arms, derelict toilets, Palestinian boys throwing stones, contorted Chinese gymnasts, Karl Lagerfeld, models preparing for fashion shows backstage, painted faces, bodies covered in mud, monks smoking cigarettes, pigeons silhouetted against the sky, Indian Sardus, children leaping into rivers, pigs being slaughtered.

The twelve-strong jury must endure a barrage of photographic clichés over a period of seven days and nights, in order to locate one single image, the World Press Photo of the year. There are also prizes for photographs in a variety of categories, but it is this single image that gets the real attention. How do twelve people reach a consensus? And what criteria could possibly be used to nominate just one image?

First we were assembled into a windowless room in Amsterdam, squeezed between a digital projector and a coffee machine, and sworn to secrecy. We are six photographers specializing in war, nature, sports, editorial and art photography, plus five photo editors and a curator.

The World Press Photo awards have been running for over five decades and in that time a clear procedure has evolved. It is a highly disciplined, mathematical system designed by psychologists to elicit consensus from a group of diverse, opinionated individuals. The total number of images had already been reduced to 17,000 the previous week by the first-round jury. Most of the pornography and pictures of domestic cats had been removed. Our job was to reduce that number to one. Each of us clasped a voting button in the half darkness, and as the images flashed across the screen we voted anonymously to keep it in the competition or 'to kill it'. As we progressed the long serving secretary and master of ceremonies, Stephen Mayes, announced in dry tones the results of each round of votes, a stream of INs and OUTs, occasionally elaborating, 'birds of paradise IN, snakes OUT, suicide bomb IN, dead children OUT, women with acid burns IN, Chairman Mao impersonator OUT, Guantánamo Bay detainee IN, sumo wrestlers OUT ...' The mechanism used for voting, nine buttons connected to a central computer display, was originally developed for a Dutch TV game show.

At this stage caption information is not available; each image must be judged on aesthetic grounds, outside of the context for which it was created, severed from words of explanation. This is simply practical; the sheer volume of images precludes more intense scrutiny. But without names, dates, locations or interviews with the photographers the decision making process regresses into using only formal considerations; composition, lighting and focus. At times this feels obscene. We are asked to judge whether for example a photograph of a child suffocating to death in a mudslide is sufficiently beautiful to win a prize. On this occasion it seems not.

In the tradition of the World Press Photo awards, a photograph that relies on its caption to create meaning is impotent. This is a strange prejudice, considering every one of the images in the competition would have been accompanied by text in its original context. Susan Sontag warns against the decontextualization of images in her book *Regarding the Pain of Others*, when she describes how during fighting between Serbs and Croats at the beginning of the Balkan wars, the same photographs of children being killed in the shelling of a village were passed around at both Serb and Croat propaganda briefings.[4]

The issue of context was highlighted by one particular submission that showed a group of spectators holding up their mobile phones in order to photograph something out of frame, something going on behind the photographer. It could have been taken at any sporting event or music concert. It turned out to be a public execution in Iran. This photograph is not simply reporting an event but alerts us to something more disturbing, our desire to look at the spectacle of a man being executed, and the role of photography as a facilitator. It is precisely the image's ambiguity, its reliance on its caption, that makes it so much more interesting than the image of the prisoner himself, hanging from a rope, which the photographer also captured, and which made it into a later round before being eliminated. [...]

The [World Press Photo Awards] submissions attest to our insatiable hunger for images of suffering. 'Sight can be turned off; we have lids on our eyes', says Sontag.[5] But sometimes we just can't resist taking a look. Since its inception photojournalism has traded in images of human suffering. If one of its motivations for representing tragedy has been to change the world then it has been unsuccessful. Instead the profession has turned us into voyeurs, passively consuming these images, sharing in the moment without feeling implicated or responsible for what we are seeing. Roland Barthes summed up the analgesic effect of looking at images of horror when he wrote 'Someone has shuddered for us; reflected for us, judged for us; the photographer has left us nothing – except a simple right of intellectual acquiescence.'[6] Put another way, we look at events in photographs and feel relieved that they're not happening anywhere near us. [...]

One winning picture, a portrait of an exhausted soldier, was taken during a battle in Afghanistan against Taliban forces. It is a stolen image, catching the young American off guard as he wipes the sweat from his forehead with one hand. The blurred focus and pixelated JPEG compression make this image feel accidental and urgent, aesthetic codes that translate as 'Real'. For some members of the jury it was also 'painterly'– a vague term often used to describe photographs that reference certain painting techniques; the lighting of a Rembrandt portrait or Caravaggio's techniques of chiaroscuro, the sublime light of a Turner or a Friedrich. All conventions that help us to identify the photograph as something 'beautiful'.

As with the Madonna and child photograph this is a predictable World Press winner; an amalgam of all the images of war and death that we have embedded in our memory. It recalls the terror of Don McCullin's marine during the Battle of Hue in 1968, the resignation of the wounded marine in Larry Burrows' image taken in South Vietnam in 1966, the urgency of Capa's Republican soldier dying in 1936. The image referents go further back; the shape and stance of the soldier clearly reminds us of Goya's *Disasters of War* etchings of 1863. It seems we are casting the world in the same mould over and over again.

Tim Hetherington, who took this photograph, later told us the following illuminating anecdote. His photographs were first published by *Vanity Fair* who also happened to be running a feature on Francis Ford Coppola in the same edition. Both Tim's photographs from Afghanistan and stills from Coppola's *Apocalypse Now* were being printed on the office Xerox machine. A staff writer came to collect the fictional stills and accidentally walked away with the real thing.

A resemblance to the famous Vietnam images by Burrows and McCullin is not coincidental – this image represents a nostalgia for the days of photojournalism at its sexiest, most lucrative and effective; the days when the press image was morally significant. In order to take a photograph like this these days the photographer must be embedded with the American forces. Although censorship has eased since the Gulf War, the US military still attempts to control representation of American casualties, body bags, the funerals of servicemen and prisoners. Publications are offered access to troops with a tacit understanding that certain images will not be reproduced. Indeed, a study in the *Los Angeles Times* found that between 11 September 2004 and 28 February 2005, neither that paper, nor the *New York Times*, *The Washington Post*, *Time Magazine* or *Newsweek*, published a single picture of a dead American soldier.[7] News corporations always concerned to keep major advertisers happy, operate what has been termed 'privatized censorship'.

This is important because war photographers have a tendency to think of themselves as anti-war photographers, operating outside of the machinery of conflict. James Nachtwey, who has photographed in conflict zones for almost three decades, qualifies this as follows. 'At the very beginning, I think I was still interested in the dynamics of war itself as a kind of fascinating study. And it evolved into more of a mission whereby I think to present pictures of situations that are unacceptable in human terms became a form of protest. So I found that my pictures were actually specifically trying to mitigate against the war itself ...'[8] Sadly the photographers' intention does not always inform the meaning of a photograph and it is hard to see how the images produced by Nachtwey or this year's winning picture can be perceived as critical of war. What makes the profession a secure one, and what ultimately nullifies the political force of any of the images, is its reliance on one pretty dependable thing – the world's permanent state of war. As Sontag remarks, 'War-making and picture-taking are congruent activities'.[9] [...]

Yet comparing so many diverse images and ultimately declaring one of them a winner feels meaningless. Do we even need to be producing these images any more? Do we need to be looking at them? We have enough of an image archive within our heads to be able to conjure up a representation of any manner of pleasure or horror. Does the photographic image even have a role to play any more? Video footage, downloaded from the internet, conveys the sounds and textures of war like photographs never could. High definition video cameras create high-resolution images twenty-four photographs a second, eliminating the need to click the shutter. But since we do still demand illustrations to our news then there is a chance to make images that challenge our preconceptions, rather than regurgitate old clichés.

There is one more photograph to consider. It was knocked out of the competition late in the bargaining then brought back at the end for an honourable mention. The photograph depicts a hand-painted shooting target, probably made by a member of a German army unit, depicting a lush, green landscape placed in the arid Afghanistan landscape. The photographer highlights the juxtaposition and through this visual strategy suggests that this is perhaps a portrait of a European psychological landscape projected onto the foreign, barren one. An interesting question about the nature of the war starts to form. Compared with the photograph taken during Bhutto's assassination, this mode of image-making transforms the photojournalist from an event-gathering machine, into something slightly more intelligent, more reflective and more analytical about our world, the world of images and about the place where these two worlds collide. As Tod Papageorge, photographer and professor of photography at Yale University, recently remarked in a live debate at the New York Public Library, 'If your pictures are not good enough, you aren't reading enough'.[10] Perhaps this reworking of Capa's oft repeated mantra offers a clue towards a new language in photojournalism – one that presents images that are more aware of what they fail to show; images that communicate the impossibility of representing the pain and horror of personal tragedy.

1 The epitaph on Man Ray's grave.

2 Wim Wenders, *The Act of Seeing* (London: Faber & Faber, 1997) cited in David Levi Strauss, *Between The Eyes: Essays on Photography and Politics* (New York: Aperture, 2003) 1.

3 From the tenth anniversary issue of *A-I-Z* magazine, in Douglas Kahn, *John Heartfield: Art and Mass Media* (New York: Tanam Press, 1985) 64.

4 Susan Sontag, *Regarding the Pain of Others* (London: Penguin, 2003) 9.

5 Ibid., 105.

6 Roland Barthes, 'Shock Photos' (1979), in *The Eiffel Tower and Other Mythologies* (New York: Hill and Wang, 1979) 71.

7 *Beautiful Suffering: Photography and the Traffic of Pain*, ed. Mark Reinhardt, Holly Edwards and Erina Duganne (Williamstown, Massachusetts: Williams College Museum of Art/Chicago: University of Chicago Press) 18.

8 From a transcript of James Nachtwey in conversation with Elizabeth Farnsworth, a NewsHour with Jim Lehrer production for PBS.

9 Sontag, op. cit., 66.

10 'Collapsing images', talk hosted by Blind Spot at The New York Public Library, 3 November 2007, part 3 of the series 'Truth and Authenticity in Photography'.

Adam Broomberg and Oliver Chanarin, extracts from 'Unconcerned But Not Indifferent', *Foto8* (5 March 2008).

David Levi Strauss
The Documentary Debate//2003

So, what does a photograph expose? It exposes, says Derrida, the relation to the law. What he means is that every photo poses itself as this question: Are we allowed to view what is being exposed?
– Avital Ronell, interviewed by Andrea Juno in *Angry Women*, 1991

It is excellent that people should be starting to argue about this again.
– Opening line of Ernst Bloch's defence of Expressionism (contra Georg Lukács), 1938

The relation between aesthetics and politics was a matter of great contention at the end of the twentieth century. Although too much of the discussion about it consisted of apodictic pronouncements and invective dismissals, it was good to have people arguing about it again. From where there is heat there may occasionally come some light.

When the 'Culture Wars' in the United States spread to censorship battles over the photographs of Robert Mapplethorpe, Andres Serrano and David Wojnarowicz, the documentary veracity and political content of aesthetic images were put on public trial. From the beginning of these conflicts, the right recognized what the real stakes were in this 'war between cultures and ... about the meaning of "culture"' (per Indiana Republican Representative Henry Hyde); they recognized the subversive nature of art and responded accordingly. On the other hand, one of the left's most articulate antecedents to this trial was the 'anti-aesthetic' branch of postmodern criticism, which Hal Foster characterized in 1983 as questioning 'the very notion of the aesthetic, its network of ideas', including 'the notion of the aesthetic as subversive', claiming that 'its criticality is now largely illusory'.[1]

During this same time, the theory and criticism of photography was being transformed by the emergence of a new, strong materialist analysis of photography by writers such as Martha Rosler, Allan Sekula, Abigail Solomon-Godeau and John Tagg, among others. One of the most trenchant and persistent critiques arising from this tendency was that of 'social documentary' photography, focusing especially on the aestheticization of the documentary image. One measure of the success of this critique is the extent to which its assumptions and conclusions were accepted and absorbed into mainstream writing about photography.

The 9 September 1991 issue of the *New Yorker* carried an article by Ingrid Sischy, titled 'Good Intentions', on the work of Brazilian photographer Sebastião Salgado. Sischy upbraids Salgado for being too popular and too successful, and also for being too 'uncompromisingly serious' and 'weighty'; for being opportunistic and self-aggrandizing, and also too idealistic; for being too spiritual, and also for being 'kitschy' and 'schmaltzy'. But Sischy's real complaint about Salgado's photographs is that they threaten the boundary between aesthetics and politics. The complaint is couched in the familiar terms of a borrowed political critique:

> Salgado is too busy with the compositional aspects of his pictures – and with finding the 'grace' and 'beauty' in the twisted forms of his anguished subjects. And this beautification of tragedy results in pictures that ultimately reinforce our passivity toward the experience they reveal. To aestheticize tragedy is the fastest way to anaesthetize the feelings of those who are witnessing it. Beauty is a call to admiration, not to action.[2]

The substantive critique upon which this by now conventional criticism is based can be found in the classic debate within German Marxism that occurred from the 1930s to the 1950s, involving Ernst Bloch, Georg Lukács, Bertolt Brecht, Walter Benjamin and Theodor Adorno.[3]

The principal source for the 'aestheticization of tragedy' argument is Walter Benjamin's essay 'The Author As Producer', in which he speaks of 'the way certain modish photographers proceed in order to make human misery an object of consumption.'[4] What is often forgotten by those who appropriate this critique is its historical context within this debate. Benjamin's criticisms here specifically refer to certain products of the Neue Sachlichkeit (New Objectivity) movement in literature and art, which was itself a reaction against Expressionism, professing a return to objectivity of vision. When Benjamin charges that 'it has succeeded in turning abject poverty itself, by handling it in a modish, technically perfect way into an object of enjoyment,' he is referring to the well-known picture book by Albert Renger-Patzsch titled *Die Welt ist schön* (The world is beautiful). And he is expressly referring to the New Objectivity as a literary movement when he says that 'it transforms political struggle so that it ceases to be a compelling motive for decision and becomes an object of comfortable contemplation'. There are contemporary photographers who are heirs to the New Objectivity, but Salgado is not one of them, and to apply these criticisms to his work is a politically pointed inversion.

The distinction is made eloquently, and in a way that Benjamin would surely have appreciated, by Uruguayan writer Eduardo Galeano in his essay 'Salgado, 17 Times', which appeared in the San Francisco Museum of Modern Art's catalogue to the 1990 Salgado show:

> Salgado photographs people. Casual photographers photograph phantoms.
>
> As an article of consumption poverty is a source of morbid pleasure and much money. Poverty is a commodity that fetches a high price on the luxury market. Consumer-society photographers approach but do not enter. In hurried visits to scenes of despair or violence they climb out of the plane or helicopter, press the shutter release, explode the flash: they shoot and run. They have looked without seeing and their images say nothing. Their cowardly photographs soiled with horror or blood may extract a few crocodile tears, a few coins, a pious word or two from the privileged of the earth, none of which changes the order of their universe. At the sight of the dark-skinned wretched, forsaken by God and pissed on by dogs, anybody who is nobody confidentially congratulates himself: life hasn't done too badly by me, in comparison. Hell serves to confirm the virtues of paradise.
>
> Charity, vertical, humiliates. Solidarity, horizontal, helps. Salgado photographs from inside, in solidarity.[5]

Are Galeano and Sischy looking at the same images? What is the political difference in the way they are looking? In another part of his essay, Galeano (who was forced into exile from his native Uruguay for having 'ideological ideas', as one of the dictator's functionaries put it) locates Salgado's transgression: 'From their mighty silence, these images, these portraits, question the hypocritical frontiers that safeguard the bourgeois order and protect its right to power and inheritance.'[6]

This is the disturbing quality of Salgado's work that so divides viewers. Like all politically effective images, the best of Salgado's photographs work in the fissures, the wounds, of the social. They cause those who see them to ask themselves: Are we allowed to view what is being exposed? In an essay on 'Active Boundaries', the poet Michael Palmer relates Salgado's work to that of Paul Celan, and notes:

> The subject of Salgado's photojournalism, we must continually remind ourselves, is not there, is not in fact the visible but the invisible: what has been repressed and will not be spoken. It appears always at the edge of the frame or in the uneasy negotiation among the space of origin, the framed space of the work, and the social space to which it has been removed, which is also a cultural space, of the aesthetic.[7]

The anti-aesthetic tendency can easily become an anaesthetic one, an artificially induced unconsciousness to protect oneself from pain, and to protect the 'hypocritical frontiers' of propriety and privilege. It is unseemly to look right into the face of hunger, and then to represent it in a way that compels others to look right into it as well. It is an abomination, an obscenity, an ideological crime.

When one, anyone, tries to represent someone else, to 'take their Picture' or 'tell their story', they run headlong into a minefield of real political problems. The first question is: what right have *I* to represent *you*? Every photograph of this kind must be a negotiation, a complex act of communication. As with all such acts, the likelihood of success is extremely remote, but does that mean it shouldn't be attempted? In his magnificent defence of modern art against Lukács, Brecht wrote:

> In art there is the fact of failure, and the fact of partial success. Our metaphysicians must understand this. Works of art can fail so easily; it so difficult for them to succeed. One man will fall silent because of lack of feeling; another, because his emotion chokes him. A third frees himself, not from the burden that weighs on him, but only from a feeling of unfreedom. A fourth breaks his tools because they have too long been used to exploit him. The world is not obliged to be sentimental. Defeats should be acknowledged; but one should never conclude from them that there should be no more struggles.[8]

A documentary practice that tries to avoid the difficulties of such communication is not worthy of the name. After the aestheticization argument made social documentary photography of any kind theoretically indefensible, a number of articles appeared calling for its recuperation as 'new documentary'. In his essay 'Toward a New Social Documentary', Grant Kester wrote:

> If social documentary can be recuperated as a new documentary, it is precisely because it was never entirely aestheticized in the first place. There must be a core of authentic practice in documentary. It seems clear that this authenticity rests in its ability to act not only as art, but also in the kind of concrete social struggles that gave it its original character.[9]

The assumptions here are clear: the 'aestheticized' (art) is not 'authentic', but always already supplementary, added on to the 'core of authentic practice'. It is also supplementary – perhaps even antithetical – to 'concrete social struggles'. Isn't this just the flip side of the right's view of art: that art is inauthentic and supplementary and politically suspect? The doctrinaire right contends that politics has no place in art, while the doctrinaire left contends that art has no place in politics. Both takes are culturally restrictive and historically inaccurate.

The idea that the more transformed or 'aestheticized' an image is, the less 'authentic' or politically valuable it becomes, is one that needs to be seriously questioned. Why can't beauty be a call to action? The unsupported and careless use of 'aestheticization' to condemn artists who deal with politically charged subjects recalls Brecht's statement that '"the right thinking" people among us, whom Stalin in another context distinguishes from creative people, have a habit of spell-binding our minds with certain words used in an extremely arbitrary sense'.[10]

To represent is to aestheticize; that is, to transform. It presents a vast field of choices but it does not include the choice not to transform, not to change or alter whatever is being represented. It cannot be a pure process, in practice. This goes for photography as much as for any other means of representation. But this is no reason to back away from the process. The aesthetic is not objective and is not reducible to quantitative scientific terms. Quantity can only measure physical phenomena, and is misapplied in aesthetics, which often deals with what is not there, imagining things into existence. To become legible to others, these imaginings must be socially and culturally encoded. That is aestheticization.

When Benjamin wrote that 'the tendency of a work of literature can be politically correct only if it is also correct in the literary sense', he meant that the way something is made (its poetics) is political. Carried over into photography, that might mean that being politically correct doesn't signify much unless the work is also visually and conceptually compelling, or rather that these two things are not mutually exclusive, nor even separate. To be compelling, there must be tension in the work; if everything has been decided beforehand, there will be no tension and no compulsion to the work. In the latter kind of imagery, the viewer's choice is reduced to acceptance or rejection of the 'message', without becoming involved in a more complex response. Such images may work as propaganda (the effectiveness of which is quantitatively measurable), but they will not work at other points on the spectrum of communication.

Aestheticization is one of the ways that disparate peoples recognize themselves in one another. Photographs by themselves certainly cannot tell 'the whole truth' – they are always only instants. What they do most persistently is to register the relation of photographer to subject – the distance from one to another – and this understanding is a profoundly important political process, as Marx himself suggested: 'Let us suppose that we had carried out production as human beings ... Our products would be so many mirrors in which we saw reflected our essential nature.'[11]

1 Hal Foster, 'Postmodernism: A Preface', in idem, ed., *The Anti-Aesthetic: Essays on Postmodern Culture* (Port Townsend, Washington: Bay Press, 1983) xv.

2 Ingrid Sischy, 'Good Intentions', *New Yorker* (9 September 1991) 92. [...]

3 *Aesthetics and Politics*, trans. Ronald Taylor (London and New York: Verso, 1980).

4 Walter Benjamin, 'The Author As Producer' (1934), in Victor Burgin, ed., *Thinking Photography* (London: Macmillan, 1982) 24.

5 Eduardo Galeano, 'Salgado, 17 Times,' trans. Asa Zatz, in *Sebastião Salgado: An Uncertain Grace* (New York: Aperture, in association with the San Francisco Museum of Modern Art, 1990) 11.

6 Ibid., 12.

7 Michael Palmer, 'Active Boundaries: Poetry at the Periphery' (1992), in *Onward: Contemporary Poetry and Poetics*, ed. Peter Baker (New York: Peter Lang Publishing, 1996) 265.

8 *Aesthetics and Politics*, op. cit., 74.

9 Grant Kester, 'Toward a New Social Documentary', *Afterimage*, vol. 14, no. 8 (March 1987) 14.

10 *Aesthetics and Politics*, op. cit., 76.

11 Karl Marx, 'Comments on James Mill' (1844) in the *Collected Works*; quoted by W.J.T. Mitchell in *Iconology: Image, Text, Ideology* (Chicago: University of Chicago Press, 1986) 186.

David Levi Strauss, 'The Documentary Debate: Aesthetic or Anaesthetic? Or, What's So Funny About Peace, Love, Understanding, and Social Documentary Photography?', *Between the Eyes: Essays on Photography and Politics* (New York: Aperture, 2003) 3–11.

Alfredo Jaar
Interview with Phong Bui, Dore Ashton and David Levi Strauss//2009

Phong Bui What strikes me the most about the film installation *The Sound of Silence* (2006) is that, based on the available news report and the photographer Kevin Carter's own writing, you were able to construct your own text that was concise and effective. In exactly eight minutes, not only do we get the entire story of Carter and his eventual suicide, we're also reminded of the greater political struggle and human tragedy, which has been more or less the central focus of your preoccupation as an artist ever since you did your first project, *Studies on Happiness* in 1979. Could you tell us how it came about, since there were a few years between when you first learned of the subject and when the piece was made?

Alfredo Jaar When I first saw the photograph by Kevin Carter published along with the article 'Sudan is Described as Trying to Placate the West', on 26 March 1993 in the *New York Times*, I was struck and taken by its problematic power immediately. My first impulse was to cut it out and save it in my archives. Then, a year later, came the news that Carter had received the Pulitzer Prize, which, only a few months later, led to his suicide. And that was when I felt strongly that I had to do something about this event. It took me roughly a year to write the piece, and so I wrote it in 1995, and knew exactly what I wanted to do with it, but there was no technical way of doing it at the time – computers had yet to become available. I first thought of it being like a performance or a play. Then I thought about doing it with a slide projector, as I had done once for a similar piece for the Rwanda Project called *Slide and Sound Piece*, but it became too complicated, so I abandoned the whole project and let it stay dormant for exactly ten years. Then, in 2005, I met Ravi Rajan, who is a technological genius, and during one of our conversations I told him about the technological difficulties I had with the piece, and he said he could design a new programme that would control the text, the projector, the green and red lights, as well as the flashlights, and that it could easily be converted into one operable installation. [...]

Dore Ashton I always have found in your work an ethical component, or critique of human behaviour. I remember in Andrzej Wajda's *Love at Twenty*, which begins with a photographer who witnesses a little boy who falls into the bear pit at the zoo, he hesitates for a minute. Instead of saving the little boy he takes the photograph; similarly, the ethic of the eyewitness photographer is engaged in your piece. Could you tell us what you think about that predicament?

Jaar Well, it is a very complex question, and it is really at the heart of the piece. As we all know, the objective and mission of the photojournalist is to show us the reality of the world. And in order to capture that reality, they go to dangerous and tragic places at the expense of their lives. I see them as the conscience of our humanity; they represent for me what is left of our humanity. And I think of them in these situations as signs of solidarity, first of all, because they are there. They truly understand that they are there to show these realities that the rest of us would rather ignore. I have great admiration for what they do. In fact I am a friend of quite a few of them. I would say that most photojournalists clearly understand their limitations, which doesn't mean that they don't intervene. But it is also dangerous when they do, simply because when they take a position in the middle of any of those situations, they will most likely get shot at, and there will be no witnessing possible. So you can imagine, they have to be able to balance between bringing the images home, and their natural humanist impulses. And believe me, when they witness these tragedies and do not intervene directly, they inevitably have to deal with that physical and mental justification. But for them, to document these realities is their way of intervening. I can assure you that the rate of suicides among photojournalists is one of the highest in the world.

Ashton I read that there were 300 photojournalists killed in the last five to six years, while many are still missing.

Jaar Exactly. They are there trying to do work that very few people are willing to do. They are trying to balance between these two impulses, and they suffer from it. Most people do not experience this, and I am not a photojournalist, but after my Rwanda experience when I was there among other photojournalists witnessing the genocide, I wanted to kill myself. I was ashamed of being a human being; I had to seek psychiatric counsel in order to cope with this situation. And this was just one experience. Imagine that now these people live with it constantly. They go from one conflict, one tragedy, to another. This is a very, very complex issue. I do not have an answer myself, and I am not sure any of us do.

Bui I remember seeing the documentary made by Dan Krauss, *The Death of Kevin Carter*, at Cinema Village in 2006, which dealt with details of Carter's own anguish as well as his own humanity. The reason why that photo was heavily criticized by Western audiences, as most of us agree, is largely because they saw all of Africa encapsulated within that small frame. And the conflict arose due to, on the one hand, that lack of understanding of the context in which the photo was taken, and on the other, the benefit of its message. Don't you also think that it was an iconic image, like those we've seen during the Vietnam War? I'm thinking of Nick Ut's horrific photo of the young naked Vietnamese girl (Pham Thi Kim Phúc) running from the napalm attack on the road near Trang Bang in 1972 with her extended arms. [...]

Jaar Exactly. First of all, I think Carter's photo is one of the most extraordinary images I've ever seen as a human being and as an artist. And I totally agree with you that the reason why it became so controversial is because it is too easy to blame Carter for being the vulture, where in fact we are the vultures, the vulture is us. We are the ones who are guilty of such criminal, barbaric indifference. And the vulture didn't need to open its wings to make that point.

Bui Which he waited for.

Jaar Yes, for twenty minutes. The truth is I've never seen an image translate so much and so well the guilt of what is called Western civilization. I am always reminded of Gandhi when he was asked, 'What do you think about Western civilization?' to which he answered, 'It would be a good idea.' [*laughter*.] Again, that image, for me, encapsulates that guilt and criminal indifference, because it really reveals our real relationship with the African continent, which is continued indifference. If you just look at the AIDS issue, for example, nearly 75 per cent of the AIDS population are African, and less than 100,000 of them are getting treatment per year. It is unbelievable. And criminal.

David Levi Strauss So much of photojournalism has to do with getting into position. That's what photojournalists do; they spend a lot of time getting into position. Once they're in position, they need to have everything working and be on: to react, to get what they're there to get. And in this particular installation, you put the viewer in that position, in relation to the Kevin Carter image. I noticed people coming into that space, and instead of sitting on either edge of the bench, they sat in the middle, as if they were getting into position to have an experience. I think the whole design and structure of the installation emphasized that position.

Jaar Right. That's why some people think that when the two lights on both ends of the screen flash, they're designed to shock them, and there's some truth to that, but my intention is that I am putting light on you, and you are being looked at, you are being photographed. I am making a kind of transfer of looking into while being looked at.

Ashton André Breton talked about the mirrors of inconstancy, without the silver wall, for which all those startling images of human catastrophe are perhaps no more than images. I often feel that your work has a similar transparency; when people are confronted with the work, they'll see what they see.

Jaar Everything is part of the visual apparatus. Nothing is hidden. The tempo or rhythm, which is one second faster than the normal comfortable reading pace, helped to create the subtle tension that still makes the viewer somewhat uncomfortable. They have to follow quite closely and fairly fast in order to read what's happening on the screen. [...]

Ashton What do you think about the fact that there is always resistance to a photojournalist, to such an extent that, not long ago, they tried to say that the famous Robert Capa photograph, 'The Falling Soldier', taken during the Spanish Civil War, was staged?

Jaar This *mise-en-scène*, that staging that some people do, is problematic. But now, most of them have a very clear vision of what they want to communicate, and sometimes they take this licence to affect the final result. And, of course, there is a limit to what all of us should do. For example, if I want to convey x feeling in one image to my audience which is thousands of miles away, drowning in a sea of consumption from newspapers, magazines, the Internet, etc, etc, and I feel that by moving this object one inch to the left, I will achieve my objective, I think that is what they are thinking about. It is not gratuitous. It is not just because it is a beautiful composition. It is more about how I am here, risking my life to photograph this reality, knowing that it will never convey even an inch of that reality. I am just making a representation of it. But while making a representation of that reality, I am creating a new reality. Every photograph is about making decisions. It is therefore a creative act, always. That is why some photojournalists think that, in making these kinds of minor interventions, it will help them to convey what they are trying to convey. But, of course, sometimes it can be read as a manipulation, as insensitive to the realities that they are experiencing.

Levi Strauss That's what happened with the *Los Angeles Times* photographer Brian Walski, who digitally altered an image of a British soldier and a group of Iraqi civilians with Photoshop, which cost him his job. In any case, with Carter's iconic image, what viewers project onto it is their sense of feeling betrayed, not just by Carter, who took the photograph which they object to, but by the entire apparatus. The apparatus has conspired to reveal their (our) true position of complicity.

Bui Yet they're compelled by what they see because it amplifies their safety.

Jaar You can look at all of these pictures and realize that there is always some kind of set-up, either way. I mean, if we are a little cynical, what is the difference between a photographer who is there on his own, trying to document an event, and moves something to convey better a certain reality, and the photographer who accepts being embedded with troops that will take him and show him exactly what they want to show him, only designated places which reveal only what is important according to their own agendas. Which one is the bigger set-up? I am giving you an extreme example, but the truth is that set-up is a reality. [...]

Levi Strauss Can you tell us about the façade of the structure [of *The Sound of Silence*], which is fully lit by vertical rows of bright, white fluorescents?

Ashton Some of my students interpreted that as bars of a jail cell, which I thought was pretty good.

Jaar That's a nice interpretation; I never thought of it in such a way. What I wanted was first to blind the viewer as soon as they entered the space. I gave myself a conceptual programme: I will blind you inside even more. Then when they sit and start watching the film, as the text emerges in and fades away almost as if it pulses with life, as if it lives and dies, they hopefully would notice that the light which the text is illuminated from is going out to the world, trying to illuminate the world. It is a kind of reverse *camera lucida*, where instead of letting light in, it throws light out. [...]

Bui Can you talk about how *Searching for Africa in LIFE* came about? [...]

Jaar What I've done for a long time is compile materials from various media, what I call press works, coverage of certain issues. *Searching for Africa in LIFE* shows *LIFE* magazine's lack of coverage of the African continent from 1936 to 1996, and when they do cover it, which is five or six times, it's mostly animals. This is the most influential magazine in terms of making photography accessible to the rest of the world.

Levi Strauss It certainly set up a lot of tropes that continue to this day in press images – I mean images that become iconic still have to look like those that appeared in *LIFE*.

Jaar Exactly, and, most importantly, it gave most people in the US and the rest of the world an image of the world. So, two or three generations were educated by school, by their parents, and by the media, and the media was mostly *LIFE* magazine. I created this piece in 1996, but it had never been shown till last year, and in this current show, I felt that it paired well with *The Sound of Silence*.[...]

Ashton Your Rwanda project, which was such a hugely incommensurate event – very much like what I'm just reading now in Claude Lanzmann's autobiography where he talks about when he did the epic *SHOAH* (1985), how hostile the reactions were from the audience, partly because they didn't want to deal with what he was trying to bring to their attention ... I'm curious, how did you deal with yours?

Jaar I don't know if I ever really dealt with it, and that's why the project went on for six years, which was the longest project that I ever created, largely because I wasn't satisfied with the answers I was finding. I simply didn't have the right language to say what I felt when I witnessed the genocide. Normally I would say barbaric, indifferent, but these are just two words that do not begin to convey what I want to convey about what we did as a world community. Primo Levi thought of this as criminal indifference.

Levi Strauss This is something that you really showed me, by encouraging me to go back and read the story of Rwanda as it was printed daily in the *New York Times*. And it was all there in black and white, from the beginning. It wasn't a surprise. It wasn't as if people didn't know what was going to happen. All you had to do was read the newspaper. That's terrifying.

Jaar It's the Security Council who did it, really. They were told that if they just gave the okay, it could be stopped immediately. But, unfortunately, it would never happen because of two factors: 1. Sadly, there is no oil in Rwanda, so why bother, and 2. I think racism is still with us.

[Audience questions]

Una Minnagh It's one thing to take photographs on site like those of the photojournalists, but when you transport that experience into a gallery space, which essentially has to be orchestrated, aestheticized or manipulated in order to draw the attention of the viewers to the screen, how do you balance between the content of what you want to communicate and the way it is made?

Jaar There is no way to represent anything without aestheticization. In other words, there is no representation without aestheticization.

Miriam Atkin I interpret the piece as a sort of series of deaths that occur on many different levels. There's the suicide of Carter, the deaths of the victims of the Sudanese famine, and there is the termination of the images as the potential provocation of change once it was appropriated by the media industry; then, finally, the negation of object, once it is displaced by the image. Let's say, if *The Sound of Silence* is a eulogy for these many losses, does it attempt to re-establish a living relationship with the dead or to create the stage for a productive discourse around these irretrievable losses?

Jaar It was Roland Barthes who said that every photograph is about death. One way or another, it's always about death. I think that the one I lament the most is our own death as human beings. What I mean is that I am afraid we have lost most of our humanity, we are already dead, or almost, as human beings.

Alfredo Jaar, Phong Bui, Dore Ashton and David Levi Strauss, extracts from round table interview published in *The Brooklyn Rail* (April 2009).

I hung from the arch extending across the street from the post office in downtown Guatemala City, a heavily trafficked area, and read my poems without a microphone, alluding to the fact that no one listens to women's voices, that they're effectively

lost

in

t h e

w i n d

Regina José Galindo, Interview with Francisco Goldman, 2006

ACTIVE AND PASSIVE SPECTATORS

Susan Sontag
On Photography//1977

[...] The political understanding that many Americans came to in the 1960s would allow them, looking at the photographs Dorothea Lange took of Nisei on the West Coast being transported to internment camps in 1942, to recognize their subject for what it was – a crime committed by the government against a large group of American citizens. Few people who saw those photographs in the 1940s could have had so unequivocal a reaction; the grounds for such a judgement were covered over by the pro-war consensus. Photographs cannot create a moral position, but they can reinforce one – and can help build a nascent one.

Photographs may be more memorable than moving images, because they are a neat slice of time, not a flow. Television is a stream of underselected images, each of which cancels its predecessor. Each still photograph is a privileged moment, turned into a slim object that one can keep and look at again. Photographs like the one that made the front page of most newspapers in the world in 1972 – a naked South Vietnamese child just sprayed by American napalm, running down a highway toward the camera, her arms open, screaming with pain – probably did more to increase the public revulsion against the war than a hundred hours of televised barbarities.

One would like to imagine that the American public would not have been so unanimous in its acquiescence to the Korean War if it had been confronted with photographic evidence of the devastation of Korea, an ecocide and genocide in some respects even more thorough than those inflicted on Vietnam a decade later. But the supposition is trivial. The public did not see such photographs because there was, ideologically, no space for them. No one brought back photographs of daily life in Pyongyang, to show that the enemy had a human face, as Felix Greene and Marc Riboud brought back photographs of Hanoi. Americans did have access to photographs of the suffering of the Vietnamese (many of which came from military sources and were taken with quite a different use in mind) because journalists felt backed in their efforts to obtain those photographs, the event having been defined by a significant number of people as a savage colonialist war. The Korean War was understood differently – as part of the just struggle of the Free World against the Soviet Union and China – and, given that characterization, photographs of the cruelty of unlimited American firepower would have been irrelevant.

Though an event has come to mean, precisely, something worth photographing, it is still ideology (in the broadest sense) that determines what constitutes an event. There can be no evidence, photographic or otherwise, of an event until the event itself has been named and characterized. And it is never photographic evidence which can construct – more properly, identify – events; the contribution of photography always follows the naming of the event. What determines the possibility of being affected morally by photographs is the existence of a relevant political consciousness. Without a politics, photographs of the slaughter-bench of history will most likely be experienced as, simply, unreal or as a demoralizing emotional blow.

The quality of feeling, including moral outrage, that people can muster in response to photographs of the oppressed, the exploited, the starving and the massacred also depends on the degree of their familiarity with these images. Don McCullin's photographs of emaciated Biafrans in the early 1970s had less impact for some people than Werner Bischof's photographs of Indian famine victims in the early 1950s because those images had become banal, and the photographs of Tuareg families dying of starvation in the sub-Sahara that appeared in magazines everywhere in 1973 must have seemed to many like an unbearable replay of a now familiar atrocity exhibition.

Photographs shock in so far as they show something novel. Unfortunately, the ante keeps getting raised – partly through the very proliferation of such images of horror. One's first encounter with the photographic inventory of ultimate horror is a kind of revelation, the prototypically modern revelation: a negative epiphany. For me, it was photographs of Bergen-Belsen and Dachau which I came across by chance in a bookstore in Santa Monica in July 1945. Nothing I have seen – in photographs or in real life – ever cut me as sharply, deeply, instantaneously. Indeed, it seems plausible to me to divide my life into two parts, before I saw those photographs (I was twelve) and after, though it was several years before I understood fully what they were about. What good was served by seeing them? They were only photographs – of an event I had scarcely heard of and could do nothing to affect, of suffering I could hardly imagine and could do nothing to relieve. When I looked at those photographs, something broke. Some limit had been reached, and not only that of horror; I felt irrevocably grieved, wounded, but a part of my feelings started to tighten; something went dead; something is still crying.

To suffer is one thing; another thing is living with the photographed images of suffering, which does not necessarily strengthen conscience and the ability to be compassionate. It can also corrupt them. Once one has seen such images; one has started down the road of seeing more – and more. Images transfix. Images anaesthetize. An event known through photographs certainly becomes more real than it would have been if one had never seen the photographs – think of the Vietnam War. (For a counter-example, think of the Gulag Archipelago, of which we have no photographs.) But after repeated exposure to images it also becomes less real.

The same law holds for evil as pornography. The shock of photographed atrocities wears off with repeated viewings, just as the surprise and bemusement felt the first time one sees a pornographic movie wear off after one sees a few more. The sense of taboo which makes us indignant and sorrowful is not much sturdier than the sense of taboo that regulates the definition of what is obscene. And both have been sorely tried in recent years. The vast photographic catalogue of misery and injustice throughout the world has given everyone a certain familiarity with atrocity, making the horrible seem more ordinary – making it appear familiar, remote ('it's only a photograph'), inevitable. At the time of the first photographs of the Nazi camps, there was nothing banal about these images. After thirty years, a saturation point may have been reached. In these last decades, 'concerned' photography has done at least as much to deaden conscience as to arouse it.

The ethical content of photographs is fragile. With the possible exception of photographs of those horrors, like the Nazi camps, that have gained the status of ethical reference points, most photographs do not keep their emotional charge. A photograph of 1900 that was affecting then because of its subject would, today, be more likely to move us because it is a photograph taken in 1900. The particular qualities and intentions of photographs tend to be swallowed up in the generalized pathos of time past. Aesthetic distance seems built into the very experience of looking at photographs, if not right away, then certainly with the passage of time. Time eventually positions most photographs, even the most amateurish, at the level of art.

The industrialization of photography permitted its rapid absorption into rational – that is, bureaucratic – ways of running society. No longer toy images, photographs became part of the general furniture of the environment – touchstones and confirmations of that reductive approach to reality which is considered realistic. Photographs were enrolled in the service of important institutions of control, notably the family and the police, as symbolic objects and as pieces of information. Thus, in the bureaucratic cataloguing of the world, many important documents are not valid unless they have, affixed to them, a photograph-token of the citizen's face.

The 'realistic' view of the world compatible with bureaucracy redefines knowledge – as techniques and information. Photographs are valued because they give information. They tell one what there is; they make an inventory. To spies, meteorologists, coroners, archaeologists and other information professionals, their value is inestimable. But in the situations in which most people use photographs, their value as information is of the same order as fiction.

The information that photographs can give starts to seem very important at that moment in cultural history when everyone is thought to have a right to something called news. Photographs were seen as a way of giving information to people who do not take easily to reading. The *Daily News* still calls itself 'New York's Picture Newspaper': its bid for populist identity. At the opposite end of the scale, *Le Monde*, a newspaper designed for skilled, well-informed readers, runs no photographs at all. The presumption is that, for such readers, a photograph could only illustrate the analysis contained in an article.

A new sense of the notion of information has been constructed around the photographic image. The photograph is a thin slice of space as well as time. In a world ruled by photographic images, all borders ('framing') seem arbitrary. Anything can be separated, can be made discontinuous, from anything else: all that is necessary is to frame the subject differently. (Conversely, anything can be made adjacent to anything else.) Photography reinforces a nominalist view of social reality as consisting of small units of an apparently infinite number – as the number of photographs that could be taken of anything is unlimited. Through photographs, the world becomes a series of unrelated, freestanding particles; and history, past and present, a set of anecdotes and *faits divers*. The camera makes reality atomic, manageable and opaque. It is a view of the world which denies interconnectedness, continuity, but which confers on each moment the character of a mystery. Any photograph has multiple meanings; indeed, to see something in the form of a photograph is to encounter a potential object of fascination. The ultimate wisdom of the photographic image is to say: 'There is the surface. Now think – or rather feel, intuit – what is beyond it, what the reality must be like if it looks this way.' Photographs, which cannot themselves explain anything, are inexhaustible invitations to deduction, speculation and fantasy.

Photography implies that we know about the world if we accept it as the camera records it. But this is the opposite of understanding, which starts from not accepting the world as it looks. All possibility of understanding is rooted in the ability to say no. Strictly speaking, one never understands anything from a photograph. Of course, photographs fill in blanks in our mental pictures of the present and the past: for example, Jacob Riis's images of New York squalor in the 1880s are sharply instructive to those unaware that urban poverty in late nineteenth-century America was really that Dickensian. Nevertheless, the camera's rendering of reality must always hide more than it discloses. As Brecht points out, a photograph of the Krupp works reveals virtually nothing about that organization. In contrast to the amorous relation, which is based on how something looks, understanding is based on how it functions. And functioning takes place in time, and must be explained in time. Only that which narrates can make us understand.

The limit of photographic knowledge of the world is that, while it can goad conscience, it can, finally, never be ethical or political knowledge. The knowledge gained through still photographs will always be some kind of sentimentalism, whether cynical or humanist. It will be a knowledge at bargain prices – a semblance of knowledge, a semblance of wisdom; as the act of taking pictures is a semblance of appropriation, a semblance of rape. The very muteness of what is, hypothetically, comprehensible in photographs is what constitutes their attraction and provocativeness. The omnipresence of photographs has an incalculable effect on our ethical sensibility. By furnishing this already crowded world with a duplicate one of images, photography makes us feel that the world is more available than it really is.

Needing to have reality confirmed and experience enhanced by photographs is an aesthetic consumerism to which everyone is now addicted. Industrial societies turn their citizens into image-junkies; it is the most irresistible form of mental pollution. Poignant longings for beauty, for an end to probing below the surface, for a redemption and celebration of the body of the world – all these elements of erotic feeling are affirmed in the pleasure we take in photographs. But other, less liberating feelings are expressed as well. It would not be wrong to speak of people having a *compulsion* to photograph: to turn experience itself into a way of seeing. Ultimately, having an experience becomes identical with taking a photograph of it, and participating in a public event comes more and more to be equivalent to looking at it in photographed form. [...]

Susan Sontag, extract from *On Photography* (New York: Farrar, Straus and Giroux, 1977) 16–24.

Martha Rosler
in, around, and afterthoughts (on documentary photography)//1981

[...] In *The Making of an American*, Jacob Riis wrote:

> We used to go in the small hours of the morning to the worst tenements ... and the sights I saw there gripped my heart until I felt that I must tell of them, or burst, or turn anarchist, or something ... I wrote, but it seemed to make no impression. One morning, scanning my newspaper at the breakfast table, I put it down with an outcry that startled my wife, sitting opposite. There it was, the thing I had been

> looking for all those years. A four-line dispatch from somewhere in Germany, if I remember right, had it all. A way had been discovered, it ran, to take pictures by flashlight. The darkest corner might be photographed that way.[1]

In contrast to the pure sensationalism of much of the journalistic attention to working class, immigrant and slum life, the meliorism of Riis, Lewis Hine and others involved in social-work propagandizing argued, through the presentation of images combined with other forms of discourse, for the rectification of wrongs. It did not perceive those wrongs as fundamental to the social system that tolerated them – the assumption that they were tolerated rather than *bred* marks a basic fallacy of social work. Reformers like Riis and Margaret Sanger strongly appealed to the worry that the ravages of poverty – crime, immorality, prostitution, disease, radicalism – would threaten the health and security of polite society as well as to sympathy for the poor, and their appeals were often meant to awaken the self-interest of the privileged. The notion of charity fiercely argued for far outweighs any call for self-help. Charity is an argument for the preservation of wealth, and reformist documentary (like the appeal for free and compulsory education) represented an argument within a class about the need to give a little in order to mollify the dangerous classes below, an argument embedded in a matrix of Christian ethics.

Documentary photography has been much more comfortable in the company of moralism than wedded to a rhetoric or programme of revolutionary politics. Even the bulk of work of the US version of the (Workers') Film and Photo League of the Depression era shared in the muted rhetoric of the popular front. Yet the force of documentary surely derives in part from the fact that the images might be more decisively unsettling than the arguments enveloping them. Arguments for reform – threatening to the social order as they might seem to the unconvinced – must have come as a relief from the potential arguments embedded in the images: with the manifold possibilities for radical demands that photos of poverty and degradation suggest, any coherent argument for reform is ultimately both polite and negotiable. Odious, perhaps, but manageable; it is, after all, *social discourse*. As such, these arguments were surrounded and institutionalized into the very structures of the government; the newly created institutions, however, began to prove their inadequacy – even to their own limited purpose – almost as soon as they were erected.

II

[...] The liberal New Deal State has been dismantled piece by piece. The War on Poverty has been called off. Utopia has been abandoned, and liberalism itself has been deserted. Its vision of moral idealism spurring general social concern has been replaced with a mean-minded Spencerian sociobiology that suggests, among other things, that the poor may be poor through lack of merit (read Harvard's Richard Herrnstein as well as, of course, between Milton Friedman's lines).[2] There is as yet no organized national Left, only a Right. There is not even drunkenness, only 'substance abuse'– a problem of bureaucratic management. The exposé, the compassion and outrage, of documentary fuelled by the dedication to reform has shaded over into combinations of exoticism, tourism, voyeurism, psychologism and metaphysics, trophy hunting – and careerism.

Yet documentary still exists, still functions socially in one way or another. Liberalism may have been routed, but its cultural expressions still survive. This mainstream documentary has achieved legitimacy and has a decidedly ritualistic character. It begins in glossy magazines and books, occasionally in newspapers, and becomes more expensive as it moves into art galleries and museums. The liberal documentary assuages any stirrings of conscience in its viewers the way scratching relieves an itch and simultaneously reassures them about their relative wealth and social position; especially the latter, now that even the veneer of social concern has dropped away from the upwardly mobile and comfortable social sectors. Yet this reminder carries the germ of an inescapable anxiety about the future. It is both flattery and warning (as it always has been). Documentary is a little like horror movies, putting a face on fear and transforming threat into fantasy, into imagery. One can handle imagery by leaving it behind. (*It is them, not us.*) One may even, as a private person, support causes.

Documentary, as we know it, carries (old) information about a group of powerless people to another group addressed as socially powerful. In the set piece of liberal television documentary, Edward R. Murrow's *Harvest of Shame* broadcast the day after Thanksgiving in 1960, Murrow closes with an appeal to the viewers (then a more restricted part of the population than at present) to write to their congressmen to help the migrant farm workers, whose pathetic, helpless, dispirited victimhood had been amply demonstrated for an hour – not least by the documentary's aggressively probing style of interview, its 'higher purpose' notwithstanding – because *these people* can do nothing for themselves. But which political battles have been fought and won by someone for someone else? Luckily, César Chávez was not watching television but rather, throughout that era, was patiently organizing farm workers to fight for themselves. This difference is reflected in the documentaries made by and for the Farm Workers' Organizing Committee (later the United Farm Workers of America, AFL-CIO), such works as *Sí, Se Puede* (Yes, We Can) and *Decision at Delano*; not radical works, perhaps, but militant works.

In the liberal documentary, poverty and oppression are almost invariably equated with misfortunes caused by natural disasters: Causality is vague, blame is not assigned, fate cannot be overcome. Liberal documentary blames neither the victims nor their wilful oppressors – unless they happen to be under the influence of our own global enemy, World Communism. Like photos of children in pleas for donations to international charity organizations, liberal documentary implores us to look in the face of deprivation and to weep (and maybe to send money, if it is to some faraway place where the innocence of childhood poverty does not set off in us the train of thought that begins with denial and ends with 'welfare cheat').

Even in the fading of liberal sentiments one recognizes that it is impolite or dangerous to stare in person, as Diane Arbus knew when she arranged her satisfyingly immobilized imagery as a surrogate for *the real thing*, the real freak show. With the appropriate object to view, one no longer feels obligated to suffer empathy. As sixties' radical chic has given way to eighties' pugnacious self-interest, one displays one's toughness in enduring a visual assault without a flinch, in jeering or in cheering. Beyond the spectacle of families in poverty (where starveling infants and despairing adults give the lie to any imagined hint of freedom and become merely the currently tedious poor), the way seems open for a subtle imputation of pathetic-heroic choice to victims-turned-freaks, of the seizing of fate in straitened circumstances. The boringly sociological becomes the excitingly mythological/psychological. On this territory a more or less overt sexualization of the photographic image is accomplished, pointing, perhaps, to the wellspring of identification that may be the source of this particular fascination.

III

It is easy to understand why what has ceased to be news becomes testimonial to the bearer of the news. Documentary testifies, finally, to the bravery or (dare we name it?) the manipulativeness and savvy of the photographer, who entered a situation of physical danger, social restrictedness, human decay, or combinations of these and saved us the trouble. Or who, like the astronauts, entertained us by showing us the places we never hope to go. War photography, slum photography, 'subculture' or cult photography, photography of the foreign poor, photography of 'deviance', photography from the past – Eugene Smith, David Douglas Duncan, Larry Burrows, Diane Arbus, Larry Clark, Danny Lyon, Bruce Davidson, Dorothea Lange, Russell Lee, Walker Evans, Robert Capa, Don McCullin ... these are merely the most currently luminous of documentarian stars.

W. Eugene Smith and his wife, Aileen Mioko Smith, spent the early 1970s on a photo-and-text exposé of the human devastation in Minamata, a small Japanese fishing and farming town, caused by the heedless prosperity of the Chisso chemical firm, which dumped its mercury-laden effluent into their waters. They included an account of the ultimately successful but violence-ridden attempt of victims to gain redress. When the major court fight was won, the Smiths published a text and many photos in the American magazine *Camera 35*.[3] Smith had sent in a cover photo with a carefully done layout. The editor, Jim Hughes, knowing what sells and what doesn't, ran a picture of Smith on the cover and named him 'Our Man of the Year' ('*Camera 35*'s first and probably only' one). Inside, Hughes wrote: 'The nice thing about Gene Smith is that you know he will keep chasing the truth and trying to nail it down for us in words and pictures; and you know that even if the truth doesn't get better, Gene will. Imagine it!'[4] The Smiths' unequivocal text argues for strong-minded activism. The magazine's framing articles handle that directness; they convert the Smiths into Smith; and they congratulate him warmly, smothering his message with appreciation. [...]

Or consider a photo book on the teeming masses of India – how different is looking through it from going to an Indian restaurant or wearing an Indian shirt or sari? We consume the world through images, through shopping, eating ...

> Your world is waiting and Visa is there. / 120 countries / 2.6 million shops, hotels, restaurants and airlines / 70,000 banking offices / For travelling, shopping and cash advances ... / Visa is the most widely recognized name in the world. / We're keeping up with you.

This current ad campaign includes photographs taken here and there in the world, some 'authentic', some staged. One photo shows a man and a boy in dark berets on a bicycle on a tree-lined road, with long baguettes of bread tied across the rear of the bike: rural France. But wait – I've seen this photo before, years ago. It turns out that it was done by Elliott Erwitt for the Doyle Dane Bernbach ad agency on a job for the French office of tourism in the fifties. Erwitt received fifteen hundred dollars for the photo, which he staged using his driver and the man's nephew: 'The man pedalled back and forth nearly 30 times till Erwitt achieved the ideal composition ... Even in such a carefully produced image, Erwitt's gift for documentary photography is evident', startlingly avers Erla Zwingle[5] in the column 'Inside Advertising' in the December 1979 issue of *American Photographer.* [...]

In 1978 there was a small news story on a historical curiosity: the real-live person who was photographed by Dorothea Lange in 1936 in what became *the world's most reproduced photograph*. Florence Thompson, seventy-five in 1978, a Cherokee living in a trailer in Modesto, California, was quoted by the Associated Press as saying, 'That's my picture hanging all over the world, and I can't get a penny out of it.' She said that she is proud to be its subject but asked, 'What good's it doing me?' She has tried unsuccessfully to get the photo suppressed. About it, Roy Stryker, genius of the photo section of the Farm Security

Administration, for which Lange was working, said in 1972: 'When Dorothea took that picture, that was the ultimate. She never surpassed it. To me, it was the picture of Farm Security ... So many times I've asked myself what is she thinking? She has all of the suffering of mankind in her but all of the perseverance too ... You can see anything you want to in her. She is immortal.'[6] In 1979, a United Press International story about Mrs Thompson said she gets $331.60 a month from Social Security and $44.40 for medical expenses. She is of interest solely because she is an incongruity, a photograph that has aged; of interest solely because she is a postscript to an acknowledged work of art. [...]

A good, principled photographer I know, who works for an occupational health and safety group and cares about how his images are understood, was annoyed by the articles about Florence Thompson. He thought they were cheap, that the photo *Migrant Mother*, with its obvious symbolic dimension, stands over and apart from her, is not-her, has an independent life history. (Are photographic images, then, like civilization, made on the backs of the exploited?) I mentioned to him that in the book *In This Proud Land*,[7] Lange's field notes are quoted as saying, 'She thought that my pictures might help her, and so she helped me.' My friend the labour photographer responded that the photo's publication caused local officials to fix up the migrant camp, so that although Mrs Thompson didn't benefit directly, others like her did. I think she had a different idea of their bargain.

I think I recognize in his response the well-entrenched paradigm in which a documentary image has two moments: (1) the 'immediate', instrumental one, in which an image is caught or created out of the stream of the present and held up as testimony, as evidence in the most legalistic of senses, arguing for or against a social practice and its ideological-theoretical supports, and (2) the conventional 'aesthetic historical' moment, less definable in its boundaries, in which the viewer's argumentativeness cedes to the organismic pleasure afforded by the aesthetic 'rightness' or well-formedness (not necessarily formal) of the image. The second moment is ahistorical in its refusal of *specific* historical meaning yet 'history minded' in its very awareness of the pastness of the time in which the image was made. This covert *appreciation* of images is dangerous in so far as it accepts *not* a dialectical relation between political and formal meaning, not their interpenetration, but a hazier, more reified relation, one in which topicality drops away as epochs fade, and the aesthetic aspect is, if anything, enhanced by the loss of specific reference (although there remains, perhaps, a cushioning backdrop of vague social sentiments limiting the 'mysteriousness' of the image). I would argue against the possibility of a non-ideological aesthetic; any response to an image is inevitably rooted in social knowledge – specifically, in social understanding of cultural products. (And from her published remarks one must suppose that when Lange took her pictures she was after just such an understanding of them, although by now the cultural appropriation of the work has long since removed it from this perspective.)

A problem with trying to make such a notion workable within actual photographic practice is that it seems to ignore the mutability of ideas of aesthetic rightness. That is, it seems to ignore the fact that historical interests, not transcendental verities, govern whether any particular form is seen as adequately revealing its meaning – and that you cannot second-guess history. This mutability accounts for the incorporation into legitimate photo history of the work of Jacob Riis alongside that of the incomparably more careful Lewis Hine, of Weegee (Arthur Fellig) alongside Danny Lyon. It seems clear that those who, like Lange and the labour photographer, identify a powerfully conveyed meaning with a primary sensuousness are pushing against the gigantic ideological weight of classical beauty, which presses on us the understanding that in the search for transcendental form, the world is merely the stepping-off point into aesthetic eternality.

The present cultural reflex of wrenching all artworks out of their contexts makes it difficult to come to terms with this issue, especially without seeming to devalue such people as Lange and the labour photographer, and their work. I think I understand, from the inside, photographers' involvement with *the work itself*, with its supposed autonomy, which really signifies its belongingness to their own body of work and to the world of photographs. But I also become impatient with this perhaps-enforced protectiveness, which draws even the best intentioned of us nearer and nearer to exploitiveness.

The *Sunday New York Times Magazine*, bellwether of fashionable ideological conceits, in 1980 excoriated the American documentary milestone *Let Us Now Praise Famous Men* (written by James Agee and photographed by Walker Evans in July and August of 1936, in Hale County, Alabama, on assignment from *Fortune* magazine, rejected by the magazine and only published in book form in 1941). The critique[8] is the same as that suggested in germ by the Florence Thompson news item. We should savour the irony of arguing before the ascendant class fractions represented by the readership of the *Sunday New York Times* for the protection of the sensibilities of those marginalized sharecroppers and children of sharecroppers of forty years ago. The irony is greatly heightened by the fact that (as with the Thompson story) the 'protection' takes the form of a new documentary, a 'rephotographic project', a reconsignment of the marginal and pathetic to marginality and pathos, accompanied by a stripping away of the false names given them by Agee and Evans – Gudger, Woods, Ricketts – to reveal their real names and 'life stories'. This new work manages to institute a new genre of victimhood – the victimization by *someone else's* camera of helpless persons, who then hold still long enough for the indignation of the new writer to capture them, in words and images both, in their current state of decrepitude. The new photos appear alongside the old, which provide a historical dimension, representing the moment in past time in which these people were first dragged into history. As readers of the *Sunday Times*, what do we discover? That the poor are ashamed of having been exposed as poor, that the photos have been the source of festering shame. That the poor remain poorer than we are, for although they see their own rise in fortunes, their escape from desperate poverty, we *Times* readers understand that our relative distance has not been abridged; we are still doing much better than they. Is it then difficult to imagine these vicarious protectors of the privacy of the 'Gudgers' and 'Ricketts' and 'Woods' turning comfortably to the photographic work of Diane Arbus?

The credibility of the image as the explicit trace of the comprehensible in the living world has been whittled away for both 'left' and 'right' reasons. An analysis that reveals social institutions as serving one class by legitimating and enforcing its domination while hiding behind the false mantle of even-handed universality necessitates an attack on the monolithic cultural myth of objectivity (transparency, unmediatedness), which implicates not only photography but all journalistic and reportorial objectivity used by mainstream media to claim ownership of all truth. But the Right, in contradistinction, has found the attack on credibility or 'truth value' useful to its own ends. Seeing people as fundamentally unequal and regarding elites as natural occurrences, composed of those best fitted to understand truth and to experience pleasure and beauty in 'elevated' rather than 'debased' objects (and regarding it as social suicide to monkey with this natural order), the Right wishes to seize a segment of photographic practice, securing the primacy of authorship, and to isolate it within the gallery-museum-art-market nexus, effectively differentiating elite understanding and its objects from common understanding. The result (which stands on the bedrock of financial gain) has been a general movement of legitimated photography discourse to the right – a trajectory that involves the aestheticization (consequently, formalization) of meaning and the denial of content, the denial of the existence of the political dimension. Thus, instead of the dialectical understanding of the relation between images and the living world that I referred to earlier – in particular, of the relation between images and ideology – the relation has simply been severed in thought. [...]

1 [footnote 2 in source] Jacob A. Riis, *The Making of an American* (1901) (New York: Harper Torchbooks, 1966) 267.

2 [5] [...] See Karl W. Deutsch and Thomas B. Edsall, 'The Meritocracy Scare', *Society* (September/October 1972), and Richard Herrnstein, Karl W. Deutsch and Thomas B. Edsall, 'I.Q: Measurement of Race and Class', in Bertram Silverman and Murray Yanowitz, eds, *The Worker in 'Post-Industrial' Capitalism: Liberal and Radical Responses* (New York: Free Press, 1974). [...]

3 [7] April 1974. (I thank Allan Sekula for calling this issue to my attention.) The Smiths subsequently

published a book whose title page reads *Minamata: Words and Photographs by Eugene Smith and Aileen M. Smith* (New York: Holt, Rinehart and Winston, 1975).

4 [8] *Camera 35* (April 1974) 3. [...]

5 [14] Zwingle's story seems to derive almost verbatim from the book *Private Experience: Elliott Erwitt: Personal Insights of a Professional Photographer*, with text by Sean Callahan and the editors of Alskog, Inc. (Los Angeles: Alskog/Petersen, 1974). [...]

6 [15] Roy Emerson Stryker and Nancy Wood, *In This Proud Land: America, 1935–1943, as Seen in the FSA Photographs* (Greenwich, Connecticut: New York Graphic Society, 1973/New York: Galahad Books, 1973) 19. [...]

7 [17] Stryker and Wood, *In This Proud Land*, op. cit., 19. [...]

8 [20] Howell Raines, 'Let Us Now Praise Famous Folk', *New York Times Magazine* (25 May 1980) 31–46. [...]

Martha Rosler, extracts from 'in, around, and afterthoughts (on documentary photography)' in *3 Works* (Halifax, Nova Scotia: The Press of the Nova Scotia College of Art and Design, 1981); reprinted in Martha Rosler, *Decoys and Disruptions: Selected Writings, 1975–2001*, (Cambridge, Massachusetts: The MIT Press, 2004) 176–7; 178–81; 183; 184–8.

Ariella Azoulay
Citizenship Beyond Sovereignty: Towards a Redefinition of Spectatorship//2008

The industrialization and dissemination of photography near the middle of the nineteenth century created a new citizenry – the citizenry of photography – whose citizens were equipped with the necessary tools for producing photographs, interpreting them, and acting on what they disclose. Although given to the modern citizen as another means of becoming a citizen in the nation-state, photography provided the possibility of becoming a citizen in this new citizenry of photography. Whereas the nation-state is based on the principles of sovereignty and territorialization, the citizenry of photography, of which the civil contract of photography is the constitutional foundation, is based on an ethical duty, and on patterns of deterritorialization. In principle, photography is an instrument given to everyone, making it possible to deterritorialize physical borders and redefine limits, communities and places (processes of reterritorialization).[1] The citizenry of photography is a simulation of a collective to which all citizens belong. Neither taking precedence over citizenship nor making it conditional, the citizenry of photography is fundamentally and solely defined by citizenship: membership in the citizenry means citizenship, and citizenship means membership in the citizenry. The citizenry of photography has no sovereign and therefore no apparatus of exclusion. Each and everyone is, in principle, a member of the collective. Membership in the collective is based on each one's renunciation of exclusive ownership of his or her image and on each one's willingness and right to be photographed and become a photograph.

The fact that the civil contract has only now been explicitly formulated does not contradict the fact that it exists and has existed as long as photography itself. That I am presently able to formulate its conditions rests on the abundant evidence we have of their existence. As early as the 1840s, the photographers David Octavius Hill and Richard Adamson, in tandem with their photographed subjects, saw photography as an instrument that establishes, on the ad hoc basis of each photograph, a universal tribunal that goes beyond local interests to see clearly what photography has to show.

These two men went to take photographs of the fishermen and fisherwomen of New Haven in an attempt to assist them at a time when their fisheries were failing. The gathering of photographers and the photographed around the camera was not contingent on a pragmatic answer to the question of whether photography could help them. Instead, it was motivated by the scopic regime that photography established – a photograph produced in the course of an encounter between photographer and photographed is created and inspired by a relation to an external eye, the eye of the spectator. It is not the same eye that is present in the situation, but one for the sake of which the photographed is willing to be photographed and the photographer is willing to take photographs: 'She looked as if she knew my photographs might help her, so she helped me. There was a kind of equality between us', wrote Dorothea Lange in her diary about Florence Thompson.[2]

This spectator's eye deterritorializes photography, transforming it from a simple, convenient, efficient, (relatively) inexpensive and easily operable tool for the production of pictures into a social, cultural and political instrument of immense power. The gap between these two dimensions of photography is newly expressed in each photographic act, summoning a supplementary eye, or at least alluding to the existence of an empty place, a potential place that enables the act of photography to occur while the participants acknowledge that they are not alone in front of the other. Photography thus enables its users to produce images that go beyond the simple technical actions required to produce them, attaining something that transcends the here and now. The reason they enjoy such a status is due to the fact that as soon as they have appeared in the world, it is impossible to dismiss them. Their presence cannot be subsumed under the reign of a higher authority. They are independent. The limits of their interpretation are not determined in advance and are always open to negotiation. They are not restricted to the intentions of those who would claim to be their authors or of those who participate in their production.

This particular characteristic of photographs tends to mislead the spectators who view them. A newspaper editor, for example, will add laconic captions to photographs, as if a denotative relation had been established between them. Such denotative relations assume that what is visible in the photograph exists there – somewhere – awaiting the precise verbal formulation that would make it a proper object. However, contrary to what Susan Sontag has claimed in her own writings on photography, the transcendent status of photographs does not require what is visible in them to be given, or assumed intrinsically to have a 'grammar' of its own.[3] Although they write on the social context of photography, both Sontag and Barthes preserve the notion of a stable meaning for what is visible in the photograph and reduce the role of the spectator to the act of judgement, eliminating his or her responsibility for what is seen in the photograph. That judgement assumes a passive attitude toward the image and is primarily interested in questioning the extent to which the photograph succeeds in arousing a desired effect or experience. Sontag focuses on the photographer and sees him or her as responsible both for the photograph and for the fact that the photographed is represented one way and not another or conveys one experience rather than another. 'Moralists who love photographs' writes Sontag, not without a small measure of contempt, 'always hope that words will save the picture.'[4] According to Sontag, the picture's fate as good or bad is sealed as soon as it is printed on photographic paper. Any attempt to start speaking for the photo is akin to an effort to revive the dead. Her 'ethics of seeing' is based on an aesthetic judgment and gives no attention to the civil contract of photography. It turns photographs into works of art that can be judged. Her ethics of seeing, in effect, reifies the new visual field created with the appearance of photography, leaving the photograph in possession of a special 'grammar' that allows it to remain independent of its spectator.

The civil contract of photography shifts the focus away from the ethics of seeing or viewing to an ethics of the spectator, an ethics that begins to sketch the contours of the spectator's responsibility toward what is visible. The individual is not confined to being posited as the photograph's passive addressee, but has the possibility of positing herself as the photograph's addressee and by means of this address is capable of becoming a citizen in the citizenry of photography by making herself appear in public, coming before the public, and entering a dialogue with it by means of photographs, which, despite their power are often both silent and silenced.

Once photographs are spoken of, however, they are spoken of among many, in regard to many; and obtain the power to remind citizens that what brings them together, what motivates them to look at photographs, is the common interest, the *res publica*. In an era when speaking in terms of the *res publica* is becoming more and more rare,[5] photography is one remaining site, a place of refuge, from which the discourse on the *res publica* may be revived. Neither a local, sectarian or national politics nor a politics of identity, photography remains part of the *res publica* of the citizenry and is or can become one of the last lines of defence in the battle over citizenship for those who still see citizenship as something worth fighting for.

This struggle links those who have citizenship, and those who are threatened by the denial of citizenship or expropriation of the rights of others, with those who have been robbed or denied citizenship, for whom photography and the citizenry of photography are often their first chance to become citizens despite being stateless.[6] In the Israeli context, for instance, the Palestinians became citizens of the citizenry of photography long before there was any possibility of their becoming citizens in the ordinary meaning of the word. The Palestinians are at one and the same time citizens of photography's global citizenry and non-citizens of the state that governs them. Photography enables them – along with many others – to make politically present the ways in which they have been dominated, making visible the more and less hidden modes in which they are exposed to Israeli power. Without the spectator participating in the construction of the photographic *énoncé*, the harm to citizenship will not be perceived. Photography does not put an end to their position as non-citizen, but it does enable them and others who take part in the reconstruction of their civil grievances to exercise the legitimate violence of photography's citizens, regardless of their status as non-citizens deprived of rights who cannot use their citizenship to negotiate with the sovereign power.

Photography thus has formed a citizenry, a citizenry without sovereignty, without place or borders, without language or unity, having a heterogeneous history, a common praxis, inclusive citizenship and a unified interest. The citizenry of photography is a global form of relation that is not subject to national regimes, despite existing within their borders, and that is not entirely obedient to global logic, even as it enjoys the channels of exchange and association the latter creates. Photography is a means of employing legitimate violence that is – or, in principle, that can be – in the hands of all of the members of the citizenry of photography, whether or not they are citizens of the space they inhabit. In the citizenry of photography, citizenship is rehabilitated and regains its essence. Not all of its citizens necessarily give active expression to their citizenship, and only a few have ever given their explicit consent to take part. However, even those who explicitly attempt to position themselves outside its bounds, or those who have never encountered a camera, are indeed a part of it.

In the ethics that photography requires of those who view photographs, it requests that its citizens – who are equally *not* governed in the citizenry of photography – not only try to avoid situations of degeneration into which the nation state and the market often sink, but actively to resist them. For the citizen of photography, national citizenship is not the ultimate realization of citizenship and does not see property and ownership as the principle achievements of human existence.

Instead, photography, while personal, is a mobile and global recording kit for contesting injuries to citizenship. Official UN data estimates the existence of 175 million non-citizens worldwide. This figure does not take into account the millions who, despite being officially granted citizen rights, are far from able to assume their citizen status. Photography can be put forward and read as a non-meditated complaint attesting to situations in which citizenship has been violated. Simply flip through any history book from the last hundred years, any NGO pamphlet, any publication written by a human rights or civil rights group, or any humanitarian organization report, and you will see that photography marks the beginning of a demand to become citizens, even when that demand is hidden behind a demand for the protection of human rights. These collections of photograph-complaints would be worthless, however, if it were not for the citizenry of photography and its citizens who produce these photographs-complaints, as photographers or as spectators. When a photograph turns into a grievance, whoever articulates it becomes its civic subject.

Often, photography has been used, in one way or another, by the sovereign power. Photographers were rapidly integrated into routine tasks, ongoing documentation, the collection, classification and storage of data, the use of data to enforce the law, and other governmental duties. Disciplinary and closed sites, in Foucault's terms, proved to be ideal places for the installation and regular employment of cameras.[7] Supervision and control, refinement and improvement, study and research – these have been the motivating goals behind camera operators and those who command them, even when they are themselves the ones exposed to the cameras.[8] Yet the formulation of these objectives, even in the form of written declarations, has not prevented the creation of a gap between the stated aims and what has actually taken place in the encounter between photographer, photographed and camera. Every photograph is a living testimony to this gap, even if some photographs may still lack an ethical spectator to notice them. In many instances, this gap is the place from which the spectator can become a citizen of photography, making it possible for the photographer or photographed to become a citizen, as well. [...]

1 [footnote 63 in source] On deterritorialization and reterritorialization see Gilles Deleuze and Félix Guattari, *A Thousand Plateaux: Capitalism and Schizophrenia*, trans. Brian Massumi (Minneapolis: University of Minnesota Press, 1987).

2 [64] See Dorothea Lange, 'The Assignment I'll Never Forget', in Liz Heron and Val Williams, eds, *Illuminations: Women's Writings on Photography from the 1850s to the Present* (London: I.B.Tauris, 1996).

3 [65] Susan Sontag, *On Photography* (New York: Picador, 1977) 3.

4 [66] Ibid., 107.

5 [67] See Hannah Arendt, *The Human Condition* (New York: Charles Scribner, 1958).

6 [68] For more on the flawed citizenship of citizens living beside non-citizens, see Azoulay and Ophir, *Bad Days* (Tel Aviv: Resling Press, 2002).

7 [69] See Michel Foucault, *The Birth of the Clinic: An Archaeology of Medical Perception* (1963) (New York: Random House, 1975).

Ariella Azoulay, extract (retitled by the author) from 'Citizenship Beyond Sovereignty: Towards an Ethics of the Spectator', *The Civil Contract of Photography* (New York: Zone Books, 2008) 128–35.

Judith Butler
Torture and the Ethics of Photography//2009

[...] [T]he mandated visual image produced by 'embedded reporting', the one that complies with state and Defense Department requirements, builds an interpretation. We can even say that what Susan Sontag calls 'the political consciousness' motivating the photographer to yield up the compliant photograph is to some extent structured by the photograph itself, even embedded in the frame. We do not have to be supplied with a caption or a narrative in order to understand that a political background is being explicitly formulated and renewed through and by the frame, that the frame functions not only as a boundary to the image, but as structuring the image itself. If the image in turn structures how we register reality, then it is bound up with the interpretive scene in which we operate. The question for war photography thus concerns not only what it shows, but also how it shows what it shows. The 'how' not only organizes the image, but works to organize our perception and thinking as well. If state power attempts to regulate a perspective that reporters and cameramen are there to confirm, then the action of perspective in and as the frame is part of the interpretation of the war compelled by the state. The photograph is not merely a visual image awaiting interpretation; it is itself actively interpreting, sometimes forcibly so. [...]

If, as the philosopher Emmanuel Levinas claims, it is the face of the other that demands from us an ethical response, then it would seem that the norms that would allocate who is and is not human arrive in visual form. Those norms work to *give face* and to *efface*. Accordingly, our capacity to respond with outrage, opposition and critique will depend in part on how the differential norm of the human is communicated through visual and discursive frames. There are ways of framing that will bring the human into view in its frailty and precariousness, that will allow us to stand for the value and dignity of human life, to react with outrage when lives are degraded or eviscerated without regard for their value as lives. And then there are frames that foreclose responsiveness, where this activity of foreclosure is effectively and repeatedly performed by the frame itself – its own negative action, as it were, toward what will not be explicitly represented. For alternative frames to exist and permit another kind of content would perhaps communicate a suffering that might lead to an alteration of our political assessment of the current wars. For photographs to communicate in this way, they must have a transitive function, making us susceptible to ethical responsiveness.

How do the norms that govern which lives will be regarded as human enter into the frames through which discourse and visual representation proceed, and how do these in turn delimit or orchestrate our ethical responsiveness to suffering? I am not suggesting that these norms determine our responses, such that the latter are reduced to behaviourist effects of a monstrously powerful visual culture. I am suggesting only that the way these norms enter into frames and into larger circuits of communicability are vigorously contestable precisely because the effective regulation of affect, outrage and ethical response is at stake.

I want to suggest that the Abu Ghraib photographs neither numb our senses nor determine a particular response. This has to do with the fact that they occupy no single time and no specific space. They are shown again and again, transposed from context to context, and this history of their successive framing and reception conditions, without determining, the kinds of public interpretations of torture we have. In particular, the norms governing the 'human' are relayed and abrogated through the communication of these photos; the norms are not thematized as such, but they broker the encounter between first-world viewers who seek to understand 'what happened over there' and this visual 'trace' of the human in a condition of torture. This trace does not tell us what the human is; but it provides evidence that a break from the norm governing the subject of rights has taken place and that something called 'humanity' is at issue here. The photo cannot restore integrity to the body it registers. The visual trace is surely not the same as the full restitution of the humanity of the victim, however desirable that obviously is. The photograph, shown and circulated, becomes the public condition under which we feel outrage and construct political views to incorporate and articulate that outrage.

I have found Susan Sontag's last publications to be good company as I consider what the photos of torture are and what they do, including both her *Regarding the Pain of Others* and 'Regarding the Torture of Others', which was released on the internet and published in the *New York Times* after the release of the Abu Ghraib photographs. The photos showed brutality, humiliation, rape, murder, and in that sense were clear representational evidence of war crimes. They have functioned in many ways, including as evidence in legal proceedings against those pictured as engaging in acts of torture and humiliation. They have also become iconic for the way that the US government, in alliance with Britain, spurned the Geneva Conventions, in particular the protocols governing the fair treatment of prisoners of war. It quickly became clear in the months of April and May 2004 that there was a pattern to the photographs and that, as the Red Cross had contended for many months before the scandal broke, there was a systematic mistreatment of prisoners in Iraq, paralleling a systematic mistreatment at Guantánamo. Only later did it become clear that protocols devised for Guantánamo had been deployed by the personnel at Abu Ghraib, and that both sets of protocols were indifferent to the Geneva accords. The question of whether governmental officials called what is depicted in the photos 'abuse' or 'torture' suggests that the relation to international law is already at work; abuse can be addressed by disciplinary proceedings within the military, but torture is a war crime, actionable within international courts. They did not dispute that the photographs are real, that they record something that actually happened. Establishing the referentiality of the photographs was, however, not enough. The photos are not only shown, but named; the way that they are shown, the way they are framed, and the words used to describe what is shown, work together to produce an interpretive matrix for what is seen.

But before we consider briefly the conditions under which they were published and the form in which they were made public, let us consider the way the frame works to establish a relation between the photographer, the camera and the scene. The photos depict or represent a scene, the visual image preserved within the photographic frame. But the frame also belongs to a camera that is situated spatially in the field of vision, thus not shown within the image, though still functioning as the technological precondition of an image, and indicated indirectly by the camera. Although the camera is outside the frame, it is clearly 'in' the scene as its constitutive outside. When the photographing of these acts of torture becomes a topic of public debate, the scene of the photograph is extended. The scene becomes not just the spatial location and social scenario in the prison itself, but the entire social sphere in which the photograph is shown, seen, censored, publicized, discussed and debated. So we might say that the scene of the photograph has changed through time.

Let us notice a few things about this larger scene, one in which visual evidence and discursive interpretation play off against one another. There was 'news' because there were photos, the photos laid claim to a representational status, and travelled beyond the original place where they were taken, the place depicted in the photos themselves. On the one hand, they are referential; on the other, they change their meaning depending on the context in which they are shown and the purpose for which they are invoked. The photos were published on the internet and in newspapers, but in both venues selections were made: some photos were shown, others were not; some were large, others small. For a long time, *Newsweek* retained possession of numerous photos that it refused to publish on the grounds that doing so would not be 'useful'. Useful for what purpose? Clearly, they meant 'useful to the war effort' – surely they did not mean 'useful for individuals who require free access to information about the current war in order to establish lines of accountability and to form political viewpoints on that war'. In restricting what we may see, do the government and the media not then also limit the kinds of evidence the public has at its disposal, to make judgments about the wisdom and course of the war? If, as Sontag claims, the contemporary notion of atrocity requires photographic evidence, then the only way to establish that torture has taken place is through presenting such evidence, at which point the evidence constitutes the phenomenon. And yet, within a frame of potential or actual legal proceedings the photo is already framed within the discourse of law and of truth.

In the US, the prurient interest in the photographs themselves seemed to pre-empt a fair amount of political response. The photo of Lynndie England with the leash around a man's head was front and centre in the *New York Times*; yet other papers relegated it to the inside pages, depending on whether they sought a more or less incendiary presentation. Within military court proceedings, the photo is considered evidence from within a frame of potential or actual legal proceedings and is already framed within the discourse of law and of truth. The photo presupposes a photographer – a person never shown in the frame. The question of guilt has been restricted to the juridical question of who committed the acts, or of who was ultimately responsible for those who did commit them. And the prosecutions have been limited to the most well-publicized cases.

It took some time before the question was raised as to who actually took the photos, and what could be inferred from their occluded spatial relation to the images themselves.[1] Did they take them in order to expose the abuse, or to gloat in the spirit of US triumphalism? Was the taking of the photo a way to participate in the event and, if so, in what way? It would seem that the photos were taken as records, producing, as the *Guardian* put it, a pornography of the event[2] – but at some point, someone, or perhaps several people, aware now of a potential investigation, realized that there was something wrong with what the photos depicted. It may be that the photographers were ambivalent at the time they took the photos or that they became ambivalent in retrospect; it may be that they feasted on the sadistic scene in some way that would invite a psychological explanation. Although I would not dispute the importance of psychology for understanding such behaviour, I do not think it should be used to reduce torture exclusively to individual pathological acts. Since we are clearly confronted with a group scene in these photographs, we need something more like a psychology of group behaviour, or, better yet, an account of how the norms of war in this instance neutralized morally significant relationships to violence and injurability. And since we are also in a specific political situation, any effort to reduce the acts to individual psychologies alone would return us to familiar problems with the notion of the individual or the person conceived as the causal matrix for the understanding of events. Considering the structural and spatial dynamics of the photograph offers an alternative point of departure for understanding how the norms of war are operating in these events – and even how individuals are taken up by these norms and, in turn, take them up.

The photographer is recording a visual image of the scene, approaching it through a frame before which those involved in the torture and its triumphal aftermath also stood and posed. The relation between the photographer and the photographed takes place by virtue of the frame. The frame permits, orchestrates and mediates that relation. And though the photographers at Abu Ghraib had no Defense Department authorization for the pictures they took, perhaps their perspective can also rightly be considered a form of embedded reporting. After all, their perspective on the so-called enemy was not idiosyncratic, but shared – so widely shared, it seems, that there was hardly a thought that something might be amiss here. Can we see these photographers not only as reiterating and confirming a certain practice of decimating Islamic cultural practice and norms, but as conforming to – and articulating – the widely shared social norms of the war?

So what are the norms according to which soldiers and security personnel, actively recruited from private firms contracted to supervise prisons in the US, acted as they did? And what are the norms that reside in the active framing by the camera, since these form the basis of the cultural and political text at issue here? If the photograph not only depicts, but also builds on and augments the event – if the photograph can be said to reiterate and continue the event – then it does not strictly speaking postdate the event, but becomes crucial to its production, its legibility, its illegibility, and its very status as reality. Perhaps the camera promises a festive cruelty: 'Oh, good, the camera's here: let's begin the torture so that the photograph can capture, and commemorate our act!' If so, the photograph is already at work prompting, framing and orchestrating the act, even as it captures the act at the moment of its accomplishment.

The task, in a way, is to understand the operation of a norm circumscribing a reality that works through the action of the frame itself; we have yet to understand this frame, these frames, where they come from and what kind of action they perform. Given that there is more than one photographer, and that we cannot clearly discern their motivation from the photos that are available, we are left to read the scene in another way. We can say with some confidence that the photographer is catching or recording the event, but this only raises the issue of the implied audience. It may be that he or she records the event in order to replay the images to those perpetrating the torture, so they can enjoy the reflection of their actions on the digital camera and disseminate their particular accomplishment quickly. The photos may also be understood as a kind of evidence, conceived as proof that just punishment was administered. As an action, taking a photograph is neither always anterior to the event, nor always posterior to it. The photograph is a kind of promise that the event will continue, indeed it is that very continuation, producing an equivocation at the level of the temporality of the event: Did those actions happen then? Do they continue to happen? Does the photograph continue the event into the future?

It would seem that photographing the scene is a way of contributing to it, providing it with a visual reflection and documentation, giving it the status of history in some sense. Does the photograph or, indeed, the photographer, contribute to the scene? Act upon the scene? Intervene upon the scene? Photography has a relation to intervention, but photographing is not the same as intervening. There are photos of bodies bound together, of individuals killed, of forced fellatio, of dehumanizing degradation, and they were taken unobstructed. The field of vision is clear. No one is seen lunging in front of the camera to intercept the view. No one is shackling the photographer and throwing him or her in jail for participating in a crime. This is torture in plain view, in front of the camera, even for the camera. It is centred action, with the torturers regularly turning toward the camera to make sure their own faces are shown, even as the faces of the tortured are mainly shrouded. The camera itself is ungagged, unbound, and so occupies and references the safety zone that surrounds and supports the persecutors in the scene. We do not know how much of the torture was consciously performed for the camera, as a way of showing what the US can do, as a sign of its military triumphalism, demonstrating its ability to effect a complete degradation of the putative enemy, in an effort to win the dash of civilizations and subject the ostensible barbarians to our civilizing mission which, as we can see, has rid itself so beautifully of its own barbarism. But to the extent that the photograph communicates the scene, potentially, to newspapers and media sources, the torture is, in some sense, *for* the camera; it is from the start meant to be communicated. Its own perspective is in plain view, and the cameraman or woman is referenced by the smiles that the torturers offer him, as if to say, 'thank you for taking my picture, thank you for memorializing my triumph.' And then there is the question of whether the photographs were shown to those who might yet be tortured, as a warning and a threat. It is clear they were used to blackmail those depicted with the threat that their families would see their humiliation and shame, especially sexual shame.

The photograph depicts – it has a representational and referential function. But at least two questions follow. The first has to do with what the referential function does, besides simply referring: what other functions does it serve? What other effects does it produce? The second, which I will deal with below, has to do with the range of what is represented. If the photo represents reality, which reality is it that is represented? And how does the frame circumscribe what will be called reality in this instance?

If we are to identify war crimes within the conduct of war, then the 'business of war' itself is ostensibly something other than the war crime (we cannot, within such a framework, talk about the 'crime of war'). But what if the war crimes amount to an enactment of the very norms that serve to legitimate the war? The Abu Ghraib photos are surely referential, but can we tell in what way the photos not only register the norms of war, but also came to constitute the visual emblem of the war in Iraq? When the business of war is subject to the omnipresence of stray cameras, time and space can be randomly chronicled and recorded, and future and external perspectives come to inhere in the scene itself. But the efficacy of the camera works along a temporal trajectory other than the chronology it secures. The visual archive circulates. The date function on the camera may specify precisely when the event happened, but the indefinite circulability of the image allows the event to continue to happen and, indeed, thanks to these images, the event has not stopped happening. [...]

Though we feel shock at these photographs, it is not the shock that finally informs us. In the last chapter of *Regarding the Pain of Others*, Sontag seeks to counter her earlier critique of photography. In an emotional, almost exasperated outcry, one that seems quite different from her usual measured rationalism, Sontag remarks: 'Let the atrocious images haunt us.'[3] Whereas earlier she diminished the power of the photograph to that of merely impressing upon us its haunting effects (whereas narrative has the power to make us understand), now it seems that some understanding is to be wrought from this very haunting. We see the photograph and cannot let go of the image that is transitively relayed to us. It brings us close to an understanding of the fragility and mortality of human life, the stakes of death in the scene of politics. She seemed to know this already in *On Photography* when she wrote: 'Photographs state the innocence, the vulnerability of lives heading toward their own destruction, and this link between photography and death haunts all photographs of people.'[4]

Perhaps Sontag is influenced by Roland Barthes at such a moment, since it was Barthes, in *Camera Lucida*, who argued that the photographic image has a particular capacity to cast a face, a life, in the tense of the future anterior.[5] The photograph relays less the present moment than the perspective, the pathos, of a time in which 'this will have been.' The photograph operates as a visual chronicle: it 'does not necessarily say *what is no longer*, but only and for certain *what has been*.'[6] But every photographic portrait speaks in at least two temporal modes, both a chronicle of what has been and protentive certainty about what will have been. Barthes writes famously of what the photograph bespeaks of Lewis Payne in jail waiting to be hanged: '*he is going to die*. I read at the same time: *This will be* and *this has been*. I observe with horror an anterior future of which death is the stake (*dont le mort est l'enjeu*). By giving me the absolute past of the pose (*aorist*), the photograph tells me death in the future.'[7] But this quality is not reserved for those overtly condemned to death by courts of law, or indeed for those already dead, since for Barthes 'every photograph is this catastrophe', installing and soliciting a perspective on the absolute pastness of a life.[8]

Under what conditions does this quality of 'absolute pastness' counter the forces of melancholy and open up a more explicit form of grieving? Is this quality of 'absolute pastness' that is conferred on a living being, one whose life is not past, precisely the quality of grievability? To confirm that a life was, even within the life itself, is to underscore that a life is a grievable life. In this sense, the photograph, through its relation to the future anterior, instates grievability. It makes sense to wonder whether this insight is not related to Sontag's imperative: 'Let the atrocious images haunt us.'[9] Her imperative suggests that there are conditions in which we can refuse to be haunted, or where haunting cannot reach us. If we are not haunted, there is no loss, there has been no life that was lost. But if we are shaken or 'haunted' by a photograph, it is because the photograph acts on us in part through outliving the life it documents; it establishes in advance the time in which that loss will be acknowledged as a loss. So the photograph is linked through its 'tense' to the grievability of a life, anticipating and performing that grievability. In this way, we can be haunted in advance by the suffering or deaths of others. Or we can be haunted afterwards, when the check against grief becomes undone. It is not only or exclusively at an affective register that the photograph operates, but through instituting a certain mode of acknowledgment. It 'argues' for the grievability of a life: its pathos is at once affective and interpretive. If we can be haunted, then we can acknowledge that there has been a loss and hence that there has been a life: this is an initial moment of cognition, an apprehension, but also a potential judgment, and it requires that we conceive of grievability as the precondition of life, one that is discovered retrospectively through the temporality instituted by the photograph itself. 'Someone will have lived' is spoken within a present, but it refers to a time and a loss to come. Thus the anticipation of the past underwrite the photograph's distinctive capacity to establish grievability as a precondition of a knowable human life – to be haunted is precisely to apprehend that life before precisely knowing it.

Sontag herself makes less ambitious claims. She writes that the photograph can be an 'invitation ... to pay attention, reflect ... examine the rationalizations for mass suffering offered by established powers.'[10] It is my sense that the curated exhibition of the Abu Ghraib photos at the International Center for Photography did precisely that. But what is most interesting to me about the increasing outrage and exasperation Sontag expressed in her writings on 9/11 and in her article 'Regarding the Torture of Others' is that it continued to be directed against the photograph not only for making her feel outrage, but for failing to show her how to transform that affect into effective political action. She acknowledges that she has in the past turned against the photograph with moralistic denunciation precisely because it enrages without directing the rage, and so excites our moral sentiments at the same time as it confirms our political paralysis. And even this frustration frustrates her, since it seems a guilty and narcissistic preoccupation with what one can do as a first-world intellectual, and so fails again to attend to the suffering of others. Even at the end of that consideration, it is a museum piece by Jeff Wall that allows Sontag to formulate this problem of responding to the pain of others, and so, we might surmise, involves a certain consolidation of the museum world as the one within which she is most likely to find room for reflection and deliberation. At this moment, we can see her turn both from the photograph and from the political exigencies of war to the museum exhibition that gives her the time and space for the kind of thinking and writing she treasures. She confirms her position as an intellectual, but shows us how this piece might help us to reflect more carefully about war. In this context, Sontag asks whether the tortured can and do look back, and what they see when they look at us. She was faulted for saying that the photographs from Abu Ghraib were photographs of 'us', and some critics suggested that this was again a kind of self-preoccupation that paradoxically and painfully took the place of a reflection on the suffering of others. But what she asked was 'whether the nature of the policies prosecuted, by this administration and the hierarchies deployed to carry them out, makes such acts [of torture] likely. Considered in this light, the photographs are us.'[11]

Perhaps she was saying that in seeing the photos, we see ourselves seeing, that we are those photographers to the extent that we share the norms that provide the frames in which those lives are rendered destitute and abject, and are sometimes clearly beaten to death. In Sontag's view, the dead are profoundly uninterested in us – they do not seek our gaze. This rebuff to visual consumerism that comes from the shrouded head, the averted glance, the glazed eyes, this indifference to us performs an auto-critique of the role of the photograph within media consumption. Although we might want to see, the photograph tells us clearly that the dead do not care whether we see or not. For Sontag, this is the ethical force of the photograph, to mirror back the final narcissism of our desire to see and to refuse satisfaction to that narcissistic demand.

She may be right, but perhaps it is also our inability to see what we see that is also of critical concern. To learn to see the frame that blinds us to what we see is no easy matter. And if there is a critical role for visual culture during times of war it is precisely to thematize the forcible frame, the one that conducts the dehumanizing norm, that restricts what is perceivable and, indeed, what can be. Although restriction is necessary for focus, and there is no seeing without selection, this restriction we have been asked to live with imposes constraints on what can be heard, read, seen, felt and known, and so works to undermine both a sensate understanding of war, and the conditions for a sensate opposition to war. This 'not seeing' in the midst of seeing, this not seeing that is the condition of seeing, became the visual norm, a norm that has been a national norm, one conducted by the photographic frame in the scene of torture. In this case, the circulation of the image outside the scene of its production has broken up the mechanism of disavowal, scattering grief and outrage in its wake.

1 [footnote 16 in source] A key exception is the excellent film *Standard Operating Procedure*, dir. Errol Morris (2008).
2 [17] Joanna Bourke, 'Torture as Pornography', *Guardian* (7 May 2004).
3 [29] Sontag, *Regarding the Pain of Others* (London: Penguin, 2003) 65.
4 [30] Sontag, *On Photography* (New York: Picador, 1977) 70.
5 [31] Barthes, *Camera Lucida: Reflections on Photography* (New York: Hill & Wang, 1981) [...]
6 [32] Barthes, *Camera Lucida*, op. cit. 85.
7 [33] Ibid., 96.
8 [34] Ibid.
9 [35] Sontag, *Regarding the Pain of Others*, op. cit. 115.
10 [36] Ibid., 117.
11 [37] Sontag, 'Regarding the Torture of Others', *New York Times* (23 May 2004).

Judith Butler, extracts from 'Torture and the Ethics of Photography', in *Frames of War: When is Life Grievable?* (London and New York: Verso, 2009) 71–86; 96–100.

Hito Steyerl
A Language of Practice//2008

In Jonathan Swift's novel *Gulliver's Travels*, an academy plans to give up human language in favour of a thing language, which is supposed to consist of the things themselves. If people wish to have a conversation about something, they are supposed to show the thing as such. According to Swift's academy, this language has great advantages, since it is understood everywhere and is thus useful for commerce and general communication. We can state without exaggeration that documentary languages have succeeded in taking on the role of this thing language. Their understanding is largely independent from national languages and cultures. Their radius of comprehension is larger than the one of individual languages. The documentary mode is a transnational language of practice. Its standard narratives are recognized all over the world and its forms are almost independent of national or cultural difference. Precisely because they operate so closely on material reality, they are intelligible wherever this reality is relevant.

This aspect was recognized as early as the 1920s, when Dziga Vertov euphorically praised the qualities of the film of facts. In the preface of his film *Man with a Movie Camera*, he claimed that documentary forms were able to organize visible facts in a truly international absolute language, which could establish an optical connection between the workers of the world. He imagined a sort of communist visual adamic language, which should not only inform or entertain, but also organize its viewers. It would not only transmit messages, but also connect its audience to a universal circulation of energies, which literally shoot through their nervous systems. By articulating visible facts, Vertov wanted to short-circuit his audience with the language of things itself, with the pulsating drives of matter.

In a sense, his dream has become true, if only in inverted form under the rule of global information capitalism. A transnational documentary jargon is now connecting people within global media networks. The standardized language of newsreels, with its economy of attention based on fear, the racing time of flexible production and hysteria, is as fluid and affective, as immediate and immersive as Vertov could have imagined. It creates global public spheres whose participants are linked almost in a physical sense by mutual excitement and anxiety. Thus the documentary form is now more potent than ever; it conjures up the most spectacular aspects of the language of things and amplifies their power.

But while Vertov aimed at unleashing the social forces which were congealed in things by capitalist commodification, contemporary documentary jargons have, on the contrary, exploited the occult potentials of documentary expression. They short-circuit fear and superstition with the realm of information. There is sometimes only a minimal difference between a piece of documentary information and a stereotype, between a guide for orientation in a complex world and wholesale judgements about whole regions and populations. Information and disinformation, rationalism and hysteria, sobriety and exaggeration are not clearly separated within these networks. The border between description and confabulation blurs, and fact and fiction fuse into 'factions'. The docu-jargons of the present immerse their public into a barrage of intense affects, an incoherent mix of tragedy and grotesqueness, which catapults the old curiosity of the vaudeville into the digital age. Ever more coarse and blurry images – which show less and less content – evoke a permanent state of crisis. These images create the norm by reporting the exceptional, even unimaginable; they transform the exception into the rule.

Documentary forms partake in the arousal of fear and feelings of ubiquitous threat. They inform panicked subjects as well as hostile and mutually suspicious collectives. In times of a presumed war between cultures, they become active players defining those cultures in the first place. The general uncertainty catalysed by recent political upheavals is channelled into simplifying clichés about others. Those pseudo-documentary images do not represent any reality in the first place. They tend to realize themselves instead within the political dynamics they originally helped to unleash. Stereotypical assumptions about so-called cultures can catalyse dangerous social dynamics and align reality step by step to its caricature.

But the documentary languages of the present also have a different function. In an age of globalization, when traditional forms of the social are shattered and national languages are downsized to local idioms, they offer orientation in an ever-expanding world. Paolo Virno recently remarked that clichés or jargons were not exclusively misleading. Rather than blatant misinformation, they may also turn out to be just empty commonplaces.[1] If we understand this term literally, it also designates a site of common communication. A language based on such *common-places* is able to transcend borders and enable a public debate across them. But the real existing documentary public spheres are underlying severe restrictions. As Virno also remarked, commodified public spheres are not public at all.[2] These public spheres remain lopsided; they speak in a standardized industrial international jargon, but do not allow any participation. The non-public public sphere isolates while it connects people to each other; it locates people in the world by fanning fears of homelessness; it communicates by simplifying; it is affective but only in so far as it serves instincts and a feeling of general menace.

The non-public public sphere can be fearsome. Let us be honest, though; it can also be fun. It connects us in real-time to the most improbable things, but prescribes the form and the speed of these connections. It is based on effects of immediacy, on innervation, the thrill of voyeurism or the complacency of bias. The languages of news media transport the conformism of things, not their potential of transformation. The more extraordinary, catastrophic and eccentric things behave within them, the more everything else can stay the same.

Private Public Spheres

The formula of the general transformation of documentary forms under the conditions of globalization can be expressed by the notion of privatization. From an economical perspective, documentary production in Europe came under pressure from the privatization of national and state-funded public spheres; from a content perspective, this pressure intensified the demand for private and intimate subject matter. The consequence of this double privatization is the development of an increasingly private public sphere – metaphorically condensed within voyeuristic docu-soaps broadcast on private TV channels.

But there is also a very different consequence of this widespread privatization for documentary practices in the present. After digital technology trickled down to consumer good production, access to it was extremely facilitated. The means of production of documentaries are more accessible than ever; they can literally be privatized and no longer exclusively belong to the tightly guarded privilege of state controlled organizations or large media corporations. Throughout the twentieth century, the control over the means of audiovisual production was repeatedly reorganized in the wake of key advances in technology: most recently with the advent of the digital era.

The keyword for this development is: camcorder revolution. It describes the mass circulation of audiovisual equipment as well as the political upheavals – for example the Romanian revolution in 1989 – which were ambivalently entangled with these new technologies. These optical-political transformations proceeded simultaneously with a general restructuring of production, to the demise of industrial labour in the industrial centres and the emergence of new types of flexibilized workers. The production of documentary tends increasingly to merge with other fields of mass symbolic production within contemporary cultural industries, which are all characterized by creative output, freelancing and widespread flexibilization. Even the previously elitist and highly delimited realm of documentary image production was largely proletarianized. Small teams of freelancers and I-reporters replaced fully employed journalists. On the other hand the extreme reduction of costs within digital production also created a space for de-professionalized popular media experimentation.

Networked Production

The conditions of documentary productions within the art field are a case in point of such ongoing de-professionalization.[3] While experimentation is possible and often even desired in this area, it becomes possible by producing it at minimal cost. Experimental or low-budget documentary production in the art field is often performed under do-it-yourself conditions with small digital cameras and home computers. Contracts are rare and primarily in place to preserve the interests of institutions. Work place and private sphere blur, just as do the functions of author, administrator, amateur translator and technical coordinator. But although this production is increasingly individualized – the author is very often indeed the producer – it also tends to take place more and more in 'common'. A rather anonymous commons, located within databases. Images are swapped, sounds downloaded, ideas shared with aliases. P2P networks provide darkrooms for illicit archival downloads. Experimental documentary production increasingly immerses itself into malleable streams of digital data; it intercepts, appropriates, copies and distributes. The printing lab is replaced by ripping software. Authorship, copyright, intellectual property are reassessed. This type of production taps into the streams of dramas and desires that are invisibly flowing around the world and traverse our bodies in the form of WiFi signals. This is reality now. The new documentary does not picture this reality but rips off large chunks to incorporate it.

Dziga Vertov's slogan of an 'optical connection' between the workers of the world is ironically updated within these communication networks, which link volatile and geographically-dispersed groups of people in partially common operational procedures. Those linkages are transitory sites of the production of commons, channels through which images, sounds and ideas travel.

Production vs. Distribution

All these ambivalent transformations are contributing to the reorganization of documentary practices. The very processes, which have extended the reach of documentary articulations across the globe, have not only altered their conditions of production dramatically but also their channels of distribution. But while production on the whole has rather been facilitated, distribution is becoming more and more tricky.

The progressive privatization of European state media has led to a rapid commercialization of their content. Formal experiments are replaced by docutainment and serial catastrophe. This means that experimental and reflexive documentary practices have lost their base and have become homeless. This applies to some areas of classical documentary film production, as well as to more experimental and artistic works. They have dispersed into a fluid and uncertain space, which is neither exclusively governed by the claims of specific national cultures nor by any single clearly distinguishable market logic. This space extends from alternative public spheres into the art field, from university auditoria to youtube and self-organized projections, from glamorous film festivals and blockbuster art shows to the informal distribution of video tapes in activist circles. This ambivalent zone is defined by various conflicting interests. It would be extremely exaggerated to call it a zone of artistic freedom. It is based on the divergent effects of technological development, creativity hypes, social concerns and general downsizing. It is a laboratory for mainstream innovation, just as it can accommodate formal experiments and pockets of civil disobedience. But it is also a potential seed for a not yet existent sphere of common communication, which might realize Vertov's vision as an optical connection.

Optical Connection

However, documentary expressions are not only a possible arena of a public debate. Their production creates material arrangements which organize things and humans in ever-shifting combinations throughout dispersed geographical locations. They connect humans and machines, images and sounds, hard drives and desires. As common practices or as shared operational procedures, they anticipate alternative forms of social composition. To work on these conditions means to work on reality today.

1 Paolo Virno, *A Grammar of the Multitude* (New York: Semiotext(e), 2002)

2 Ibid.

3 Although there is no systematic research into these conditions as yet (and although it does not concern a low budget production either) Harun Farocki's production diary of his work *Deep Play* provides a fascinating case study.

Hito Steyerl, 'A Language of Practice', in Maria Lind and Hito Steyerl, eds, *The Green Room: Reconsidering the Documentary and Contemporary Art #1* (Berlin and New York: Sternberg Press, 2008) 225–31.

SEARCHING FOR AFRICA IN *LIFE* SHOWS *LIFE* MAGAZINE'S LACK OF COVERAGE OF THE AFRICAN CONTINENT FROM 1936 TO 1996, AND WHEN THEY DO COVER IT, WHICH IS FIVE OR SIX TIMES, IT'S MOSTLY ANIMALS

Alfredo Jaar, Interview with Phong Bui, Dore Ashton and David Levi Strauss, 2009

THE LIMITS OF THE VISIBLE

Georges Didi-Huberman

Images in Spite of All: Four Photographs from Auschwitz//2003

[...] [Four photographs], snatched from the hell of Auschwitz, address two spaces, two distinct periods of the unimaginable. What they refute, first of all, is the unimaginable that was fomented by the very organization of the 'Final Solution'. If a Jewish member of the Resistance in London, working as such in supposedly well-informed circles, can admit that at the time he was incapable of imagining Auschwitz or Treblinka, what can be said of the rest of the world? In Hannah Arendt's analysis, the Nazis 'were totally convinced that one of the greatest chances for the success of their enterprise rested on the fact that no one on the outside could believe it'. The fact that terrible information was sometimes received but 'repressed because of the sheer enormity' would follow Primo Levi to his nightmares. To suffer, to survive, to tell, and then not to be believed because it is unimaginable. It is as though a fundamental injustice continued to follow the survivors all the way to their vocation of being witnesses.

Numerous researchers have carried out detailed analyses of the machinery of *disimagination* that made it possible for an SS officer to say: 'There will perhaps be suspicion, discussion, research by historians, but there will be no certainties, because we will destroy the evidence together with you. And even if some proof should remain and some of you survive, people will say that the events you describe are too monstrous to be believed.' The 'Final Solution', as we know, was kept in absolute secrecy – silence and smothered information. But as the details of the extermination began to filter through, 'almost from the beginning of the massacres', silence needed a reciprocal discourse. It involved rhetoric, lying, an entire strategy of words that Hannah Arendt defined in 1942 as the 'eloquence of the devil'.

The four photographs snatched from Auschwitz by members of the Sonderkommando were also, therefore, four *refutations* snatched from a world that the Nazis wanted to obfuscate, to leave wordless and imageless. Analyses of the concentration camp have long converged on the fact that the camps were laboratories, experimental machines for a *general obliteration*. It was the *obliteration of the psyche* and the disintegration of the social link, as Bruno Bettelheim's analysis showed as early as 1943, when he was just out from eighteen months in Buchenwald and Dachau: 'The concentration camp was the Gestapo's laboratory for subjecting ... free men ... to the process of disintegration from their position as autonomous individuals.' In 1950, Hannah Arendt spoke of the camps as 'laboratories of an experience of total domination ... this objective being attainable only in the extreme circumstances of a hell of human making'. [...]

The end of the 'Final Solution' – in all senses of the word 'end': its aim, its last stage, but also its interruption by the military defeat of the Nazis – called for a new enterprise, which was the *obliteration of the tools of the obliteration*. Thus, crematorium V was destroyed in January 1945 by the SS itself. No less than nine explosive charges were needed, one of which, being very powerful, was placed in the fireproof ovens. Yet another attempt to make Auschwitz unimaginable. After the Liberation, you could find yourself in the very place from which the four photographs were snatched a few months earlier, and see nothing but ruins, devastated sites, or 'non-places'.

Filip Müller, moreover, specified that up to its destruction, crematorium V continued 'burning the corpses of prisoners who had died in the main and auxiliary camps' while the gassing of the Jews had already been interrupted. Members of the Sonderkommando then had to burn, under strict surveillance, all 'prisoners' documents, card indexes, death certificates and scores of other documents'. It was with the tools of obliteration that *archives – the memory of the obliteration – had to be obliterated*. It was a way of keeping the obliteration forever in its *unimaginable* condition.

There is a perfect coherence between Goebbels' discourse, analysed in 1942 by Hannah Arendt according to its central motif, 'No one will say Kaddish' – in other words, we will murder you without remains and without memory – and the systematic destruction of the archives of the destruction by the SS itself at the end of the war. Indeed 'the forgetting of the extermination is part of the extermination'. The Nazis no doubt believed they were making the Jews invisible, and making their very destruction invisible. They took such pains in this endeavour that many of their victims believed it too, and many people still do today. But 'reason in history' is always subjected to the refutation – however minor, however dispersed, however unconscious, or however desperate it be – of particular facts that remain most precious to memory, its imaginable possibility. The archives of the Shoah define what is certainly an incomplete, fragmentary territory – but a territory that has survived and truly exists. [...]

Photography, from this angle, shows a particular ability – illustrated by certain well- or lesser-known examples – to curb the fiercest will to obliterate. It is technically very easy to take a photograph. It can be done for so many different reasons, good or bad, public or private, admitted or concealed, as the active extension of violence or in protest against it, and so on. A simple piece of film – so small that it can be hidden in a tube of toothpaste – is capable of engendering an unlimited number of prints, of generations and enlargements in every format. Photography works hand in glove with image and memory and therefore possesses their notable *epidemic power*. For this reason, photography was as difficult to eradicate in Auschwitz as was memory in the bodies of the prisoners.

What do we mean when we refer to 'Reason in history'? It is the state secret decreed at the place where the mass extermination occurred. It is the absolute prohibition of photographing the Einsatzgruppen's enormous acts of abuse in 1941. It is the notices put up on the walls and fences around the camps: '*Fotografieren verboten*! No entry! You will be shot without prior warning!' It is the circular sent around by Rudolf Höss, the commander at Auschwitz, dated 2 February 1943: 'I would like to point out once again that taking photographs within the camp limits is forbidden. I will be very strict in treating those who refuse to obey this order'.

But to prohibit was to want to stop an epidemic of images that had already begun and that could not stop. Its movement seems as sovereign as that of an unconscious desire. The ruse of the image versus reason in history: photographs circulated everywhere – those *images in spite of all* – for the best and the worst reasons. They began with the ghastly shots of the massacres committed by the Einsatzgruppen, photographs generally taken by the murderers themselves. Rudolf Höss did not hesitate either, in spite of his own circular, to present Otto Thierack, the minister of justice, with an album of photographs taken at Auschwitz. On the one hand, the Nazi administration was so anchored in its habits of recording – with its pride, its bureaucratic narcissism – that it tended to register and photograph everything that was done in the camp, even though the gassing of the Jews remained a 'state secret'.

Two photography laboratories, no less, were in operation at Auschwitz. It seems astonishing in such a place. However, everything can be expected from a capital as complex as Auschwitz, even if it was the capital of the execution and obliteration of human beings by the millions. In the first laboratory, attached to the 'identification service' (*Erkennungsdienst*), ten to twelve prisoners worked permanently under the direction of SS officers Bernhardt Walter and Ernst Hofmann, suggesting an intense production of images here. These consisted mainly of descriptive portraits of political prisoners. Photos of executions, of people being tortured, or of charred bodies were shot and developed by SS members themselves. The second laboratory, which was smaller, was the 'office of construction' (*Zentralbauleitung*). Opened at the end of 1941 or the beginning of 1942, it was directed by the SS officer Dietrich Kamann, who put together an entire photographic archive on the camp installation. Nor must we forget the whole 'medical' iconography of the monstrous experiments by Josef Mengele and his associates on the women, men and children of Auschwitz.

Toward the end of the war, while the Nazis were burning the archives en masse, the prisoners who served them as slaves for that task availed themselves of the general confusion to save – to divert, hide, disperse – as many images as they could. Today, around forty thousand photographs of this documentation of Auschwitz remain, despite its systematic destruction. Their survival says much about the probable size and horror of the iconography that filled the files when the camp was in operation.

A single look at this *remnant of images*, or erratic corpus of *images in spite of all*, is enough to sense that Auschwitz can no longer be spoken of in those absolute terms – generally well intentioned, apparently philosophical, but actually lazy – 'unsayable' and 'unimaginable'. The four photographs taken in August 1944 by the members of the Sonderkommando address the unimaginable with which the Shoah is so often credited today – and this is the second period of the unimaginable: tragically, the Shoah refutes it. Auschwitz has been called *unthinkable*. But Hannah Arendt has shown that it is precisely where thought falters that we ought to persist in our thought or, rather, give it a new turn. So, if we say that Auschwitz exceeds any existing juridical thought, any notion of fault or of justice, then political science and law must be rethought entirely. And if we believe that Auschwitz exceeds all existing political thought, even anthropology, then we must rethink the very foundations of the human sciences as such. [...]

Georges Didi-Huberman, extracts from *Images malgré tout* (Paris: Éditions de Minuit, 2003); trans. Shane B. Ellis, *Images in Spite of All: Four Photographs from Auschwitz* (Chicago: University of Chicago Press, 2008) 19–20; 21–5 [footnotes not included].

Harun Farocki
Reality Would Have to Begin//2004

In 1983, as preparations were underway to install even more nuclear weapons in the Federal Republic of Germany, [the Jewish philosopher] Günther Anders wrote: 'Reality has to begin. This means that the blockade of the entrances to the murder installations, which continue to exist, must also be continuous ... This idea is not new. It reminds me of an action – or rather a non-action – more than forty years ago, when the Allies learned the truth about the extermination camps in Poland. The proposal was immediately made to block access to the camp, which meant bombing the railroad tracks leading to Auschwitz, Majdanek, etc. extensively in order to sabotage, though this blockade, the delivery of new victims – that is, the possibility of further murder.'[1]

Nuclear weapons stationed in the Federal Republic of Germany arrive by ship in Bremerhaven where they are put on trains, whose departure time and destination are kept secret. About a week before the departure, army aircraft fly the entire length of the route and photograph it. This status report is repeated half an hour before the train is to pass, and the most recent set of images is compared with the first set. Through their juxtaposition one can discern whether any significant changes have occurred in the interim. If, for example, a construction vehicle has recently been parked along the tracks, the police will drive to or fly over the spot to investigate whether it is providing camouflage for saboteurs. Whether such sabotage has been attempted is not made public.

Reconnaissance of enemy territory by means of photographs taken from aeroplanes was already in use during World War I. And even before there were aeroplanes, balloons and rockets carrying cameras aloft and even carrier pigeons were outfitted with small cameras. In World War II, it was the English who were the first to begin equipping their bombers with photographic apparatus. Since they had to fly through enemy flak (anti-aircraft artillery fire) and enemy fighters, the bomber pilots always tried to drop their bomb load as quickly as possible (often a third of the planes were lost on flights from England to Germany). In their fear, the pilots believed all too readily that they had delivered their bombs on target. The introduction of cameras on board aircraft significantly diminished the space previously accorded to their oral reports. The English bomber pilots had the first workplace in which the camera was installed to monitor performance. Up to that point, men in war did work that was much less monitored and capable of being monitored than all industrial, commercial or agricultural activity, since the object of their labour, enemy territory, was not under surveillance. In the case of the bomber pilot, the workers' perceptions and descriptions still counted for something. Photographs would destroy this last remaining sense of authority.

A photographic image is a cut, a section through the bundle of light rays reflected off objects in a circumscribed space. Photography reproduces the three-dimensional object on a flat plane, based on the laws of projective geometry. In 1858, it occurred to Albrecht Meydenbauer, the director of the Government Building Office, to make use of this optical principle and to think of photographs as images for scale measurement. Faced with the task of measuring the façade of the cathedral in Wetzlar, he traversed the length of the façade in a basket suspended from block and tackle (in the same way that window-washers do), in order to avoid the expense of erecting scaffolding. One evening, in order to save time, he tried to climb from the basket into a window of the tower, when the basket swung away from the façade and put him in danger of plummeting to the ground. 'In the nick of time I grabbed the curved edge of an arch with my right hand, and with my left foot I kicked the basket far into the air; the counteraction sufficed to push my body into the opening and I was saved ... As I came down, the thought occurred to me: is it not possible to replace measurement by hand by the reversal of that perspectival seeing which is captured in a photographic image? This thought, which eliminated the personal difficulty and danger involved in measuring buildings, was father to the technique of scale measurement.'[2]

Meydenbauer often repeated this story from the nineteenth century. It is a narrative of endangerment and redemptive insight: the hero is in the process of making a construction into a calculation, is engaged in the labour of abstraction, at which point the measured space wants once more to prove its actuality. The greatest danger is posed by the objectivity and actuality of things. It is dangerous to remain physically near the object, to linger at the scene. One is much safer if one takes a picture and evaluates it later at one's desk. Immediately following the initial publication of Meydenbauer's idea, the military, an organization with many desks, offered to cover the cost of a practical experiment, but this could not be undertaken right away, as there was a war on at the time. The first scale measurement based on photographs took place in 1868 at the fortress of Saarlouis. The military immediately recognized in the technique of photographic scale measurements the possibility of capturing objects and spaces at a distance, numerically, spaces which soldiers otherwise could only traverse and measure at the risk of life and limb. The military took Meydenbauer's formulation of death or measurement literally.

The first image taken by the Allies of the concentration camp at Auschwitz was shot on 4 April 1944. American planes had taken off from Foggia, Italy, heading towards targets in Silesia: factories for extracting gasoline from coal (gasoline hydrogenation) and for producing buna (synthetic rubber). While approaching the I.G. Farben complex, still under construction, an airman turned on the camera and took a series of twenty-two aerial photographs, three of which also captured the 'main camp' located in the vicinity of the industrial plants. These images, along with others, arrived at the centre for aerial photography analysis in Medmenham, England. The analysts identified the industrial complexes pictured, recorded in their reports the state of their construction and the degree of their destruction, and made estimates of the production capacities of the buma plants – they did not mention the existence of the camps. Again and again, even in 1945, after the Nazis had cleared out the Auschwitz camps, having dismantled some of the murder complexes and either killed, abandoned or transferred the prisoners to other camps in the West, Allied planes flew over Auschwitz and captured the camps in photographs. They were never mentioned in a report. The analysts had no orders to look for the camps, and therefore did not find them. [...]

It was the success of the television series *Holocaust* – a programme that tried to make suffering and dying imaginable through visual narratives, thereby turning it into kitsch – that gave two CIA employees the idea of looking for aerial photographs of Auschwitz. They fed the geographic coordinates of all camps that were located in the vicinity of bombing targets into the CIA computer, and thus also those of the I.G Farben factory in Monowitz. I.G. Farben had built large plants in Monowitz and allowed the SS to provide them with slave labourers. For a time, they operated a camp (Auschwitz III, also known as Buna) located immediately adjacent to the factory grounds. Here, Jewish prisoners from across Europe, prisoners of war from the Soviet Union, and others who had been declared enemies of the Reich were worked to death. Sometimes, one-seventh, or thirty out of two hundred, of a particular group perished in one day. Those who did not die from overwork or undernourishment, and those who were not beaten to death by the SS or kapos, soon became too weak to work and were transferred to Birkenau, the extermination camp (Auschwitz II). The I.G. Farben Monowitz factories served the aircraft industry and consequently were of strategic interest to the Allies, which is what attracted the bombers and cameras and later helped lead to the rediscovery of the images.

Thirty-three years after the pictures were shot, two CIA men undertook a new analysis of the images. In the first image from 4 April 1944, they identified the house of Auschwitz's commandant and marked the wall between Blocks 10 and 11 where executions regularly took place. They also identified and marked the gas chambers of Auschwitz I and wrote: 'A small vehicle was identified in a specially secured annexe adjacent to the Main Camp gas chamber. Eyewitness accounts describe how prisoners arriving in Auschwitz-Birkenau, not knowing they were destined for extermination, were comforted by the presence of a "Red Cross ambulance".' In reality, the SS used that vehicle to transport the deadly Zyklon-B crystals. Could this be that notorious vehicle? The analysts are not entirely certain since, while they are able, at a distance of seven thousand metres, to make out the spot as a vehicle, they can establish neither what type of vehicle it is nor discern any markings on it. What distinguishes Auschwitz from other places cannot be immediately observed from these images. We only recognize in these images what others have already testified to, eyewitnesses who were physically present at the site. Once again, there is an interplay between image and text in the writing of history: texts that should make image accessible, and images that should make texts imaginable.

'On the night of 9 April we suddenly heard the distant rumble of heavy aircraft, something which we had never known in all the time we had been in Auschwitz ... Was the secret out? Were high explosives going to rip away the high-tension wires and the watchtowers and the guards with their dogs? Was this the end of Auschwitz?'[4] The two prisoners listening for the sounds of aircraft on this 9 April were attempting to escape from Auschwitz. One of them, Rudolf Vrba, then nineteen years old, had already been in the camp for two years, first working on the construction of the buna factory and later in the 'effects' detachment. When a train with deportees arrived at the camp, the new arrivals had to have their possessions dropped in by air, which were collected and sorted by a special detail, a Sonderkommando. The Nazis called these possessions 'effects', and among them Vrba found food, which helped him to sustain his strength and stay alive. The other prisoner, Alfred Wetzler, like Vrba, a Jew from Slovakia, worked in the camp administration office. There, he committed to memory the arrival dates, places of origin and the number of deportees newly arrived at the camp. And since he was in contact with men in the special details forced to work at the gas chambers and the crematoria, he also learned the statistics of those murdered – and memorized long lists of numbers. Vrba and Wetzler decided to flee when it became clear to them that the resistance groups in the camp would not be able to revolt, but could at best fight for their own survival. They wanted to flee because they could not imagine that the existence of the camp was known to the Polish resistance and the Allies. Vrba was convinced that Auschwitz was possible only 'because the victims who came to Auschwitz didn't know what was happening there'.[5]

'Some may find it hard to believe, but experience has proven that one can see, not everything, but many things, better in the scale measurement than on the spot', wrote Meydenbauer in a text in which he sought to lay the groundwork for the historic preservation of archives. Again, he described how unnecessary a long stay at the site was, even for the purpose of measurement. 'At his mentally and physically strenuous occupation, the architect is exposed to the weather; sunshine or rainfall on his sketchbook, and when he looks up, dust in his eyes.' In these passages, a horror of the objectivity of the world is noticeable. Meydenbauer's meditation gave rise in 1885 to the foundation of the Royal Prussian Institute for Scale Measurement, the world's first. The military took up the idea of measuring from photographs, as did the historic preservationists of monuments – the former destroys, while the latter preserves. Since 1972, the UNESCO Convention concerning the Protection of the World Cultural and Natural Heritage obligates all member states to document special buildings photographically. Using these archived photographs, one ought to be able to read and calculate the building's floor plan, in the case of its destruction – a destruction already conceived in these protective measures. The mathematical artists of the Renaissance stretched transparent papers in frame and traced on the plane the outlines of the spatial objects shining through. With the invention of photography these founders of the perspectival method seem to be the precursors of photographers; with the invention of scale measurement, they seem to be early scale measurement engineers. Erwin Panofsky wrote that one could understand perspective observation both in terms of ratio and objectivism, and in terms of chance and subjectivism. 'It is an ordering, but an ordering of visual phenomena.'[7] If one considers an image as a measuring device, then one should ignore chance and subjectivity. To conceive of a photographic image as a measuring device is to insist on the mathematicality, calculability, and finally the 'computability' of the image-world. Photography is first of all analogue technology; a photographic image is an impression of the original, an impression at a distance, made with the help of optics and chemistry. Vilém Flusser has remarked that digital technology is already found in embryonic form in photography, because the photographic image is built up out of dots and decomposes into dots.[8] [...] The human eye synthesizes these dots of information into an image. A machine can capture the same image, without any consciousness or experience of the form, by situating the image points in a co-ordinate system. The continuous sign-system image thereby becomes divisible into 'discrete' units; it can be transmitted and reproduced. A code is thus obtained that comprehends images. This leads one to activate the code and to create new images out of the code language. Images without originals become possible and, hence, generated images.

Vrba and Wetzler hid themselves outside the high voltage fence around the camp; under a pile of hoards they had doused with a mix of tobacco and petroleum. An experienced fellow prisoner had advised them to do so, because this would keep the tracker dogs at bay. After three days, the SS gave up their research and reported the escape of both men in a telegram addressed to Himmler; this indicates the extent to which they must have feared an eyewitness account from the concentration camps. Vrba and Wetzler made it to the Slovakian border by marching at night, crossed it, and made contact with the Jewish Council in the city of Zilina. Over the next days they reported on the death camp at Auschwitz. They drew the ground plan of the complexes, and recounted the lists of statistics on the people delivered and murdered. What they reported they had to reconfirm time and again, as they were cross-examined and the questions rephrased. The Jewish Council wanted conclusive, irrefutable material, in order to prove to the world the barely-believable crime. The unimaginable was repeated to make it imaginable. Three copies of the Vrba-Wetzler report were drawn up and sent out.[9] The first was supposed to go to Palestine. It was sent to Istanbul, but it never arrived there since the courier was probably a spy paid by Nazis. The second copy was sent to a rabbi who had contacts in Switzerland, and reached London via Switzerland. The British government passed the report on to Washington. A third copy was sent to the papal nuncio and arrived in Rome approximately five months later. When Vrba and Wetzler fled in April, the deportation and murder of about one million Hungarian Jews was imminent. It was only in July of 1944 that the Horthy government sought an arrangement with the West, which now had accurate knowledge of Auschwitz and demanded, through diplomatic channels, an end to the mass extermination. Vrba and Wetzler's report had thus helped save hundreds of thousands of lives. On 25 and

27 June, the *Manchester Guardian* reported on the Nazi death factory and for the first time mentioned the place name, Oswiecim. The mass extermination of the Jews by the Nazis was now occasionally mentioned in the newspapers; however only as one among many stories of dramatic war events, as news that soon disappeared into oblivion. A year later, when the Germans had lost the war and the concentration camps were liberated, the Allies photographed and filmed the camps, the survivors, and the traces that pointed to the millions murdered. It was above all the images of piles of shoes, glasses, false teeth, the mountains of shorn hair, that have made such a profound impression. Perhaps we need images, so that something that is hardly imaginable can register: photographic images as the impressions of the actual at distance. [...]

When on 25 August 1944, American planes once more flew over Auschwitz, one of them again took a picture from which we notice that a train has just arrived in Auschwitz II (Birkenau). One of its freight cars can be identified near the left edge of the image. A group of deportees is walking along the tracks toward the gas chambers at crematorium complex 2 where the entrance gate is open. Behind the gate a decorative flowerbed ('landscaping'), a courtyard and buildings are meant to convey the impression that this is a hospital or a sanatorium. Over the flowerbed a flat building, barely recognizable through the shadow of its front wall ('undressing room'). In this room, the arrivals were told to undress in preparation for showering. Diagonally across the room are the gas chambers. The details were meant to simulate a shower room. It could hold up to two thousand people, who were often forced in violently. Then the SS would lock the doors. Four openings can be spotted on the roof ('vents'). It was through these openings that, after a short waiting period to allow the temperature in the gas chamber to rise, SS men in gas masks dropped the Zyklon-B pellets. Everyone in the gas chambers died within three minutes. Others, who did not have to go to their deaths immediately, can be seen here waiting in line being registered. They are waiting to be tattooed, to have their heads shaved and assigned work and a place to sleep. The doubly curved figure of their waiting line extends all the way to the trees on the lower right.

The Nazis did not notice that someone had taken note of their crimes, and the Americans did not notice that they had captured them on film. The victims also failed to notice. Notes that seemed to be written into God's book alone.

Meydenbauer's fear of death established departments and administrative authorities that began to process images. Today, one speaks of image processing when machines are programmed to screen and classify photographs according to given criteria. A satellite continuously takes pictures of a specific region, a computer programme examines all the images to determine whether their details betray differences with earlier images. Another machine examines all the sequential images to detect traces of moving vehicles. Yet another is programmed to recognize any forms that may indicate a rocket silo. This is called image processing; machines are supposed to evaluate images made by machines. The Nazis talked about the eradication of cities, which means the suspension of their symbolic existence on the map. Vrba and Wetzler wanted to put the names Oswiecim/Auschwitz on the map. At that time, images of the Auschwitz death factory already existed, but no one had yet evaluated them. 'In the fall of 1944, Jewish women who worked at a munitions factory inside Auschwitz managed to smuggle small amounts of explosives to members of the camp's underground. The material was relayed to male prisoners who worked in the gas chamber and crematoria area. Those few wretched Jews then attempted what the Allied powers, with their vast might, would not. On October 7, in a suicidal uprising, they blew up one of the crematorium buildings.'[10] None of the insurgents survived. An aerial photograph displays the partial destruction of crematorium IV.

1 Günther Anders, 'Schinkensemmelfrieden – Rede zum Dritten Forum der Krefelder Friedensinitiative', *Konkret* (Hamburg, November 1983).

2 Cited in Albrecht Grimm, *720 Jahre Photogrammetrie in Deutschland: Das Tagebuch von Albrecht Meydenbauer* (Munich: R. Oldenbourg Verlag)' 1977) 15–16.

3 Dino A. Brugioni and Robert G. Poirier, *The Holocaust Revisited: A Retrospective Analysis of the Auschwitz-Birkenau Extermination Complex* (Washington, DC: Central Intelligence Agency, February 1979) 5.

4 Rudolf Vrba and Alan Bestic, *I Cannot Forgive* (London: Sidgwick and Jackson Ltd./Anthony Gibbs and Phillips, 1963); reprinted, with additional material, as *44070: The Conspiracy of the Twentieth Century* (Bellingham, Wash.: Star and Cross Publishing House, 1989) 233.

5 Rudolf Vrba, in a statement from *SHOAH*, in Claude Lanzmann, *Shoah: An Oral History of the Holocaust: The Complete Text of the Film* (New York: Pantheon Books, 1985) 166.

6 Albrecht Meydenbauer, *Das Denkmäler-Archiv* (Berlin, 1884).

7 Erwin Panofsky, *Perspective as Symbolic Form* (1974) (New York: Zone Books, 1991) 71.

8 Vilém Flusser, *Towards a Philosophy of Photography* (1983) (Göttingen: European Photography, 1984).

9 The full text of the report is reprinted in Vrba and Bestic, op. cit., 279–317.

10 [footnote 13 in source] David S. Wyman, *The Abandonment of the Jews: America and the Holocaust, 1937–1945* (New York: Pantheon Books, 1984) 307.

Harun Farocki, extracts from 'Reality Would Have to Begin', trans. Marek Wieczorek, Tom Keenan, Thomas Y. Levin, in Thomas Elsaesser, ed., *Working on the Sight-Lines* (Amsterdam: Amsterdam University Press, 2004) 193–202.

Lisa F. Jackson
Interview with Melissa Silverstein//2008

Melissa Silverstein Why did you want to make this movie [*The Greatest Silence: Rape in the Congo*, 2008]?

Lisa Jackson It's an invisible story as a lot of women's stories are, the horrific tale of the systematic rape and mutilation of hundred and thousands of women. It's just stunning to me that nobody was reporting it. The *New York Times* did one story on this angle of the war. But what they are doing to women ... not only the militias from the neighbouring countries but the Congolese army itself. I interviewed soldiers who were raping the very women they were supposed to be protecting.

Silverstein It was amazing that when you were talking to the rapists how they had a complete and total disconnection from the harm they were actually causing.

Jackson They [the Congolese army] see themselves as just 'raping' whereas the militias are the ones who mutilate the women and fire guns into their vaginas. But the end result is exactly the same. The women are shunned, turned out from their villages and abandoned. So the end result is exactly the same and that they parse the difference is just ridiculous, the disconnection is pretty profound.

Silverstein You made yourself a character in the film. Why did you do that?

Jackson It wasn't something I was initially going to do but people who saw rough cuts said that I absolutely had to because it was through telling them my story [of being raped] that the barriers between us came down.

Silverstein What compelled you to go to the Congo?

Jackson Here was this story, the stories of these women and no one was telling it. It seemed important to me not to have some hand-wringing piece but to actually listen to the women's stories. These are women who are silent and to be able to share their story with someone who was not judging them was an experience none of them ever had. [...]

I am continuing the theme and have been to Colombia twice in the last three months doing a film on displaced women. It is said that 60 per cent of the women in Colombia have suffered either physical or sexual violence. This is another one of those invisible stories, and it is a requirement of a documentary to find stories that otherwise you would never hear about.

Silverstein How did it feel being a first-world white woman going into a third world country?

Jackson I thought that through before I went. I was a white woman in the bush with a camera. I might as well have been dumped from a spaceship. I thought that as much as I could it was important to let them know I was one of them so I brought photographs to demystify where I was coming from and I shared my story of rape. They kept asking me about the war [thinking that rape only occurs in times of war]. They asked lots of questions including, did your family know you were raped? How was it is you got married? They were fascinated that I had a boyfriend, and they were stunned to hear that I chose not to have children.

Their questions pointed to how different we really were. I feel an intense responsibility to them. It was the rare woman who would tell me her story without pleading for help for her and her sisters. [...]

Silverstein What can people do to help?

Jackson We are putting together an outreach strategy around the culture of impunity, hopefully to pressure the Congo government into prosecuting rapists. We will provide resources where people can donate money. But also it's important for the first world to look at its role. This is an economic war. The blood of Congolese women is on our cell phones. It's important to understand that it's not just a bunch of crazy Africans killing each other. There is an economic imperative behind the pillaging, killing and rape.

To strike at the women is to strike at the heart of the culture. If you destroy women the civilization collapses.

Lisa F. Jackson and Melissa Silverstein, 'Interview with Lisa F. Jackson, Director of *The Greatest Silence: Rape in the Congo*' (2008) (womenandhollywood.com).

Lisa F. Jackson
Interview with Ben Kharakh//2008

Ben Kharakh How did you feel watching the footage as you were editing it?

Lisa F. Jackson The raw footage took a while to get translated and subtitled, but a lot of the interviews that I did in the Congo, I had a translator there sort of giving me suggestions of what people were saying, so to have it right there in front of me and with the letters on the screen, I was removed a little. The hardest part was listening in the first place and having direct eye contact with these women as they poured their hearts out to me. Doing that day after day after day was a tremendous emotional burden. I wept every day that I was in the Congo. The real shock was actually having the rapists subtitled – the soldiers – because when I was doing those interviews, I only got a rough idea from Bernard about what they were saying and, to tell you the truth, I was in some sort of zone where I was in a little bit of denial about being in the middle of the Bush with these kind of drunk guys with their guns. So when I actually looked at their faces on the screen and saw them looking at me, that was hard material to work with. It truly was difficult, and it still fills me with rage and loathing when I watch it.

Kharakh You couldn't understand directly what they were saying, but what did you pick up from the way they spoke – just the tone and their cadence ...?

Jackson I got incredible arrogance – a sense that this was their right. There was a pridefulness and a preening sense of self-regard, and a sort of malevolence. They tried to intimidate me, but ultimately I knew that they very much wanted their 15 seconds of fame and that if anything were to happen to me or my camera, they wouldn't get that, so I actually felt that the camera, while it wasn't the equivalent of their guns, it was my protection. It definitely was my protection. And the fact that they truly did want to brag about what they had done was evident in just their posture and the way they spoke.

Kharakh Was it the fact that it would be a film that people would see that got many of them to give their interviews?

Jackson Yeah, I think so. Nothing happens in the Congo without money. I gave everybody five dollars, but that was hardly the motivation. I think the motivation was to be seen, bragging about what they had done because they didn't consider it a crime, and they definitely didn't consider it a war crime, and they knew that they might have been confessing to unspeakable acts, but they would never be held accountable. And that was also a very hard moment, when the interviews were over and they just sort of melted back into the trees. I realized that I had videotaped soldiers confessing to war crimes and crimes against humanity, and I would never see them in court. They just disappeared, off to claim their next victims. [...]

Kharakh You asked one soldier if they were doing it because of power or sex, and the translator said, 'These are complicated questions. He will not understand.' Might any of these soldiers have been able to answer such a question?

Jackson I don't think that they tend to be very self-reflective individuals, but it's kind of understood that it is about power. These soldiers, they may have guns, but in a very real sense, they are powerless. The army is a pragmatic mess. There's no chain of command; there's no discipline. They don't get paid, so they take out their frustrations on the population. They claim it's about sex, but I think it's more about power. That's an interesting question that I really can't answer. I've had men in screenings ask me about the soldiers, 'Why do they do it? Why do men do these things?' and I say, 'You're a guy. You tell me.' But I can't answer this, and I don't think that they could either. [...]

Kharakh How did you establish connections with the women of Congo?

Jackson The simple universal act of exchanging personal narrative. You're simply telling them a story about your life and you're asking them to tell you a story about their lives. It's the simplest of connections and it's the most profound of bonds. I told my story to all the women I interviewed because there were a couple of situations, especially in the village, where they would line up to talk to me. The need to tell their story was evident, and it was something that was closeted within their own community. Maybe they talked about it within a very close circle of other women who have experienced the same thing, but they didn't have therapists and they definitely could not talk about it with their husbands. And that's if their husbands were even still around. It was thought of as something that should be hidden. The ability to talk to somebody who would listen to them without any judgement and with sympathy was, for many of them, a new experience. [...]

Kharakh What was life like for you after leaving the Congo?

Jackson It has pretty much consumed me for about three years. I came away from there with such a profound sense of obligation to these women that had shared with me their worst nightmare, and I felt obligated to make people listen to that and make people react, and make people do something. Even though it's a film that's just fraught with deep sadness, there is still, I think, a hopefulness that the women still come together, they still help each other. And then there are those brave souls, like the policewoman and others who are working to help them, and you have the sense that all is not lost because of the dignity, grace, and resilience of the women. I hope that this film conveys some of that, because otherwise, it's just a pretty relentless summer. So I not only wanted to convey the profundity of their experience, but also the truth about their souls, which you know, are just vibrant and keep going in the midst of things that would bring most of us to our knees. [...]

Kharakh The UN had also passed a resolution saying that rape was a tool of war, and your film was one of the catalysts for that.

Jackson Yes, the US Ambassador to the UN had seen the film and was inspired to sponsor the resolution, and he told me so to my face. Yeah, it recognizes rape as a destabilizing force that destroys families, it destroys communities, and it threatens the security of nations. By acknowledging it as a security issue, it takes it a notch above a humanitarian issue, which brings in medical supplies. A security issue means you bring in troops and guns and make it stop, because the ripple effect will devastate a country. [...]

Kharakh Do you believe that a moral obligation exists for people to become aware of not only this issue, but also other issues of its kind, and to do something about them?

Jackson Yeah, I think that people should not look away. I think that there is a moral obligation, especially in the first world, to listen to others and to understand what is happening and understand our connection to it. You also have to pick your causes. The film is the 'what' and people who watch it need to figure out the 'how', if you catch my drift, because I can't tell people, 'This is what you should do.' The film motivates people in different ways. It's been part of my moral underpinning as a filmmaker to look at difficult stuff and to bring it to an audience that hadn't considered it before. [...]

Lisa F. Jackson and Ben Kharakh, 'Lisa F. Jackson Interview: *The Greatest Silence: Rape In The Congo*', Buzzine.com (2008)

Ursula Biemann
Black Sea Files//2005

[...] The *Black Sea Files* [video installation, 2005] do not share the US-centric perspective taken by most of their authors. If anything, I hope to fragment and disperse the concentration of power in current oil discourses and present an alternative to the consolidation of power into a master narrative. Often enough, petroleum history is represented as an uninterrupted sequence of portraits depicting great men at the historical moment of deciding on war and peace. The authorial narrative tends to amalgamate many different levels of documents into one smooth homogeneous text. The hardcover master narratives are always the easiest source of information to obtain. Data on more obscure events, remote places, written in untranslated languages, are far less easily accessible. And there are insights that can only be gained from being personally embedded in the field. These *FILES* contain background information, media clips, personal notes and interviews, as well as reflections in the aftermath. Above all, they consist of numerous videographies recorded in the field during two trips to the Caucasus and one to Eastern Turkey in 2003–4 resulting in the *Black Sea Files* video complex. [...] In my understanding of the practice of art, images and text are inseparably interwoven in their common purpose to produce knowledge. When I quote the *Black Sea Files*, I refer to both my video and text research. To organize the material, I opted for files because they are an open structure, a case in progress and not a rigid order. In fact, files tend to contain a unique combination of documents, whose logic often lies entirely with the author of the files. This has to do with the personal circumstances under which data are found and new images produced, encapsulating the unspoken chain of associations and links to other protagonists and happenings. The unique logic might also be the result of a research trajectory which doesn't always follow scheduled directions. Seen from the outside, certain events might seem coincidental and unrelated, but through my sheer physical movement through the region, a connection is established and together they start to make sense. The coincidence of being able to record this image rather than that image will ultimately determine the critical videogeography which is my project, bound to be profoundly subjective. For all these reasons, the file seemed the appropriate structure for bringing a minimum of order into a complex web of interrelations. The reason being that, in oil geography, every move is entangled with international politics, every incident points to a string of histories, branches out into further cross-references. The *Black Sea Files* are about the Caspian oil, and the deep incisions made through the injured Caucasus to secure the precious fluid for the West. The video research roams the oil-soaked extraction wastelands around Baku, tracks the logistic technology of the pipeline, comments on the urban and rural transformations caused by the transformational project, engages with the people who live alongside its route, and generally tries to make sense of the hidden agenda of this political area. With the promise of a bonanza in the air, the Caucasus has started to bustle with oil seekers, investors, journalists and the intelligence community for over a decade. I arrived on the scene in the summer of 2003, at that time when long-negotiated contracts started to be implemented. The construction of the pipeline had been underway for a few months, turning the region into an open ditch. My investigations began with a visit to the site and sidelines of the giant foreign intervention, in order to collect visual intelligence relevant to the case. [...]

A million barrels of crude a day will be pumped through [the pipeline] when it is fully operating. A novelty in pipeline projects of this scale is the fact that the whole extent of the 1,760-km-long infrastructure will be buried underground. Petroleum has become a strategically invisible commodity. Only at the moment of construction are the material processes noticeable. Later, the scraped and dug-up landscape will return to its rural, disconnected state while high-tech subterranean infrastructures silently and invisibly pump energy to Western markets. All you will see then are the mileposts measuring the land.

On my filming trip through the Caucasus I followed long segments of the pipeline trajectory in Azerbaijan, Georgia and South East Turkey. Video *FILE 3* captures the gigantic material and physical effort involved in building the ducts. This contradicts most current representations of data and energy flow indicating a boundless and effortless, even magic transfer of energy. The field records show otherwise. The most powerful technologies are those which are pervasive and unnoticeable. Operating in the background, they connect, inform, empower and organize our lives. To investigate the infrastructure physically, as opposed to just theoretically, from a distance, is a surprisingly difficult thing to do. Oil companies run a severe image regime. The working conditions of an embedded artist recording the construction of a mega-transnational corporate infrastructure are pretty tough. As odd as it sounds, it is risky simply to videotape a pipeline.

The difficulties in producing visual intelligence are multiple. The first problem is to find out where the construction actually takes place. This information is not readily available and the oil company is the last to tell you. The trajectory is very long and winds through difficult terrain, sometimes miles away from the insufficient and poorly maintained road system. It can take a seven-hour brainrattling trip on a 4WD Lada to reach an area where the corridor might possibly be visible. I found it one day because I happened to come across a truck carrying three giant pipes in the rural heart of Azerbaijan, a lucky day. Its route fed me straight to the construction site. To my surprise, the man who approached me was fluent in Spanish. He acted as the translator for the many Colombian workers on the site who had been employed by BP for previous pipeline projects in Latin America. The head of the operation was a laid-back Scotsman (born on Braveheart's last battlefield, he specified) who invited me for a ride along the corridor. This unusual incident could only take place far away from the watching eyes of corporate policy and decision-making centres.

More likely, one is faced with problem number two which consists of overcoming being physically prevented from approaching and documenting the site. Nissan-driving pipe patrol is always on the horizon and the operators hired an army of guards among villages to watch the construction sites, making sure unauthorized persons do not enter them, not just physically but also televisually. This is when it becomes blatantly clear that their measures have little to do with security and everything with control of perception and representation. Their concept is that, during construction, image-making is prohibited and once the pipeline is buried it will be invisible anyway. The main challenge then is not an artistic one involving choices of framing, lighting and camera movements, but how to go undetected: to generate images of oil infrastructures has become an undercover mission. Keeping a low profile by means of general scarcity of information is a major concern in a project involving such a high level of financial investment and the employment of large amounts of equipment, machinery, and technology, particularly when the project runs through a poverty-stricken region whose population is entirely disconnected from the impact of the developments. But this cannot be the whole explanation. Why is it so important to keep it a secret? The ensemble of the *FILE* is an exploration of the meaning of this tube in the hidden corporate imaginary of this area and the function it has in its own secret ordering system.

Ursula Biemann, extracts from 'Black Sea Files', in Anselm Franke, ed., *B-zone: becoming Europe and beyond* (Berlin: Kunst-Werke, 2005) 25–7; 49–51.

Marta Zarzycka
Showing Sounds: Listening to War Photographs//2012

[...] Photographs of exploding buildings, screaming bystanders and lamenting mourners are not populated by deaf and mute characters that move about in soundless space. We as viewers, moreover, do not remain insensitive to these images' sonic effects. I will argue that these photographs can suggest sounds (even though those sounds lack physicality) which may clash or merge with the actual sounds that one makes/hears while viewing them. [...]

Unlike vision, which has often been conceived of as distancing the viewer from the viewed, sound is well-suited to express and evoke the traumas of war. The physics and the phenomenology of sound in Western culture are often associated with proximity, contact and consequently violent disturbance; through the air, sound transmits the agitation resulting from collisions of objects with each other to our ears and skin. Whereas eyes have a visual range of 180 degrees and can be closed instantly, ears cover a 360-degree expanse, often immersing us in sound against our will. Though light and sound both come to us in waves, it is only the sonic blast which can knock us over and even kill us. Frances Dyson writes:

> Because hearing is not a discrete sense, to hear is also to be touched, both physically and emotionally. In listening, one is engaged in a synergy with the world and the senses, a hearing/touching that is the essence of what we mean when we talk about a 'gut reaction' – a response that is simultaneously physiological and psychological.[1]

A sound one hears in a film without seeing its originating cause is called an acousmatic sound. How can we then call a sound of which, conversely, the source is visible, but which does not reach our ears? The two case studies that I develop below will each address different types of sounds, silences and their workings. The first case study is a still photograph of a scream/lament. My approach here has been informed by studies on silent cinema, in which the image has been employed to suggest sounds: the smoke coming out of the gun or the flock of startled birds signified not just the consequences of the action of firing, but also the noise of a gunshot. My analysis pertains to the following question: how does listening to the sounds of certain photographs structure our perception of them?

Secondly, I engage with an online documentary in which still photographs are accompanied by music and a voice-over. Adding sounds to photographs in the postproduction engenders further important questions: does the aural layer enhance or rather confuse our reception of still photographs? Can a sound hijack an image? My analysis of the sensorial intersections found in this case has been informed by performance theories of the senses that address both the visual and the sonic. The concept of performativity, in this case, does more than just suggest the visibility of sound, but rather indicates a whole range of resonances between the many interactive processes involving the somatic, the physiological and the imaginative. Moreover, the specific rhythmic effect of certain fragments of the footage created by the regular recurrence of sounds and images makes it necessary to think about how the visual and the aural can (co)operate outside the cognitive threshold of representational awareness.

Both of my case studies represent women in the aftermath of violence, a choice which reflects the tendency of the contemporary media to use female bodies as sites of despair, as signifiers for the ravages of wars, genocides and racial and gender inequalities. While I point out the dangers in reducing women to the pathological and the melancholic, I am also aware of the fact that through cultural rituals connected to sound and music, women have enacted an emotional response to violence and loss. Women in many cultures have used the aural as a means of both reappropriation and empowerment; their screams and silences have formed an indispensable expression of pain, formerly constructed as private and consecutively transferred into a communal web of global and intermedial relationships. Because of the global societal implications of these screams and silences, we should be aware of them within the genre of war photography.

Sounds Figuring as Sight

A photograph by Hocine Zaourar, World Press Photograph of the Year 1997, shows 'A woman crying outside the Zmirli Hospital, where the dead and wounded were taken after the massacre in Bentalha (Algeria). Mass killings and bomb blasts dominated life since the army annulled the results of the 1992 elections, in which it appeared the Muslim fundamentalist party, FIS, would win. The conflict had claimed more than 60,000 lives in five years.'[2] The image shows the aftermath of an August night when around two hundred men, women and children in the village were methodically slaughtered in their houses, while armed forces units were stationed outside the village and stopped some of those trying to flee.

The fact that the image depicts grieving has a particular significance in regard to its aural layer. In Western culture, the responsibility of remembering the dead, formerly assigned to the mourning rituals of lamenting, singing, screaming, wailing and silence, has been gradually replaced by portrait photographs of the deceased performing the function of rites of passage. In commemoration and mourning, the aural has therefore been replaced by the visual. What interests me here is what happens if we bring back the notion of sound to the photographic rendition of lamentation.

Just as in silent cinema, where sound is conveyed through a number of physical gestures at an appointed point of maximum intensity, here the scream is suggested by the focal point of the image: the open mouth, reminiscent of the *Laocoön* sculpture or Picasso's *Guernica*. The close-up of a face produces an intense phenomenological experience of almost excessive, unbearable presence and propels us to imagine a sort of acoustic close-up. And yet the image tells us about the semiotic possibilities and cultural connotations of the scream rather than about its specific character, its pitch, duration and intensity. In fact the character of the sound itself is unknown to us; the same image may suggest a wail, a scream, a moan or a gasp.

There have been witnesses, however, who did grasp the specificity of this very scream, both within and just outside the frame of the photograph: the other woman who puts her hand on the wailing woman's breast as if to accompany the flow of air, and who holds her head as if to keep it from failing to exclaim; the shadow of a person to the left; the people on the street we do not see; and the photographer himself. However, the audiences of this mediated testimony are confronted with the silence. The silence is not a neutral emptiness, but 'the negative of sound we've heard (or imagined) beforehand.'[3] It is this silence that makes Zaourar's photograph convey an acoustic sensation that extends beyond the environment in which we might be viewing it (which is hardly silent anyway, due to the noise of our blood and our heartbeats). Just like in John Cage's composition *4'33*, one has to *see* the silence to realize there is one. Our cultural understanding of silence is ambivalent: on the one hand, silence is seen as a form of control and prescribed normativity; on the other hand, it is often the sign of abnormality and malfunction. Yet, despite these dominant ideas about silence as constraint or impoverishment, silence experienced on the basis of the visual rendition of an extremely loud event can offer new spaces of social encounter. It is the tension between the materiality of the sound we imagine and the very lack of anything audible that functions as the carrier of affective reactions.

To become fully aware of how the silence unfolds, we need to re-examine the notion of time in this image. Duration – rather than pitch, loudness or timbre – is the only parameter of sound that is shared by silence. After all, sounds need temporal space to develop, to resonate and to fall silent again. Consequently, we usually think of sound-image combinations in relation to animated footage; if we press the 'still' button while watching a film, the sound vanishes. Photographs, seen as *tableaux vivants*, as moving images that have come to an eternal standstill, are thought to have no temporal directionality unless connected to other shots. We generally understand the organization of time through movement in space.

Yet in the case of a photograph, we are presented with an image that is immobile and therefore perpetually present. That shapes our affective and ethical relationship to them. As a consequence, many of the photographs of war and conflict move into the realm of universalized human suffering located *beyond* time; their actual, politicized dimension is denied.

Consequently, photography is culturally perceived as being a soundless practice. As the issues of sound and time have a comparable position vis-à-vis the photographs, it seems fruitful to turn to critical approaches towards photographic temporality in order to bring sound(s) into this image. Benjamin conceived of photography as a dynamic, temporalized medium displaying aspects of both stasis and movement. In *Camera Lucida*, Barthes commented upon Alexander Gardner's *Portrait of Lewis Payne*, taken when Payne had been sentenced to death, and the ambiguity of the 'anterior future': we are looking at somebody who is dead already. The photograph provides unique phenomenological evidence of a prior existence; it comprises of *the here* and *the formerly*, but also the *not anymore*, and the *not yet*. Following that argument, Azoulay argues that the force of images of atrocity can only be understood if the spectator recognizes his or her temporal co-presence with a photographed body, temporarily suspended but in continuous action. If we assume that the photographed people have not been there *once*, but are there *still* at the time we are watching them, we can restore the identity, accountability and civil status previously denied to them. Azoulay argues for *watching*, rather than *looking* at photographs: usually reserved to moving images, watching entails dimensions of time and movement that allow for connections between the photographer, the photographed subject and his/her audiences. We can therefore argue that the photograph of a lamenting Algerian woman stages an encounter between a distinct historical moment in time and simultaneously produces the sense of an affective present, in which our watching takes place. In that sense, it mirrors the temporal structure of trauma which, never completed nor processed, is simultaneously *after* and *now*, in motion and at a standstill. Adding listening to the process of watching yields a similar notion of temporality. Just as it covers a moment larger than its own instant, the image may suggest sounds that last beyond the moment in which it was taken, breaking through the linearity of progressive historical time. [...]

In the afterlife of Zaourar's photographs, cultural voices and silences merge, loop, contract and open up. [...] After taking the picture, featured on the front pages of many newspapers around the world, the photographer was forbidden by the Algerian authorities to work in the country and stopped using his last name for the time being to protect his identity for safety concerns. Just like many photographic stills of crying women, one of the central visual techniques of humanitarianism, the image had a significant voice in swaying public opinion and influencing political actions. It was quickly dubbed the 'Bentalha Madonna' or 'Algerian Pieta' and controversy ensued as the Muslim woman, Umm Saad, objected to being identified with Christian symbols and sued the Agence France Presse for defamation and exploitation of human suffering. It is on this backdrop that I propose to encounter Hocine Zaourar's image not as *silenced*, where its aural layer is lost as soon as this image becomes a sound container emptied of the female voice and filled with those of others, but rather as *silent*, where the (lack of) sounds open up the potential of a more accountable engagement.

Seeing Rhythm

Ordinarily, we arrange photographs into sequences, place them in various contexts – such as the family album, the newspaper, the exhibition – and create rituals to make sense of them. Yet still photographs are also increasingly incorporated into multimedia projects. This new form of visual storytelling, either linear or interactive, is rapidly becoming a part of photography contests, museum installations and online news platforms. The project by photojournalist Jonathan Torgovnik titled *Intended Consequences* tells the stories of Tutsi women in Rwanda, who fell victim to sexual violence used as a weapon of war by Hutu militia groups in 1994. Close to 20,000 children were born as a result; most of them have contracted HIV/AIDS from their mothers. Due to the stigma of rape, the women's communities and the few surviving relatives have largely disapproved of the existence of these children. Torgovnik's project resulted in a book with interviews and photographs of thirty women and their families, a travelling exhibition, and a film available at *Media Storm* (www.mediastorm.com), an online platform featuring still photographs enhanced by videos, music, voiceovers and interviews.

Despite their culturally acknowledged 'fixity', it is important to point out that the meaning and impact of photographs can easily be shifted by changing their context of viewing, or, as happened in this case, by literally adding sounds. Seen in this respect, digital photographs encountered online emerge from a complex entanglement of perceptual and cognitive processes in which various strategies of negotiation and exchange are involved. When senses other than vision are addressed, the effects that these images have change dramatically. If we saw Zaourar's photograph as stripped bare of its sound layer, the case of *Intended Consequences* leads us to ask what happens when we re-add sounds to still images, and whether we can do this without changing their integrity. What are the losses and gains of adding sound to photographs?

Although the documentary is about long-internalized silences, it has a complex and elaborate sonic structure: there is (originally written) music, most of the time a translated account is provided, and in several instances we hear the women themselves, with a (female) voice-over, giving their accounts in translation. I would like to focus here on the opening and closing minutes of the film where the portraits of individual women (in the beginning of the film) and their children (in the end) are flashed at us rhythmically, accompanied by the same tune. The last frame of each sequence smoothly transforms into a video portrait, which may at first look like a still photograph, but on closer inspection reveals minimal movements such as blinking eyes or curling lips.

At first glance, there seems to be a disjunction between the images and the sounds. While in conventional cinema practices of sound editing streamline sound and image to give a coherent impression of the events, the sounds we hear in *Intended Consequences* are not linked to the images in an illustrative manner: the portraits appear to listen rather than be heard, their mouths are closed, their eyes focused. Although the photographs of women and children claim truth on the basis of their indexicality, there is a distinct absence of diegetic sounds – i.e. sounds inscribed within the film's action, with an apparent source. The discrepancy between the origins of the sounds and the images in *Intended Consequences* points towards a disruption of the transparent immediacy of the photographic image. This disruption is reminiscent of the mediation processes taking place and the restrictions/enhancements operative in the genre of documentary. In this sense, images and sounds (dis)organize each other.

However, watching/listening on, the audience realizes that sounds and images are closely interwoven and meticulously synchronized in the opening and closing sequence. Sounds participate directly in conveying, prolonging and amplifying the emotional impact of images: the formal qualities of the photographs (texture, contrast, lighting and composition) form a duet with the formal and temporal qualities of music. The frequency with which the images pop up is identical to the frequency of the sounds, leading to a tight coupling of vision and sound. A lot of our viewing and listening pleasure stems from this rhythmic and multisensory performance and is based on anticipation, progression to climax, release, and the symmetrical replaying of the cycle. The repetition of sounds which are similar in pitch, volume and timbre and the regular patterns of their pace and composition smooth over gaps, fissures and discontinuities between the reality of the film and that of a spectator. Vibrations and frequencies surround the viewer-listener and lead to a perceptual experience radically different than the sense of sight alone would have given. The result of this simultaneity is that at moments the film annuls the distance between itself and its viewers.

This is not to conclude, however, that sounds are always beneficent factors in the perception of photographs of war and trauma. While digital culture presents its audiences with mixed, layered and heterogeneous audiovisual images in non-linear space and time, it rarely offers the tools to challenge homogenous, linear modes of reception. Although music and sound indisputably impart a particular new intensity to certain shots, they may also frame, discipline and contain our emotional response. Sound and image often inscribe themselves into each other to such an extent that eyes and ears become a synaesthetic, trans-sensory system which perceives the concomitance of a sound event and a visual event as a single integrated phenomenon. Yet this synaesthetic experience may easily amount to a captivating feel-good consumption of images of atrocity in which the intensity of political injustice wears off as the intensity of aesthetic experience grows. [...]

1 [footnote 8 in source] Frances Dyson, *Sounding New Media: Immersion and Embodiment in the Arts and Culture* (Berkeley and Los Angeles: University of California Press, 2009) 4.

2 [16] Caption as found on www.worldpressphoto.org, accessed 15 May 2011.

3 [21] Michel Chion, *Audio-Vision: Sound on Screen* (New York: Columbia University Press, 1994).

Marta Zarzycka, extracts from 'Showing Sounds: Listening to War Photographs', in Marta Zarzycka and Bettina Papenburg, eds, *Carnal Aesthetics: Transgressive Imagery and Feminist Politics* (London: I.B. Tauris, 2012).

WE HAVE ALWAYS URGED OUR AUDIENCE TO TREAT OUR DOCUMENTS AS HYSTERICAL DOCUMENTS IN THE SENSE THAT THEY ARE NOT BASED ON ANY ONE PERSON'S ACTUAL MEMORIES BUT ON FANTASIES ERECTED FROM THE MATERIAL OF COLLECTIVE MEMORIES

Walid Raad/The Atlas Group, Interview with Alan Gilbert, 2002

DOCUMENTARY FICTIONS

Joan Fontcuberta
Interview with Christina Zelich//2005

Joan Fontcuberta [...] Among photojournalists there is still the sense that making a photomontage is far graver than adding a filter. I'm against this type of hierarchy that demonizes some options over others – in respect of what? Ideology, or moral code? A bankrupt and fundamentalist ideology without doubt. Some years ago I visited the Center for Creative Photography in Tucson. Its archive has among other things the entire legacy of Eugene Smith. The person who took me around commented that when assessing the original negatives one could see that sometimes Smith made a montage of certain images everyone had assumed to be spontaneous and direct. While making this confession she raised her hand to her lips as if to ask me to keep it quiet. It was as if the revelation of this supposed secret should be kept to a limited number of specialists, as if we had the obligation to preserve the photographer's myth in the face of public opinion. Some years later Professor Jesús de Miguel revealed that many of the most famous shots one sees in the Spanish Village series had been staged and re-shot until Smith was satisfied with the results. For me, this information does not in any way devalue Smith's humanistic or artistic merit. I've always thought that the photographer does artistic work and that art consists of working with fictional premises.

Christina Zelich [This brings to mind the moment when] you stopped using methods supposedly employed to create a separate category, and went on to use direct photography – the version of photography to which all the attributes of truth are ascribed, the one that pretends to render a faithful reproduction of reality. You did that intentionally, in order to subvert that idea, and demonstrate the deception contained in that idea.

Fontcuberta It's true that towards the end of the 1970s I began to get interested in certain 'places', shall we say, where it is no longer necessary to fabricate contradictions, because they are right there in front of you; all you have to do is uncover and reveal them. And this evolution came thanks to a series of successive anecdotes. My method of working when I was using photomontage consisted in looking for appropriate backgrounds into which I would inject the action of some actors or fragments of other images. But a moment arrived when the backgrounds themselves interested me to such a degree, were so evocative and mysterious on their own that it felt like the addition of other elements would only diminish their enigmatic, poetic qualities. So I dedicated myself to doing a series of works where the manipulation or the condensation of information was controlled by the theme, by the moment of actual shooting, the light, etc. That is, by perfectly accepted photographic techniques that in common parlance can be summed up in the notion of 'decisive space' as opposed to Cartier-Bresson's 'decisive moment'.

Little by little I moved into spaces that were not so innocent and that had certain connotations. This is when, for example, I started to dedicate myself somewhat obsessively to botanic gardens, zoos, science museums, all kinds of places where Nature appears in an artificial context. Whether these things were artificial for cultural or scientific, or didactic reasons, they were always about taking something from its place of origin and putting it somewhere else and they always created a surreal sensation much like that defined by Lautréamont, who brought about that fortuitous encounter between a sewing machine and an umbrella placed on a dissection table. When we find a dissected lion in the midst of modernist architecture, such as in the Zoological Museum of Barcelona, the situation provokes a cultural, ideological and aesthetic shock without any need for the introduction of any additional elements. It constitutes a photomontage all on its own. It's not a typical arrangement using a laboratory and juxtaposing negatives but rather a scenographic photomontage, because someone had the idea of putting those elements together.

A moment arrived when my work basically consisted of the detection of these kinds of tensions in various places and then moulding them; in this sense I became a documentary photographer, or, better put, I played at appearing as if I was a documentary photographer who made an inventory of these absurd situations. And this calls into question what it is that we call absurd. The absurd depends on the perspective from which one makes an analysis. [...]

In 1969 NASA photographs of the first astronauts to land on the moon had documentary, scientific value, accomplishing a strictly informative task. We saw them in the press, in magazines, in the media. But ten years later, in 1979, MoMA, New York, I believe, organized a photo exhibit about space because they believed these pictures opened up new fields of representation with their own minimal aesthetic that linked them to a more conceptual form of documentation than the merely formalist kind, that linked them with the New Topographics. In short, a whole theoretical presentation. But in practical terms they chose the same pictures, they matted and framed them, hung them in the institutional space of a museum and canonized them as artworks. So already they had taken one step away from the purely functional to the artistic, from the environment of an archive to a museum exhibit. Photography begins as an informational medium and is transformed into a work that people go to see, looking for aesthetic and emotional values as a way of participation in an artistic experience. [...]

My work, which is conceptual or experimental, highlights and offers commentaries about the documentary nature of photography, analysing how information is actually transmitted. So I need there to be documentary photographers, because my work is meta-documentary; it is a commentary about the documentary use of photography. [...]

Sometimes colleagues say to me that what I was doing a few years ago made sense because analogue photography did have the kind of charismatic authority as a document that I was claiming for it. Today with the electronic culture, with digital techniques, computers and the Internet, people's sensibility and awareness have changed so much. Everybody has Photoshop at home and even children have fun distorting their own snapshots, so that the notion of respect for an image as testimony does not have a leg to stand on because we have learned how easy it is to manipulate images. To this I reply that, yes, it's true that a cultural change has taken place, an authentic epistemological revolution in the field of knowledge and in the communications media, because the eruption of digital techniques for treating images tosses aside the photojournalistic values that have reigned up until now; but even so, and even looking at other areas that are not exclusively photographic, there continue to exist elements of authority that impose a determined notion of what the truth is. Don't you think? Whether these new elements come propitiated by a technological platform we call photography or whether they are generated by some other type of technology is all the same to me. I continue to focus on why we tend to believe, to deem credible, one model of information over another. What are the conditioning factors that elicit certain reactions when looking at images?

In an interview moderated by Angelo Schwartz, Rudolf Arnheim said something fundamental. Schwartz asked him: 'What is the substantial difference between photography and other types of imagery? How might one in essence define photography?'

The definition problem is something absolutely crucial. We are, after all, talking about photography but in practice we can't agree on what it is we actually consider 'photography' to be. And Arnheim said that photography is a kind of image that produces a certain experience in the viewer, that is, that it is not so much about what we do or with what sort of mechanical device, with this kind of light or that kind of lens, but rather the effect it has on the public; conveying a sensation of verisimilitude that is not questioned. It is for this simple motive that we carry photos around in our wallets to show the face of our daughter, or why we use photographs on passports, or why the police use photographs as forensic evidence, or why a biologist will use an electron microscopic photograph to show what a cell looks like. If we did not have this kind of a relation with it, it would not be photography. And so it is paradoxical because, according to Arnheim, what characterizes photography is not anything intrinsic to its own language, nothing that particular in its own technique or formation, but only an attribute that is social and cultural, something historically and ideologically stamped.

What defines photography are its own atavisms. [...]

It could be that occasionally we lose some of the confidence we normally concede to photography, but we pass it on to another element. The question is, where did the confidence we had before in photography go, and did it really merit such confidence in the first place? In the final analysis I believe my artistic role consists in being an observer of what it is that gives us that sensation of confidence, and in calling into question the mechanisms that seem to guarantee it.

Joan Fontcuberta and Christina Zelich, extracts from interview, in *Conversations with Contemporary Photographers* (New York: Umbrage Editions, 2005) 13–38.

Kutlug Ataman
Interview with Ana Finel Honigman//2004

Ana Finel Honigman You never dramatize events; instead you allow beauty and ugliness to be exposed through their narrative contrast.

Kutlug Ataman We articulate absence through presence and express a thing's presence by highlighting its absence. This process is a little like the work of Rachel Whiteread, very roughly speaking. Rather than look at a structure, you are looking at what that structure is defining. The structure is therefore implied by what it is not. Ultimately, this method makes both the structure and its absence appear more complex and essential through its purpose and relationship to other things. The empty spaces point to its existence. When my characters talk about their stories, like in *Women Who Wear Wigs* (1999), they do not offer a clear political narrative. They never say, 'I am so and so and I represent this political party or that political party.' They never say, 'I want to revolt.' They do not talk about gay rights, human rights or women's rights. They never articulate these big issues. Instead, they talk about personal, everyday, little stories. These stories are ultimately stronger than lessons and speeches. Through these stories they define their lives and point out their context. From this comes an impression of the bigger society. Without any encyclopaedic description of Turkey, you get an idea of Turkey through its imprint on these people's stories. In a way, their stories are disturbing and often devoid of a clear message, or empty of hope, because they never say, 'We will have a revolution and things will change.' But there is hope, because these stories show the hopeful act of changing or crafting an identity within a social context, which is ultimately a tool for survival.

Honigman Do you feel that you have or want to maintain an objective relationship to your subjects and their lives?

Ataman I am a curious person. I try to avoid making moral statements or distinctions, which I feel diminish the work of art. I protest, by allowing my subjects to protest, the lack of beauty. The TV presenter who speaks about her breast cancer and chemotherapy experience in *Women Who Wear Wigs* articulates an attitude about feminine identity that would be unacceptable to a lot of feminists. Her identity is rooted in her own perception of idealized feminine beauty, which also happens to be the socially clichéd combination of long, blond hair and big breasts. She derives pleasure and power from this conventional perception of a beautiful woman. She works in the media, and her profession depends on her image as well as her intellect. This is her reality but, along with her body, her ideals of beauty were attacked by breast cancer. The illness attacks her breast, which might have to be removed, and the treatment causes her to lose her hair. This is a huge intervention, a horrific interruption in her life. She talks about how she defends her ground. We all defend our defining lines by our stories.

Honigman What do you consider to be the effect of telling their stories to you and being aware that they will be seen – or in the case of one woman in *Women Who Wear Wigs* simply heard – by strangers?

Ataman I look at people like buildings. Instead of walls and rooms, we have stories and experiences. As long as we can live these stories, express these stories, tell and retell these stories, then we can stand up, the way a building stands. Talking is the only meaningful activity we have. Once we are no longer willing or allowed to tell our stories, we collapse into conformity. I like to look at my subjects in this way. My interest in recording them is not a service or anything like that. I am interested in their stories and how the telling functions in the context of their lives. [...]

Identity is an intellectual thing. You can change it. You can change who you are or your history by choosing to tell a different story each time. You can lie, like Semiha [the Turkish veteran opera singer in *Semiha B. Unplugged*, 1997]. History does not live in the past; it only lives in the present. You select your memories. You select what you tell. Lies are more real to me because they are immediate. Retelling the facts, as they are supposed to be told, means much less. The facts are not interesting. Recounting facts is like creating systems of documentary. It is creating catalogues. I am interested in a person's lies because of the reasons they lie. Those are far richer and more compelling than the reasons they would have to recite the facts. What purpose do their lies have? What result are they aiming for? I am not referring to lies as moral issues, but simply as non-truths. [...]

Honigman Do you see history as a popular consensus on fact? Do you consider history a trustworthy authority?

Ataman History, as an authoritative system, was a necessary evil, perhaps needed to keep people together. It is deeply linked to nationalism, patriotism and prejudice. We need radar telling us how we are being manipulated and how we manipulate others through telling our 'histories'. As a child, you discover that you are the lead, the star, in your own movie. After that discovery, we then need to learn the effects as well as our motivations for changing our plot.

Honigman How do these stories translate from one language to the subtitles? How do you think the experience is altered? Specifically in *Women Who Wear Wigs*, where the voices mix, leaving it unclear whose voice tells which story.

Ataman In this installation I really wanted those competing voices, so as to point out how these narratives compete with each other for space – each trying to have its own say. Each story shoulders the other. But I install it completely differently in Turkey. There I use sound sticks, so the sound emerges immediately behind your head as you watch, conflicting with the cacophony around you. In England, people mainly access the dialogue by reading the subtitles. [...]

Honigman In other interviews you have referred to your characters as Brechtian. Do their personalities evoke those in Bertolt Brecht's plays?

Ataman I was not referring to my characters as much as my method. By pointing out how the machinery works, I am following Brecht. For example, *Semiha B.* is impossible to watch in its entirety. The film is eight hours long, and in order to watch it you need to ask questions about your role in the process. Are you watching a film, and how active can you be during that experience? Are you supposed to recline and enjoy, or are you encouraged to think actively? With *Never My Soul!* (2001), for instance, you never know if it is real, if she is acting, if she is a woman, if she is a man. My role is disrupted as well. It is never comfortably clear where there is a director and whether that director is an artist or a journalist. This condition exaggerates an awareness of these definitions and their synthetic perimeters. Therefore we are no longer placated by the pleasure of watching a Hollywood flick in which we are lost in illusion; instead we are constantly forced to remain unsettled. This process is a Brechtian concern because it requires an intellectual, inquisitive engagement with the artwork. [...]

Kutlug Ataman and Ana Finel Honigman, extracts from 'What the Structure Defines: An Interview with Kutlug Ataman', *Art Journal*, vol. 63, no. 1 (Spring 2004) 78–86.

Sean Snyder
Marriot Hotel Islamabad//2008

'It's just like in a movie' is a much-heard cliché about the images of the 9/11 attack on the World Trade Center. But this is only partly true, and increasingly less so. The effects are like in a movie, the images are not. Most Hollywood films are shot on 35mm film or HD video; but many of the now familiar iconic images of the 9/11 attack were captured by amateurs and television news bureaus overlooking the skyline of New York City. In addition, the images were viewed and distributed on television and later the Internet, not on the big screen.

Hollywood has, of course, long been associated with apocalyptic images and, on more than one occasion, has even been accused of contributing to the events of 9/11. Today amateurs continue to edit and reproduce the dramatic impact of those images into existing footage, in some instances resulting in 'new' videos that generate re-readings and reinterpretation of the events of 9/11. The cumulative effort of amateur post-production posted on video sharing sites such as YouTube reconnects memory and time, while in the process potentially constructing false recollections.

I would like to emphasize that I am not directly addressing the politics of images, but rather want to engage in a subjective analysis of the visual surfaces ideology produces. As an artist I am currently working with the malleability of images and the technical mechanics of their production. As images replace textual information – taking the temporal nature of those images, to consideration – they must be increasingly unconventional to have an impact. Not to say that we are entirely desensitized to spectacular acts of terror, but we are somehow conditioned to read the various subtexts for meaning. That is to say, we search for what distinguishes these images from our familiar environment and cognition.

While watching YouTube I was reminded of the Cold War-era film *Red Dawn*. Set in a small Midwestern American town under Soviet and Cuban occupation, the film *enacts* the unthinkable under détente. Playing on the ominous threat of nuclear warfare, the film depicts an unconventional invasion initiated by disguised commercial airliners followed by ground troops. Local teenagers form a guerrilla resistance to fight in an act of self-preservation and patriotism. In this case the narrative seems obliquely to resemble the method used by the terrorists on 9/11, with no option, however, for heroics on the part of the citizens, with the planes themselves being the weapons. [...]

Shortly following the events of 9/11 we were exposed to a number of vivid descriptions of everyday life in Afghanistan under the Taliban regime invoked by the Western media: hanging televisions, trees draped in videotape pulled from cassettes and 'executed computers' in the streets of Kabul, alluding to the unthinkable actions of 'the other'.

For years following 9/11, the Western media often referred to the jihadists' release of 'videotapes,' implying their use of archaic or inferior technology in the production of their messages. It seems doubtful, however, that at a certain point any traditional audiotape, videotape or film was used in the production or distribution of Al Qaeda's materials (for instance by As Sahab, Al Qaeda's media wing).

We were constantly told by unknown 'experts' and well-known agencies what we were seeing or should be seeing. Take, for example, the continued mention of the specific positioning of Osama Bin Laden's watch on his wrist indicating 'further attacks'. In other words, experts are supposed to create a narrative, to construct a certain meaning of the image. However, there is a common and quite limited rhetoric, which could be extracted from an expert's discourse; it shows how our notion of credibility is based not on the old idea that 'seeing is believing', but rather on abstracted constructions of meaning.

A few years ago I worked on a project which entailed comparing the image production of the US Department of Defence to that of Al Qaeda. I will outline a series of speculative interpretations based on this research, exploring some aspects of these 'complicated constructions' of meaning that have to do with the amateur video production that Al Qaeda tactically implemented in its propaganda strategies.

As a side note: in 2008 there was a remarkable decrease in the release of videos by Al Qaeda which seems to imply that they don't intend to produce sequels.

A short scene from a 2005 Al Qaeda release includes footage of the operation of a video camera recorded by a second camera. Once slowed down, the camera being filmed appeared to be a Sony model, incidentally similar to one I purchased in Hong Kong in the late 1990s. After enlarging and printing out a series of still images of the camera and comparing its make to a number of similar Sony camcorders, I was able to identify the specific model as a Sony DCR PC-120E.

It turned out that this exact high-end consumer model was the first to be brought on the market with Bluetooth technology, giving the possibility, among other things, to upload video from anywhere via mobile phone. A Sony press release states the camera's capacity to transmit MPEG format data with a resolution of 240 x 320 pixels. On a television screen the image quality would appear equivalent to the resolution of VHS format videotape.

Another sequence from a 2004 Al Qaeda release shows the transference of a captured US forces' computer hard-drive and an operative using a (Sony Vaio model) computer to open a PDF file containing information about their own (that is, Al Qaeda's) tactics, underlining the jihadists' use of consumer technology as a tactical weapon.

Using do-it-yourself montage techniques, jihadist video editors employ graphics, animations and the dramatic use of sound to disseminate their message. Often assembled like music videos, their seduction is achieved by the merging of sound and image, alluding to the editors' fluency. The superimposed graphic elements and the repetition of clips from previous videos create 'iconic' moments, often including American media footage from the attacks on 9/11.

What makes a moment iconic, how does it work? It would be my hypothesis that image producers, jihadist videographers included, use common visual techniques informed by popular visual culture that constitute a similar vocabulary to that of any other YouTube contributor. [...]

If the iconic moment is something almost universal in the production, and the dissemination of imagery is part of the current imaginary, it goes beyond our visual faculty, with its grounding principle of singling out and repeating the most dramatic effect. However, that aside, the iconic moment is not necessarily only visual but a kind of constructed point of dramatic intensity. There are other tendencies in the current popular visual vocabulary, which, following the slogan of a new American Television channel, 'True-TV – Not Reality, Actuality', have to do with an amateurish quality opposed to professionalism. This quite established visual trend of attributing truth as actuality to the amateur, 'poor' quality (from certain films, or many on-line videos) refers not only to the changing technology but also to changing sensibility (in the visual field). This trend seems to work very well and in fact is one of the interpretative frames of the Western perception of media imagery after 9/11.

In the visual strategies of As Sahab over the last few years, the same tendency can be seen – the effectiveness of the conveyance of messages lies in the notion of verisimilitude, which depends less on the high level of technology and professionalism than on a certain emotive trust on the side of the subject/viewer. Furthermore, it could be said that the underlying aesthetics of current imaging techniques play a role in establishing a sense of authenticity. Data compression, resulting in the disintegration of image quality, gives the effect of actuality – an imaginary quality, which in respect to its rhetorical effects seems more valuable.

Many of the Al Qaeda videos not only provide a spectacular image of war, but are also designed to give an 'actual' view into the banal and everyday routines that lead up to the implementation of an operation. A video from 2005 follows the regiment of an operation in Afghanistan, including details of everyday life: cooking, their living quarters, instruction classes, bomb-making and field activities. The 60-minute video suggests the implementation of war as an ingenious and methodical craft. These images might equate to the antithesis of the representations of American military power and technology, say that of the Stealth bomber or the Apache helicopter.

In many of the As Sahab videos, the technical functions of the camera are fully implemented: the infrared night-shot function illuminates operations in the dark, the zoom lens extended to its maximum focal length traces the movements of the enemy in pursuit, and Bluetooth is possibly even used to upload video data. Perhaps this exploitation of the capabilities of the camera makes Al Qaeda's videographers the ultimate consumers.

The Arabic subtitling of one scene in an As Sahab video from 2005 locates an operation in an abandoned American base in Afghanistan. The jihadists wander around the site documenting their occupation of the space. A short incidental shot focuses on some paperback books on a table, presumably left behind by the US soldiers. Once slowed down and the image data enlarged, the titles of a few Tom Clancy paperback novels become legible. The plot of one of the books, *Executive Orders*, written in 1997, revolves around a terrorist attack on the US Capitol using an airliner, the unleashing of a virus on the American public, and a presidential sex scandal. A coincidental identification or not, fiction and reality here come full circle.

Sean Snyder, extracts from 'Marriot Hotel Islamabad' (20 September 2008), in Jelle Bouwhis, Ingrid Commandeur, Gijs Frieling, Domenik Ruyters, Margit Schavemaker and Christel Vesters, eds, *Now is the Time: Art and Theory in the 21st Century* (Rotterdam: NAi Publishers, 2009) 51–8.

Omer Fast
Interview with Sven Lütticken//2007

Sven Lütticken [...] How do you see *The Casting* (2007) in relation to your preceding works?

Omer Fast I guess the preceding two works focused on individuals whose personal narrative somehow floats between first-hand experience and its re-creation. *Spielberg's List* (2003) looked at extras who participated in the filming of *Schindler's List*; *Godville* (2005) presented the costumed guides who work as historical characters in Colonial Williamsburg. In both works, the idea was to exploit an ambiguity central to these persons' experiences: as narrators they can recall an impossible past in precise lived-through detail; as witnesses they've lived through real events that are nevertheless replicas. By cutting and mixing the narrator's memories with the witness's reflections to a point where they lose their signature instance and start to blur and intermingle, I was trying to open a stretch of time of the third kind, if you will, one that plays with the normally fixed notions of past and present, authentic and copy. Another feature common to the previous two works is that both looked at historical events through how they've been re-enacted in the public domain. Since the Hollywood film and the living-history museum obviously preceded my filming (both are famous and discrete spectacles in their own right) they can be handled like found objects or readymades. This gives me the split-subject I like so very much: namely the duped/duping witness. It allows me to look at historical events by looking at how they've been portrayed publicly and remembered privately, critically after the fact, by those who have 'been there,' on-location for their re-creation. [...]

In *The Casting*, I think this logic is turned on its head. To begin with, there is no big-time re-enactment to hark back to. There are certainly genre conventions and plenty of media depictions of romance and war that come to mind, ones to borrow or to avoid. Nevertheless, the young Army sergeant's storytelling is personal, spontaneous and genuine. Of course he becomes an actor in the sense that anyone who agrees to sit in front of a camera does. But the past he describes is his own, narrated in two separate stories: one takes place near Baghdad and involves a violent attack; the other is a romantic liaison with a girl in Bavaria. As a script, the two stories are woven together to produce a hybrid that swings back and forth between time, place and feeling. Still, each story retains its distinct setting and, more crucially, each draws on a chain of events whose occurrence is not questioned. Finally, since *The Casting* isn't based on an already-made re-enactment, this leaves me room to move in and produce one. I've been wanting to do this for a long time, not least because I'd grown tired of the sort of easy media critique that basing a work on a Hollywood film, for example, seems to welcome. In this respect, I think *The Casting* represents somewhat of a turn for me. It still provides the evidence of the 'documentary', the encounter with the real that's been so important to me in previous projects. But it simultaneously presents its own dramatization of that encounter: recreating the real by staging the soldier's stories as a series of silent tableaux, replete with actors in costumes, several locations and props, and (horror of horrors) even a smoke machine. [...]

The actors that I hired for the project were told they would do all their acting off camera and that they would be filmed still, like mannequins. In the beginning they all stood around stiff and had no idea what to do. (Frankly, neither did I.) After a while though, we developed a system in which they would act out the scene, according to the script and directions, and then, at some random moment, instead of 'Action!' I would yell 'Stop!' They were then supposed to freeze, to hold a pose; whatever it was, and only at that moment would the camera roll and the proper scene start. This worked out only some of the time. Very often the actors would not hear me yell, or just pretended not to. (It's amazing just how much they're into this acting thing, actors.) Some persons responded as if it's a game; others just seemed to dread the whole thing and cringed whenever their work was interrupted. I was quietly cursing the whole thing at the beginning, losing my voice from repeatedly screaming, 'Stop!' Before we began, I imagined scenes that would be magical, trance-like, still. What I more often got was coughing fits, laughter, whispering and lots of high-desert wind. Nevertheless, when I flew back home with the footage I was really surprised, especially by those particular scenes that did not seem to work out on location. Unlike previous works, editing took only several days. (And it was fun ...)

In the end, I see the project as a collection of the frozen awkward moments that exist between an actor's wish to identify with his/her subject and scene (the cathartic objective of good old drama) and the vagaries of the real: wind, gravity and the body's ever-present desire to twitch, cough, fall and rebel, always at the wrong moment. Strangely, this is probably the basic principle of comedy.

Lütticken [...] To me one of the many moments of brilliance in *Godville* – in which, as you mention, there is a constant slippage from the era of the War of Independence to that of the War on Terror – is the militia man's rant about you – this liberal artsy guy with his hidden agenda, twisting his words. In a very funny way, this articulates the divide between 'mainstream' re-enactors, whether they are hobby war re-enactors or 'interpreters' at living history museums, and artists and intellectuals with an interest in re-enactment, a divide which involves social distinctions (the word class distinctions may suggest a precision that is lacking here). We should be conscious of this even while trying to articulate what remains unsaid in mainstream re-enactment.

Fast The very idea of re-enactment strikes me as something that is fundamentally about a contradiction: literally an attempt to cheat the clock, however illusory or fleeting that attempt is, through the agency the body and its all-too-corporeal (ultimately terminal) nowness. I think it's really helpful that you point to two caveats that should probably rank high in any re-enactor's list of commandments: the danger in detail and historical texture (the myopia implicit in 'getting it right') and a kind of imperative to remain in the moment while time traveling (i.e. not to lose track of the present when re-doing the past.) The thing is, when you visit Colonial Williamsburg, their very motto – coined eighty years ago, probably by their strangely-named founder, the Right Rev. Dr W.A.R. Goodwin, is – 'that the future may learn from the past'. Almost everybody I met in the two intense weeks I spent there from the professionals working in historical drag to the amateur clubs that convened over the weekend for re-enacting the town's 1781 occupation, was impressively articulate about (A) the larger historical context that they were portraying, and (B) the weird echoes that still play out today (as you say, history erupting in our present, the past haunting the now.) For whatever it's worth, I left town with a lot more understanding and respect for what these people are doing. More importantly though, I also left town with a lot less certainty about what their audience experiences: what actually happens to them when they enter the museum and start to time travel?

Lütticken For the past two years or so I have felt that the status of re-enactment as a time-based activity needs to be investigated further. What happens when historicism is set in motion – first in theatre and pageants, then in film, in 'living history' museums and in 'modern' re-enactment since the 1960s? You mention the agency of the body and its nowness as a crucial factor; I think one has to see this bodily time as being engaged in a perpetual dialectic with mental duration, if I am permitted to sound a pop-Bergsonian note. Together both form the complicated time of the subject, which in a re-enactment is articulated by means that are proper to drama, such as the creation of suspense. Since the drama in question is historical in nature, this dramatic time is in turn short-circuited with historical time. Thus various times are superimposed, and difference is momentarily – annulled – at least in the ideal scenario posited by some war re-enactors. With film it is different; even though war re-enactors participate as extras in films such as *Saving Private Ryan*, they are often sceptical about what they see as inauthentic and merely external spectacle.

By the way, I think it is suggestive that we are using the term *time travel*, and that the motif of time travel in modern fiction (time travel with a machine to a destination of your choice) is a late nineteenth-century invention. In nineteenth-century historicism there is already the desire to make the past present, to bring it close through objects and architecture or through fictional characters that put modern sentiments into, for instance, mediaeval knights. Walter Benjamin noted that nineteenth-century interiors aimed to give the bourgeoisie the impression that a historical event such as the crowning or the murder of an emperor could have taken place in the adjoining room – historicist armchair time-travel! Such craving for experiencing the past in a fundamentally dramatic way is amplified both in parks such as Colonial Williamsburg and in war re-enactment, which cater to desire for direct experience in different ways, allowing for different degrees of socio-political contextualization. As your remark about Colonial Williamsburg suggests, such museums place much more emphasis on historical context and on contemporary relevance than fanatical hobby re-enactors who are after a 'period rush'; who really want to immerse themselves in a period and, more specifically, in a simulated war situation. On the other hand, some right-wing war re-enactors dream of having the past erupt into the present in a rather sinister way: in a recent BBC report on neo-Nazi infiltration in World War II re-enactment groups, an SS re-enactor was filmed with a hidden camera saying that if the SS still existed and if he was younger, he would join them to rid the country of Muslims. I think the fantasy of a contemporary anti-Islam SS is as telling as the two 'ifs' in this statement. It's like double time travel; he imagines traveling to an alternative present via the past. This suggests, by the way, that the time travel starts in the mind, and that physical re-enactments are attempts to actualize this mental experience, to anchor duration in the time of the body – to use the bodily experience to experience a more complete superimposition of times. Perhaps in the nineteenth century the act of reading a Walter Scott novel was the ultimate re-enactment, supremely intangible. [...]

Omer Fast and Sven Lütticken, extracts from email dialogue (2007), in *Omer Fast: The Casting* (Vienna: Museum Moderner Kunst Stiftung Ludwig Wien/Cologne: Verlag der Buchhandlung Walther König, 2007) 27–41.

Walid Raad
Interview with Alan Gilbert//2002

Alan Gilbert All the work you produce is organized under the rubric of a fictional collective called the Atlas Group that's based, as you are, in New York and Beirut. Reviews of exhibitions that include your work may mention the Atlas Group but almost never mention you by name. Recently you've begun to emphasize your individual authorship of the work without abandoning the Atlas Group conceit. Can you talk about the tension in your work between individual authorship and the idea that the Atlas Group is collectively producing and accumulating anonymous and pseudonymous documents?

Walid Raad It seems to me that this question concerns the authorship of the Atlas Group project and its archive – documents attributed to Dr Fadl Fakhouri, Souheil Bachar, Operator #17, and the Atlas Group, among others. It is not true that I have recently begun to emphasize the individual authorship of the work. In different places and at different times I have called the Atlas Group an imaginary foundation, a foundation I established in 1976 and a foundation established in 1976 by Maha Traboulsi. In Lebanon in 1999, I stated, 'The Atlas Group is a non-profit foundation established in Beirut in 1967.' In New York in 2000 and in Beirut in 2002, I stated, 'The Atlas Group is an imaginary foundation that I established in 1999.' I say different things at different times and in different places according to personal, historical, cultural and political considerations with regard to the geographical location and my personal and professional relation with the audience and how much they know about the political, economic and cultural histories of Lebanon, the wars in Lebanon, the Middle East, and contemporary art. I also always mention in exhibitions and lectures that the Atlas Group documents are ones that I produced and that I attribute to various imaginary individuals. But even this direct statement fails, in many instances, to make evident for readers or an audience the imaginary nature of the Atlas Group and its documents. This confirms to me the weighty associations with authority and authenticity of certain modes of address (the lecture, the conference) and display (the white walls of a museum or gallery, vinyl text, the picture frame), modes that I choose to lean on and play with at the same time.

It is also important for us to note that the truth of the documents we research does not depend solely on their factual accuracy. We are concerned with facts, but we do not view facts as self-evident objects that are already present in the world. One of the questions we find ourselves asking is, How do we approach facts not in their crude facticity but through the complicated mediations by which they acquire their immediacy? The Atlas Group produces and collects objects and stories that should not be examined through the conventional and reductive binary of fiction and non-fiction. We proceed from the consideration that this distinction is a false one, in many ways – not least of which is that many of the elements that constitute our imaginary documents originate from the historical world – and does not do justice to the rich and complex stories that circulate widely and that capture our attention and belief. Furthermore, we have always urged our audience to treat our documents as 'hysterical documents' in the sense that they are not based on any one person's actual memories but on 'fantasies erected from the material of collective memories'.

Gilbert You work in a variety of media (photography, collage, video, digital, performance), and individual pieces migrate among these media: a photograph may be taken of something originally pasted up in a notebook, and these photographs are then incorporated into a video that becomes part of a PowerPoint presentation shown during a performance. Similarly, the objects, individuals and histories represented in your work always elude direct representation, however obsessively you represent, follow or record them. There's a similarity in the form and content of your work to the way trauma can rarely speak directly, despite its gnawing desire to articulate itself. The obsessive and repetitious serial form of your work gives this away, as do the references to war and devastation: car bombs, hostages, disappeared persons, subjects under surveillance. Notwithstanding these details, it's impossible to reconstruct a history of the Lebanese Civil Wars from your project. If you can speak about historical and experiential traumas that remain partly unspeakable, can you talk about your work's linking of image, history and trauma and how they might interrelate for both individuals and larger social formation?

Raad You point out correctly that it is impossible to reconstruct a history of the Lebanese Civil Wars from this project. It is evident in Lebanon and elsewhere that 'The Lebanese Civil War' refers to an abstraction. We proceed with the project from the consideration that this abstraction is constituted by various individuals, groups, discourses, events, situations and, more importantly, by modes of experience. We began by stating, 'The Atlas Group aims to locate, preserve, study and make public documents that shed light on some of the unexamined dimensions of the Lebanese Civil War.' Soon thereafter, it became clear that it is difficult for us to define precisely what this proposition means, and as a consequence we stated, 'It is difficult for us to speak of the Lebanese Civil War, and we prefer to speak of the wars in Lebanon.' Today, we refer to 'the history of Lebanon of the past fifty years with particular emphasis on the history of Lebanon since 1975.' We have also realized that our concern is not with documenting the plurality of wartime experiences as they are conditioned by manifold religious, class, ideological and gender locations.

It is important to note that Dr Fadl Fakhouri's *Notebook Volume 72*, titled 'Missing Lebanese Wars', raised for us troubling questions about the possibilities and limits of writing any history of the recent wars in Lebanon. The notebook recounts the story of some Lebanese historians who bet on photo-finish horse-race photographs as they were published in the Lebanese daily *Annahar*. Apart from the historians' bets and some calculations of averages, the notebook's pages include cut-outs of the photo-finish photographs as they appeared in *Annahar*. What is fascinating about these images is that the horse is always captured either just before or beyond, but never exactly at, the finish line – the horse is never on time. This inability to be present at the passing of the present raised for us numerous questions about how to write, and more particularly about how to write the history of events that involve forms of extreme physical and psychological violence. The notebook forced us to consider whether some of the events of the past three decades in Lebanon were actually experienced by those who lived them.

Gilbert This notion of history as never on time saturates almost every aspect of your work and I think is one of the keys to the subterfuge it employs. Moving on from the exhausted postmodern trope of the uncoupling of the sign from its referent, you turn this into a larger historiographical and even political issue. While there's a sense of despair at the inability to ever finally arrive – even in retrospect – at a true historical moment, it also appears to be a liberating awareness for you; hence the strategic misdirections in your work. But it's a liberation emitting a mournful tone for a lost and impossible object. Your recording of sunsets from Beirut's seaside promenade at the end of your video *I Only Wish That I Could Weep* (2002/1997), and your haunting series of photographs *Secrets in the Open Sea* (1994/2004), are good examples. At first glance, the latter appear to be beautiful, pure blue abstractions, with a black-and-white thumbnail photograph situated in the bottom right-hand corner of their white borders. The imaginary narrative accompanying these blue photographs is that they were found in 1992 under the rubble of demolished buildings in the Souks area of Beirut and given to the Atlas Group for examination. Using a lab in France, the Atlas Group was able to extract grainy black-and-white photographs embedded within the varying fields of blue. These photographs were of small groups of women and men – all of whom, it turned out, had been found dead in the Mediterranean Sea. The sense of mourning in these photographs inflects much of your work.

Raad I think there may have been a sense of despair (even as it appears to be a liberating feeling for us, as you note), especially with the works produced between 1991 and 2001. We no longer feel this way. In this regard it has been productive for us to read and think about Jalal Toufic's books *Over-Sensitivity* (1996) and *Forthcoming* (2001). The absence of the referent in our earlier works, our treatment of the documents we were finding and producing as hysterical documents, was not the result of a philosophical conviction imposed on our object of study. It may have been due to the withdrawal of reality itself as a result of what Toufic identifies as 'the withdrawal of tradition past a surpassing disaster'. Our project titled *Sweet Talk: Photographic Documents of Beirut* is related in this regard. The blurred, never-on-time, always-to-the-side images we produced in this project between 1987 and 1999 are indicative of this withdrawal.

It is difficult for us to say where we are today, but we have noticed a shift in the documents we are finding and producing and in our conceptual, formal and critical approach to the writing of the history of Lebanon. As Toufic recently suggested, 'It may be that a resurrection has been produced.' This is clearly a question that requires further elaboration. [...]

Walid Raad and Alan Gilbert, extract from interview, *Bomb* magazine, no. 81 (Fall 2002).

I LOOK AT PEOPLE LIKE BUILDINGS.
INSTEAD OF WALLS AND ROOMS,
WE HAVE STORIES AND EXPERIENCES.
AS LONG AS WE CAN
LIVE THESE STORIES,
EXPRESS THESE STORIES,
TELL AND RETELL THESE STORIES,
THEN WE CAN STAND UP,
THE WAY A BUILDING STANDS

Kutlug Ataman, Interview with Ana Finel Honigman, 2004

COMMITMENT

Craigie Horsfield
Statement//1987

1. [...] Art as reflexive resistance acts on this exposed nerve, our hope of redemption, of meaning overfilling life. However, its action runs counter to the impulse that gives it birth, for if 'bad' art massages the ego, reassures and more tightly binds to us the world as false vision, the world of fantasy and convention; 'good' art is essentially selfless. If 'bad' art allows us to colonize the world as a reflection of the self, 'good' art does not confirm our prejudices or reassure us in a deathless dream. It shows that the world is wholly indifferent to us, to our suffering as well as to our desire. It supposes that through intensity of seeing we may cut through to reality. The goal is to show – in its unique indifference to us – the thing not freed from time, but most exactly that particle, that single unique moment, the present. By apprehending the present, we rupture the surface and continuity of time and cut through to other moments, irregular, uncharted and singular. 'Good' art therefore is utterly opposed to the attempt to create timeless and universal symbols, which join the seamless flow of history, bearing us forward through an unchanging landscape towards death.

Photography, which has a particular (though not more valuable) relation with reality and with time, can be seen as a means by which we may address questions humankind must always ask concerning life and death, compassion, pity and justice. The great danger in making photographs is of voyeurism. Passive and masochistic, it denies the responsibility of action, interceding self between the object and our aim. Reality is indifferent and our perception of it has no reward, it is in this sense selfless.

2. How does this work in practice? The pictures that I recognize or respond to are very few, they seem to follow no rule or formula, only chance.

I make pictures of people I know and places I live in. Maybe 'people I know something about' would be more truthful. It seems paradoxical to speak of a selfless way of seeing whilst making pictures that appear to be little more than a diary. This is not such an uneasy parallel. As a sequence of events or the things I did today, it is of no interest. I have never kept a diary nor have I been much concerned by others. As a fragmentary account of the world and of people, it is more interesting. However personal and intimate Chris Marker's films, their power is in the recognition of others, of the mystery of Kuomiko.

Maxim Gorky, writing about Alexander Herzen's marvellous autobiography, says that he created a whole province of people. Herzen himself emerges from his book as the most egocentric of men and yet the great power of his work is that it is inhabited by others who our gaze follows as they move by, whole and more singular even than Herzen himself. It is this acknowledgement of 'otherness' that matters. I don't believe that one is able to penetrate another's reality, or that intensity or depth of description corresponds to such revelation. On the contrary, I believe that the most that one can hope to achieve is the precise and accurate delineation of the surface of things. All else is fantasy.

There is a passage, I think from Van Gogh's letters to his brother, where he writes that he would like to make portraits that to people a century later would look like ghosts. It seems to describe that distracted and terrible looking out that occurs occasionally in photographs. Barthes describes a similar look as being terrible because it is the return of the dead. I do not see it in such a way; in my response there is a sense of pity, perhaps a sense of loss and of sheer longing, but each time it is resistance to death that lies in the recognition of another. This seems a sad litany of defeat, of failure and loss. It should not be, because in our resistance we find solidarity with others. The feeling of recognition, if only momentarily. The pictures themselves are not such sombre things, sometimes they are joyous, sometimes funny. They recall other dreams and other memories, almost familiar things just beyond reach; rather like a still from an unseen film.

The people I know seem to have about them a kind of heroism, not the heroism of great gestures, though that may be there, but of resistance, of actions; small actions in the world. It seems difficult now when I show the work to reconcile the things on the wall with this man or that woman and the ambition to tell of them. How stupidly I have made the pictures, how little they show. I believe that each photograph should be unique and discreet and yet, isolated one from another, how can they show the world entire and complex in its relation? Too often, perhaps through my inability to understand, the photographs remain at the level of allusion, of making about the world. I say that it is an inability to understand, but I think it is more than that. I don't believe that one can engineer moments of intense being, there is no drug or mantra to turn to. This intensity of being isn't a recurring phenomenon associated with a particular type of landscape or face that one might recognize and reproduce, maybe a cast of the eyes or a peculiar paleness of skin. It is none of these. All that may be said is that it is wholly unpredictable and irregular. Perhaps at the most one can be open to the world, one can work, make things – however banal – to go into the world but never to expect revelation. It is a modest aim, but this being face to face with the world seems to me now to be no easy thing.

3. Some years ago I gave a lecture with John Goto, on the Czech photographer Jan Svoboda. When later it was to be published, the editors cut out my final paragraph

as being 'too difficult'. As though it were a disreputable drunkard that had stumbled into an otherwise sedate and well mannered party. I reproduce it now without apology. Perhaps because we admire in others much that we long for in ourselves. It describes the hope of virtue I have struggled to record above. I see it as the artist's task, forsaken in our culture, simply to speak about reality; to try to break through the veil of fantasy and familiarity that shrouds reality. Svoboda, through form, through the web of relation, tries to speak clearly about reality and goodness, because it is his responsibility and his limit: this utter reality, this 'there-it-is'. He says with his voice and with the voice of men and women before him the one thing that is a guarantee of hope, though never of our escaping extinction: 'There is a land, there is a time, very far away, that is our present.'

Craigie Horsfield, statement (Antwerp, November 1987), in *Craigie Horsfield* (Cambridge: Cambridge Darkroom, 1988) 39–41.

Boris Mikhailov
Statement//1999

I'll start with a confession. Sometimes I have a feeling as if I had been run over by an ideological car and the words, like jumping frogs, are breaking free out of my mouth, independent of me: *developed socialism, evils of capitalism, vast is my native country, unity and contradiction, great experiment.*

Since the century's beginning, Russia has constantly attracted attention, due to social cataclysms. Of course, it's not entirely so. Let's admit that it is not the Russian situation itself, but the fact that a 'world' experiment took place there, based on the German philosophy of Karl Marx: the building of socialism. Now the experiment seems to be finished and we are probably witnessing its completion. And we'll consider that as a photographer I 'documented' periods of that experiment. This book [*Case History*] belongs to one of the latest periods of that 'great' experiment.

After the brown and blue series I was going to create a pink one, which would probably have corresponded to the revival of new life, like during a sunrise, when the light is evenly covering the whole surface.

Returning home after one year I saw the opposite. Devastation had stopped. The city had acquired an almost modern European centre. Much had been restored. Life became more beautiful and active, outwardly (with a lot of foreign advertisements) – simply a shining wrapper. But I was shocked by the big number of homeless (before they had not been there). The rich and the homeless – the new classes of the new society – this was, as we had been taught, one of the features of capitalism.

'Welcome to Russian capitalism!' (Sorry, again it broke free.)

For myself I call this situation of the country a 'zero' state, because besides the creation of the new classes, there is no advancement from point 'zero'. The dynamics of the processes became relatively constant. The internal energy of the society is not directed to future creation. In any case, the perceived activity is not enough to survive. (The amount of people is being reduced.) And because now nothing is created, but each individual somehow personally faces changes, I got interested in man and his surroundings. In addition, I got the feeling that the processes in society have reached the next level of concentration.

I try not to photograph sensation. On the other hand, I try to take photos of what really increased a lot. I only try to find unique things in this great number.

I have missed the moments with 'new Russians'. There was a time when they were not yet aware of their wealth and their position, as if they had remained 'normal' people. It was possible to take photos in their environment – they were open. And very soon they started to shoot at each other and surround themselves with bodyguards.

Then came a time when it was possible to start writing a book about the other main feature of the time – poverty. The best way to depict it is to take photos of the homeless. And this 'chance' (to take a picture of the homeless) could occur, as it seemed to me, only during a short moment.

First, these were the people who had recently lost their homes. According to their position they were already the *bomzhes* (*bomzh* = the homeless without any social support), according to outlook they were simply the people who got into trouble. Now they are becoming the *bomzhes* with their own class psychology and 'clan' features. For me it was very important that I took their photos when they were still like 'normal' people. I made a book about the people who got into trouble but didn't manage to harden so far.

Their feeling of social oppression and helplessness shocked me. I watched a scene, when a young strong man doing exercises, suddenly, out of the blue, kicked a *bomzh* passing him by chance. The other screamed. It seemed to me that I even heard the crunch of his bones. Nobody paid any attention, neither the people standing around nor the militiaman who was not far away.

When I was first working on the book, I suddenly felt that many people were going to die at that place. And the *bomzhes* had to die in the first rank, like heroes – as if their lives protected the others' lives. And I took the pictures displaying naked people with their things in their hands like people going to gas chambers. They agreed to pose for a so-called historical theme. They agreed that their photos would be published in magazines for others to learn about their lives.

Accidentally, for myself, I started to take pictures of the people with a criminal past, just to do this theme. Maybe their criminal aesthetics with its 'readiness' for death and perception of its inevitability helped me to explain the situation of *The Requiem*. (In addition, in a strange way, it coincides with the general criminal situation of the society.)

Changing the borders of the Soviet Union, establishing new states, all this drove many, it seems to me, to lose their identification with the place of their birth. In this situation 'art consciousness' loses the flavour of historicism. The 'fading out' of the historical process probably turns it into a non-perspective for the artists who treat the current reality as something already known, referring to it as if to the past. That's why I feel a strong sense of responsibility working on this book.

I have received many questions connected with legitimizing my work and the ethical problem related to it. I think I have mentioned why I do this kind of work. As to the ethical question, I have to say that I am not to blame. But very often, when I took pictures, I was ashamed. And in general, it is hard to speak about morality, when one is wearing long fur coats, while the others don't change their sawn and mended shoes for months, while a creditor is more often killed than he is returned money ...

When I made the previous books, I didn't have the impression that I did something wrong. As I took pictures, I did not get into contact with those whose photos I made, so everything seemed natural. And at that time the main feeling was the sense of communal unity, through it was coming to an end.

Now this community doesn't exist any more. And it turned out that I got in one social class and the *bomzhes* in another. And while before the sense of social justice was aimed at the possible future improvement of all, now the questions 'why' and 'what for' should be answered, because you are busy with the problems of others. And particularly, at this moment (at the loss of historicism) the book can cause doubts (considering that to search for nuances in the life of well-to-do people seems to be more natural).

On the one hand, for myself personally, I understood that taking pictures of poverty was my professional and civil duty. On the other hand, I accept traditional clichés about 'not using others' grief'. But what does 'others' grief' mean? And how must a photographer behave?

In the history of photography of our country we don't have photos of the famine in the Ukraine in the 1930s, when several million people died and corpses were lying around in the streets. We don't have photos of the war, because journalists were forbidden to take pictures of sorrow threatening the moral spirit of the Soviet people; we don't have non-'lacquered' pictures of enterprises, nor pictures of street events, except demonstrations. The entire photography history is 'dusted'. And we have the impression that each person with a camera is a 'spy'.

The main three rules which somehow indirectly regulated the development of photography were:

1. 'On spying activity': It was forbidden to take photos from higher than the second floor, the areas of railways, stations, military objects, at enterprises, near enterprises, at any organization, without special permission.

2. 'On biased collecting of information': This law touched the moral elements of taking photos. It was forbidden to take photos which brought into disrepute the Soviet power, the Soviet way of life.

3. 'The law on pornography': Photographing any naked body could become reason for accusation. Actually at all our art exhibitions, until 1986, pieces depicting naked bodies by modern photographers or artists could not be displayed. Only museums contained such pictures by Old Masters.

Having these laws and their consequences in my memory, I was aware that I was not allowed to let it happen once again that some periods of life would be erased.

I'd like to tell an episode. A man was lying in the street with his head on the road in frosty weather. It was night. Everybody was passing by. I came up to him, took his photo. A woman turned around and shouted: 'Why are you taking a photo of him? Do you have nothing to do?' I asked her to help me raise him, but she went away. Of course, I lifted him up and helped him home. And frankly speaking I was very happy that he didn't even get ill (I saw him the next day). But what did the shout of a woman, directed at me, mean? Better let him die than the photo would be published? She was passing by as if not noticing and not willing to see it either outside on the street or in newspapers. There is nothing bad.

Independently someone's glance selects what this person needs. My acquaintances, after having seen my photos, said: 'Now we see these people outside, while we haven't noticed them before.'

In a book by the Japanese writer Kobo Abe, *Person-as-box*, a man put a box on his head in order not to be seen by others. *Bomzhes* whom one doesn't want to notice put on clothes – their boxes – due to the evil destiny. And that has somehow crossed them out of life. This book is not about them (or rather not only about them), though metaphysically, having made them visible, it is as if it restores their rights for life.

It seems to me that my personal uncertainty (it is not clear where I live – in Kharkov or somewhere in the West, where I work, etc.), my instability in society, on the formal level, has transformed the obscurity of borders between documentary and scenery within the framework of the documentary. Different vibrations of this documentary depend on the so-called 'non-ethical impulse' which has the task to check the local 'ethical' by means of different sorts of 'ethical' already accepted in other places (cultures). For example, I send a 'non-ethical impulse' (I tell the model to undress). This impulse meets with life, excites it (when the model agrees) or doesn't excite it (when the model refuses), and it is as if life deforms, as if the suggestion to accept the level of the 'non-ethical impulse' is always ethical to me. (Let it be so.) That means that I never gave them tasks, which would have been strange for the models.

I was interested in the borders of the new morality which would suit the new borders of survival. But the main point is that I myself was tested by the 'non-ethical impulse' – and could you yourself do what you are not willing to do? Can you communicate again with *bomzhes*, after having got lice from them, can you shake their hands greeting them while your acquaintances are passing by, etc.? Yes, I had to be the first person to lose my respectability.

I go on speaking 'scientifically-like', as it were. One could say I took photos by the method of 'posing for little money'. I told people: 'I want to take your picture, you are interesting to me, I can give you a little money for that'. (But it was always more than one is paid at the Art Institute for posing.) Such a way of work resulted in the following:

1. The work was not very tiresome.
2. Quick finishing of the work.
3. Doubtful street acquaintances could be easily rejected if the suggestion seemed unnatural and aggressive.

The people didn't have a choice; either you pose or you vanish. They were not scared of any boss. They didn't do it under compulsion, I photographed usually on their territory. When I took photos at my place, either immediately or later, they could take revenge. That's why they didn't do what they didn't want to do. This situation from my point of view doesn't violate life. While posing a man tries to be different; beautiful, strong etc. Here the models didn't perform in such a theatre. At least, they were given the role of 'who they are in reality'. And presenting themselves, they didn't pose, and it was like 'life itself'. And the stasis of the pictures reflects the submissiveness of the models.

I asked my friends what they could advise about shooting photos. One said: 'Give them money and let them beat each other.'

One more episode. I asked a *bomzh* to bring a lady to take a photo of both of them. He refused saying that it was not good. I took his photos, but he was alone.

I took a long time making this book. Often I stood by my house and many *bomzhes* approached me, knowing my intentions. I felt very often ashamed that I didn't use them and that I didn't pay them.

Manipulating with money is somehow a new way of legal relations in all areas of the former USSR. And by this book I wanted to transmit the feeling that in that place and now people can be openly manipulated. In order to give this flavour of time I wanted to copy or perform the same relations which exist in society between a model and myself.

I don't know exactly why, but after *The Requiem*, the idea stuck in my mind to go on taking photos of the naked. Maybe I was driven by the old complex connected with the ban on photographing the naked, which was now connected with the notion of 'nakedness of life itself'. People got undressed, naked and took away the barrier of their dirty, ponging clothes, built between them and others. I was interested in what would happen to a face when a body gets undressed. But sometimes they, simply as people of the 'new' morality, exposed their 'values'. When naked, they stood like people.

Coming back to the terminology 'sense of life itself', I should like to give the following metaphor. Something is lying, wrapped in something, for example, in a raincoat. I touch it, the raincoat unfolds and one can see a baby there.

No, I don't want to spy on those whom nobody would like to see. My touch-request helps the model himself or the situation itself to say – 'Here I am.'

Now it is important for me to say how the West came to the East and why I used colour photos. Previously I used a toner that made a photo look like old. I received a reflection, which corresponded to the sense of disaster and war – the blue and the brown series. The colour 'express-photo' became for me the thing which mostly correlated with the new time, in each corner a photo-centre – 'Agfa', 'Konica', 'Fuji' – was opened. The appearance of Western technology made a colour album photo the thing that connects the rich and the poor. Both the rich and the poor wanted to have colour photographs and there was only one distinction: the rich could afford them, the poor couldn't. The colour photo became an image of the new life. And the poor having a beautiful photo can state: 'Now we also live nicely.'

It suddenly came to my mind that these colour photos are more like a rash on the ill body. At the end I again have to refer to old terminology of the 'evils of capitalism'.

I suddenly got the image of a slightly mad journalist in international affairs, a specialist in defining the 'evils'. Returning to the motherland from his long business trips abroad, out of habit, he goes on to search out the 'evils'. This is a research of the post-Soviet space made by the old Soviet method. The circle is closed. And the experiment?

Boris Mikhailov, untitled statement, in *Boris Mikhailov: Case History* (Zurich: Scalo, 1999) 5–10.

Renzo Martens
Interview with Joe Penney//2010

[...] In the film *Episode III – Enjoy Poverty* (2009), Renzo Martens travels to the Democratic Republic of the Congo to tell the Congolese people that the greatest resource they have is their poverty and they must take control of its means of production. After hundreds of years of slavery and colonization, the inheritors of the West's brutal history now exploit the Congo through media. At the end of the trip Martens is exasperated by his failure to make a difference in the Congo, and concludes his journey by offering a struggling plantation worker and his malnourished children what he can easily provide: a full meal with meat. Martens knows he can do no more. His mission has failed, and he leaves the DRC to return to a comparatively comfortable life in Europe. Martens' journey can be seen as a parable for the exploitive relations that characterize virtually all Western activity in the Third World, and especially the DRC. He has gone to the country to lift them out of poverty, made a film that he will earn his living from, and given nothing but a meal in return.

Martens presents a troubled, critical view of how we – directly and indirectly – interact with the Congolese, whether through aid organizations, African governmental structures, factory owners who churn out commodities and goods, and most importantly, through our selves. In his film, 'the entire picture is looking out at a scene for which it itself is the scene',[1] forcing us to stand on a moral precipice reflective of our own actions, where we must look within ourselves for the answers.

The director has blurred the line between his character, Renzo Martens the 'Imperialist White Male in Africa', and Renzo Martens the artist and social commentator, to the point that the two are nearly indistinguishable. When he touches a starving child's protruding ribcage and instructs Congolese photographers to get closer to photograph it, or when he flatly tells a subsistence farmer how poor he is to his face, the film turns into an oppressive reality that Martens the artist is responsible for. But few can argue with the idea that our dominant, Western patriarchal society ought to think more about our relationships with people we believe we are helping, for 'good intentions may do as much harm as malevolence, if they lack understanding.'[2] Our relationship with the Congolese definitely suffers from our lack of understanding of them, but perhaps it is first and foremost the victim of our profound misperceptions of ourselves. This is not a call for the end of all aid or a total damnation of 'Western media' (both heavily over-simplified ideas themselves), but an appeal for relationships built on self-awareness, love and respect. We can learn a lot from the young Angolan man in Abderrahmane Sissako's film, *Rostov-Luanda* (1997), who simply and eloquently points out that 'if I share a moment with somebody, and we laugh together with love and tenderness, then if that person rightly criticizes me, I'll accept it'. There are definitely ways to help other people, but first we need to acknowledge our role in perpetuating the abhorrent power structure. Then we can shape our actions accordingly through love and respect, which are the true forces of positive change. (Joe Penney.)

Joe Penney Although you've stated that your film is primarily an artwork, it has a strong political message to it. How does *Episode III* negotiate the relationship between politics and art, and what was your goal in making the film?

Renzo Martens Yes, it is primarily an artwork, for sure, and the reason for this is that in the film there is a guy who does all these things: he says you are now being exploited through media, and then we see that he, too, exploits people through media. He just gives people a view and returns to a relatively comfortable life in Europe. And then you say, and that's the important part, that this is like a parable for most Western activity in the Third World. So what happens in *Episode III* doesn't critique by showing something bad but by duplicating what may be bad. On the one hand it gives some critique within the film: media might be bad, it exploits you, takes possession of the means of production; on the other hand I, the guy in the film, do pretty much exactly the same thing and in the end just leave.

So the film's critique is not so much in Renzo's actions; the critique is the film as a whole, it's the duplication of existing power relationships. [...] Most documentary films critique or reveal some outside phenomenon – this is bad, or good, or tragic ... In this film, it's not the subject, like poverty in Africa, that's tragic, it's the very way that the film deals with the subject that is as tragic. So that's why it's an artwork, because it deals with its own presence, it deals with its own terms and conditions, it's not a referential piece. It's auto-referential.

Penney So the regular media does not deal with its own presence the way your work does.

Martens Hardly ever. And it's by dealing with its own presence that it's able to reveal so much more, not only of its own presence – of yet another film made in the Congo and who's benefiting from that film and who's not – but also, as you said, it forms a parable of Western behaviour in the Third World in general. And that's why – because it's an artwork – it can be political: it reveals so much more of these power relationships, these discrepancies, than just a film showing that

Western journalists in Africa make money and the poor don't. Well, a film like that would be good, but this film takes it a few steps further: it inscribes itself in these much broader discrepancies and political problems.

Penney When you're aware of yourself, then you have a more nuanced view of what's going on. Is that what you mean?

Martens Yes, more nuanced, but also deeper. When you're aware of yourself, you only have to study yourself, and you see why all these other things are going wrong, too.

Penney You said in another interview, 'I can never be the saviour or emancipator because I am defined by the structures and institutions that exploit in the first place.' You said this I guess, because your film was partly financed by grants from European countries.

Martens Sure, partially, but also because even without those grants ... I made the films with grants, but I started out without grants, with hardly any money. With around 30,000 Canadian dollars I filmed for over a year and a half. Then I got some more money for another year. So it was done with very little money in terms of what documentary films cost. But still, not only am I defined by the grants, I'm also defined by the education I have, by the racism and the feeling of agency that I've grown up with, I'm defined by the idea that I think it's normal that I have a cup of coffee every day and it's normal that other people don't drink coffee but work for me anyway. I mean, so the institutions are not just the grants. I am a representative of a world which allows people to die of hunger on the one hand and allows other people to be terribly rich. That's the institution I'm talking of.

Penney So do you think it's possible for someone like yourself to entertain relations with the Congolese outside of these roles, outside of the saviour/emancipator role?

Martens Yes. It will take a little effort from both sides, but sure, if you cut through some of the prejudices and expectations, which I, by the way, have made into the subject of the film (by making you cut through it, I guess), then yes, for sure, there is no reason why a relationship between myself and a Congolese person, on a deeply personal level – once we've transgressed all these prejudices – why it couldn't be as truthful and real, and loving and aesthetic, as any other relationship between two people.

Penney But it's just that the structures and institutions which exploit, that you speak of, make it very hard for this to happen?

Martens Yes, they make it very hard for this to happen, first of all because, for example, any European or North American working for the United Nations in the Congo works among people that maybe make 20 dollars per month – maybe their own personnel make 20 dollars per month, yet they make 10,000 dollars per month. I'm not so good at maths but this is a lot more. So, people feel guilty about it and then they have to come up with other strategies. You have to think you're very much superior, otherwise there's not much to account for this terrible difference in income. It's not just the institutions that make it difficult but very much your own attachments to privilege, and to power and superiority.

Penney So do you think that to have more egalitarian relations with the Congolese, you would basically have to throw away your privileges as a white male in a Third World country?

Martens Well, if your aim is to have a deeply personal relationship with anybody, yes, you have to let go of your privileges, in general, yes. In general.

Penney Susan Sontag wrote [in *On Photography*] that the limit of the photographic world is that, while it can goad conscience, it can, finally, never be ethical or political knowledge. The knowledge gained through still photographs will always be a kind of sentimentalism, whether cynical or humanist. It will be a knowledge at bargain prices – a semblance of knowledge, a semblance of appropriation, a semblance of rape.

When you look at pictures of the Congo, you get the sense of terrible human suffering. But your film has a critique of this relationship between photographer and subject, as well as that between the viewer of the photograph back at home and the subject. Can you speak a little about these relationships?

Martens I couldn't agree more with Sontag. She takes this further in another statement I'll cite as I remember it: Empathy as a reaction from the viewer towards the suffering of others, as portrayed in film, is possibly an inappropriate reaction, because the empathy allows you to disregard the structural violence that is at the basis of suffering.

If you have empathy as a reaction, for example, to the earthquake crisis in Haiti [in 2010], you think, these people have a terrible disaster, I should help them; it's a reactionary force. You see suffering, you want to help. Of course the people in Haiti have been suffering for ages. It was the poorest country in the western hemisphere well before this earthquake happened and it was invaded a number of times by US forces to secure business interests well before this time. So empathy as a reaction allows you not to see their suffering and your agency to look at that suffering. It allows you to not put it on the same map, as if it belongs to another world.

Penney Does it create a sort of distance between the viewer of that photograph and the subject of that photograph that's not really so distant?

Martens Well it creates a distance because it just shows you suffering, and then your reaction is either you feel empathetic toward this or maybe you don't. Maybe you reject the suffering or maybe you reject responsibility. But if you are able to put the suffering and yourself on the same map, then so much other, deeper action is necessary than just feeling empathetic. Because the suffering in this world, as in the Congo, is not an accident, an earthquake that all of a sudden happens, it's structural. And that's exactly what Sontag said. We are indebted, our riches are indebted to this suffering in, for example, the Congo. And empathy, pity, does away with all this need for structural justice.

Penney It distracts from looking at the real basis for these problems.

Martens Yes, it can offer an initial spark, and that can be good. But in the corporate media and in most art, photography and museum art, it only offers that initial spark because that's enough to please the consumer. Nothing more is needed. And going deeper than that would ask us to cut into our own flesh.

Penney And no one wants to do that because you won't make any money from it.

Martens Few people want that, yes.

Penney So, given the current state of Western media coverage of places like the DRC, how do you see other, major, non-Western media coverage of events there? While there is a lot of big, corporate Western media, there's also more and more corporate media in other parts of the world like al-Jazeera, Xinhua, Iran's PressTV, al-Arabiyya. How do you see these?

Martens I have no idea. I tried in the film to make, as I said, a duplicate, a readymade almost, or an appropriation of the media representations that I can follow on a daily basis and that I grew up with. So this is not al-Jazeera. I'm not saying al-Jazeera is less valid, or maybe it's far more valid than what I do, it's very possible, but I didn't take it as the grounds for my argument. I took as the grounds for my argument the mainstream representations that I grew up with, that I live with; I try to comment on those.

Penney So it's more of a personal ... well, it's more what you know best.

Martens No, it's not about personal or not personal. I just try to understand the big common denominator of how these things work. Of course in the Congo you will find diplomats, missionaries, journalists, who try everything they can, who do cut into their own flesh, let's put it that way. Who do try everything they can to make a difference on a structural level. These people do exist, but except for one maybe, they are not in my film. In my film you see the common denominator, you see the rule, not the exception. I try to deal with the rule.

Penney In Sissako's film *Bamako* (2006), a Malian court hands out life sentences of community service to the World Bank and the IMF ...

Martens Which is funny because that's what they should have done in the first place, right? Community service.

Penney That's for their role in implementing negative structural adjustment programmes throughout Africa. What would you see as a just response to the relationship of exploitation that has plagued the Congo for hundreds of years?

Martens Well it's good to refer to the past, as you do, and maybe as I did in the film, it's very important. But we should not forget that it's not only the past, it's right now. I'm in New York right now and if I go to a Whole Foods market, I will be able – and not only I but hundreds of thousands of people – to buy the chocolate and drink the coffee made in the plantations that figure in this film. So, I agree we should talk about history but let it not be a way to not talk about the present first of all. I don't know if the World Bank should ... It's a very smart sentence because as I said I think it's what the World Bank is supposedly there for in the first place. [...]

But what you see in my film is that, in my view, there isn't one single actor responsible for everything. It's not like the UN is responsible for everything, or the photographers, or maybe a plantation owner. The problem is that all these people take their own privileges too seriously. They attach to them. And I guess many of us do, and as you see in the film, I do too. And I think that's really the main problem, on a spiritual level. If you look at it in practical terms, it is very clear that people who deliver services should be paid for it. We supposedly live in a monetary economy, I'm fine with it, but then let's pay the people who produce goods and services. I don't see that happening so much. I see that we live in a capitalist world only for the people who have a lot of capital. The people who give other goods and services don't seem to be getting that much in return. And the guy in the film, the man that I give food in the hut, explains it very clearly. I tell him, well, chances you are going to make more money any time soon are really very limited. His response to that is, 'I don't care about your market in Europe or how high prices should or should not be. A man needs a salary'. This is the bottom line to me.

Penney So we're not even implementing the rules we established for ourselves.

Martens Oh, for sure we are not. If [our local minimum wage is] eight dollars an hour, how come our workforce abroad – because these people work for us, they are our employees – how come they don't even make eight dollars per month?

Penney Because then we would have to raise prices on the goods we sell.

Martens Not so much, because the biggest part of what we pay for a chocolate bar, for example – the per cent of wages in that chocolate bar, in for example the Congo, is very small. Most of the people who produce that chocolate bar and bring it in your shop are paid decently. The people who drive the trucks around, who operate the cash register, who do the advertising campaigns, who model, most of them are paid decently I'd think. There's only a few people in the whole production process of that chocolate bar that don't get paid at all, and those are the people who actually grow the chocolate. So if we would pay them a decent wage too, maybe it would be more expensive, maybe two cents or three cents, it's not a big deal. But there are some shareholders or corporate bosses who prefer to put those two or three cents in their own pockets. [...]

1 [footnote 10 in source] Michel Foucault, *The Order of Things: An Archaeology of the Human Sciences* (1966) (New York: Vintage Books, 1994) 14.

2 [11] Albert Camus, *The Plague* (1947) (New York: Vintage Books, 1991) 131.

Renzo Martens and Joe Penney, extracts from '"Enjoy Poverty": Interview with Renzo Martens' (16 July 2010), *Africa is a Country* (africasacountry.com) [revised for this publication].

Regina José Galindo
Interview with Francisco Goldman//2006

Francisco Goldman I imagine that we should begin with a few words about what is happening today in Guatemala. Hurricane Stan, the flooding, the terrible loss of lives, the general calamity that is going to sink people even deeper into lives of inescapable poverty. What did Guatemala do to deserve so much suffering?

Regina José Galindo To me this question feels too deep, too heart-rending. As you say, my country has suffered an eternity of calamities of all shapes and sizes: a mortal conquest, the maltreatment of indigenous villages and the negation of their rights throughout our entire history, the Gringo intervention, an infernal 36-year war, evil governments, spine-chilling levels of corruption, a murderous army, histories of violence that are a daily nightmare of inequality, hunger, misery – and now this, which unlike the aforementioned things is a natural disaster. How is such karma even possible?

But you ask what Guatemala did to deserve all this. Perhaps the proper questions would be: What *haven't* we done? Why have we been so afraid, and tolerated so much fear? Why have we not woken up and taken action? When are we going to stop being so submissive?

I feel impotent, unable to change things, but this rage has sustained me, and I've watched it grow since I first became aware of what was happening. It's like an engine – a conflict inside me that never yields, never stops turning, ever.

Goldman If someone had asked me if I thought a performance about Guatemala's violence, past or present, could be something as moving and surprising, as direct and effective and simply poetic, as your *Quién puede olvidar las huellas*? (Who Can Erase the Traces?), I guess I would have said no. (And I say that despite the fact that I can only 'see' it via the Internet – maybe that's not such a bad definition of how conceptual art works, when it works: you see an image, a trace, a link or a 'footprint' on a screen, read a bit of text, and then imagine the rest!) The other two works that you presented in Venice were of equal impact and eloquence. And they seem related to the spirit of your poetry, though your performance artworks are grand public gestures, and your poetry is intensely personal. Where did *Who Can Erase the Traces*? come from? What were your hopes for it? Who thinks of doing something like that, and why?

Galindo It emerged from rage and fear. When it was announced that Efraín Ríos

Montt had managed to win acceptance as a presidential candidate, I was in my room, and I suffered an attack of panic and depression. I cried out, I kicked and stomped my feet, I cursed the system that rules us. How was it possible that a character as dark as this would have such power with which to bend everything to his will? I decided then and there that I would take to the streets with my shout and amplify it. I had to do it.

Goldman What was the experience of performing it like? When you were walking barefoot through the streets carrying that basin of blood, stopping, dipping your feet in it, leaving your prints, going on and doing it again, what were you thinking about? Were you aware of people watching you? Is that personal experience, the interior space – even the memory of having lived it – part of the work? Did you learn anything unexpected from the public's reaction? And what did you do that night? After doing something like that, can you just sit down to dinner with your family, then go to sleep?

Galindo Every performance requires a different energy, and in each of them I have experienced distinct sensations and thoughts. The process of this performance was a bit cold, clinical. I went out to buy the human blood in the morning, and then I began the walk. It probably lasted about 45 minutes: that walk on pavement that did not burn.

I suppose my mind fell completely silent during that time. I was focused on the image of dipping my feet and leaving my footprints at every step along the way. But when I got to the Palacio Nacional and saw the line of police officers guarding it, I ignited. I walked more firmly, I reached the main doors, I saw the eyes looking back at me, and I left two final footprints side by side. I left the basin holding the blood there too. Nobody followed me, nobody said anything. I quickly walked across the street, washed my feet off in the park fountain, got something to eat, and then went back to my job that afternoon.

Goldman In the Guatemalan context, it is a profoundly political work. Did it have a political impact? And how is it different to present it, even on video, in Venice?

Galindo To present it on video is simply to show a document. In this case, whoever sees this document can come to know the history behind it.

As for the performance itself, it was all over in a moment, and I felt as I always do, that it hadn't done any good. But a group of artists began the necessary work: spreading word of the performance and the message. A curator friend of mine, Rosina Cazali, sent out images of the performance alongside a text declaring Ríos Montt's candidacy unacceptable. I say that these efforts were necessary, because

Guatemala is a country without memory. The people, with little access to education, are easy to mislead with promises and the little gifts that politicians hand out during election campaigns. The official party, to which Ríos Montt belonged and belongs, made a huge effort and had all the power to reach the Guatemalan minorities, who had difficulty connecting the actual Ríos Montt (the presidential candidate) to the past dictator-president who was guilty of the greatest crimes against their own people, their own blood. Every effort was necessary, any help at all, it was all needed to shout out the truth, by whatever means. After they were published online, the images of the performance were then published in newspapers that reached various groups.

Goldman Guatemalans, for all their collective psychosis, sometimes live in a state of negation; they've certainly become used to hearing denunciations of the human rights violations, the violence and massacres, etc., that occurred during the years of war. That doesn't lessen the valour of your work on the subject – but Regina, in Guatemala, a work like *Himenoplastia* (Hymenoplasty) must have been unprecedented. It must have hit like a bomb. Obviously it's an act of rage that many – the majority even, myself included – can't help but contemplate with a sense of incomprehension, perhaps even paralysis. It moves me almost to tears to think about what could have brought you to such an extreme. Please, talk a little bit about that work.

Galindo One day in April I was reading the newspaper, and I saw an article about reconstructing the hymen. Then I saw a classified ad purporting to restore virginity. I went to the advertised place, which was a bit seedy, and interviewed the doctor. At that time I was working on an idea for a group show organized by Belia de Vico, which was titled 'Cinismo' (Cynicism). I went back to the place with Belia, we spoke with the doctor, I showed him my work, and we broached the idea of filming the process. He agreed to do it for a certain amount of money.

I went to the clinic several times to observe the women who were patients there. I spoke with the doctor several times too, and he told me the stories of many of his patients. The majority of the patients want to regain their intactness for their wedding. They do it to gain a certain social status. In other cases, children and adolescent victims of sex trafficking are operated on so that they will fetch a better price. It is preferable to buy a virgin girl not only because of her virginity but also because it is considered better protection against STDs.

On the day of the operation, I went with Belia and Anibal Lopez, an artist and good friend. The operation was quick. Half an hour. Painful. Chaotic.

We left, feeling happy that it was over. We talked about what to have for breakfast. I wanted pancakes. In Belia's car, I began to feel a warm liquid between my legs, flowing more and more with every passing second. We drove back to her house and I put on a sort of diaper, but nothing could stop the flow. Then we went to my gynaecologist's clinic – my doctor there had been seeing me for years, and had asked to examine me after the operation – and from there to the hospital. Everything happened so fast. They dressed me in a gown, laid me on a bed, stuck an anaesthetic in my arm, and as I was fading into sleep I could hear the nurses talking among themselves, feeling sorry for me as they had for the many other girls who had been admitted to the hospital bleeding from a botched medical procedure, be it an abortion or a hymenoplasty.

The video was edited within a few days, and a week later it was exhibited as part of Belia's show. So many things must have been said about it. I didn't pay any attention to any of it, not at any time. It was already done, and I knew that I'd had to do it.

Goldman Who was this work done for?

Galindo I suppose that – like everything I do – this was done for me.

Goldman What expectations did you have for this project?

Galindo I never have any expectations after completing something. What I do have is a certain amount of nervousness and anxiety before every performance. But after that I have no expectations. It's done. [...]

Goldman There's definitely a spirit of satiric playfulness in your performance *Angelina*. When you did *Angelina*, you worked as a maid, or at least you went around dressed in a maid's uniform. It is difficult for someone from the US to understand what it means to be a domestic servant in Guatemala.

Galindo I dressed as a domestic servant and went about my normal life. The experience was extremely interesting right from the start, but as the days went by it became quite difficult indeed. Guatemala is a racist, exclusive, completely divided culture. Being a servant has many disadvantages. You're a woman, and a poor woman at that, generally with little education and dubious origins. You aren't worth a thing, and so they look down on you, and you go around with your shoulders always slumped, and they speak to you always with that disparaging tone in their voice. They barely deign to notice you, they won't let you into many places, and when they do let you enter, they stare at you disdainfully. At the end of the month, my self-esteem was in the dirt. [...]

Goldman Your poetry is written in the first person and takes on a confessional tone. How would you compare the process of the poetic act with that of the performative act?

Galindo The similarities lie along two lines. On the formal side I find it to be an obsessive search for cleanliness and for synthesis, as much in writing as in doing a performance. Conceptually, I find thematic similarities, like my dissatisfaction with the world and the system in which I happen to live. There is a cathartic effect in both my exercises, but it has different results for me, as do my experiences of life. When I write a text, I make an effort to not involve more than my brain and my emotions: my cry is not powerful enough to leave me exhausted. In the act of writing, energy is diluted into a passive being. Whereas in the moment of realizing a performance, something in which I am completely involved, it's not only the intellectual process of developing the proposal but also principally the energy that I gather to carry out the performance. In performance art, everything is real action: the energy explodes, reaches unexpected boundaries. The experience involves my entire being and sometimes even the beings of the people present.

Goldman I am very interested in a remark you made to me last week about how people on the streets react when they see your performances: whether or not they understand it as 'art' or as more of a protest, they don't find it stranger, more frightening, or more offensive than what they see in the streets every day. (And I'm not talking about 'magic realism'.) Could you say more about this?

Galindo My head is filled with hallucinated, surreal, tragic and inconceivable images. I have seen many faces, characters, moments and places in my country. It is part of what it means to be Guatemalan. It is, in part, what makes us.

In Guatemala, though spirits are generally grey, colour abounds. Blue sky, green mountains, red blood. It's not uncommon to see an armed clown holding up a bus, a yellow canary picking slips of paper out of a pocket, a body drowning in its own blood on the asphalt.

I did a performance in 1999 called *Lo voy a gritar al viento*. I hung from the arch extending across the street from the post office in downtown Guatemala City, a heavily trafficked area, and read my poems without a microphone, alluding to the fact that no one listens to women's voices, that they're effectively lost in the wind. With this piece I was confident that I would be seen and analysed from a general, popular perspective, not a formal, artistic one. This was a woman on the verge of throwing herself into space, a woman protesting against violence, one more crazy person. My long walk of the bloody footprints was not initially understood as a performance, but every step was indeed understood as memory and death. As Guatemalans we know how to decipher any image of pain, because we have all seen it up close.

Goldman Everyone has heard about the horrific, unpunished and largely unexplained murders of women in Ciudad Juárez, Mexico. But it seems that nearly as many women die violently in one year in Guatemala as have over ten years in Ciudad Juárez, but almost nobody pays any attention to this. (Though just last week there was a strong editorial in the *New York Times* about the murder of women in Guatemala and the utter lack of an official or police response.) What is happening in Guatemala, and why? But maybe that's too big a question ... Your response as an artist, in your performance *279 Golpes* (279 Blows), was very moving. You enclosed yourself inside a grey cube and flagellated yourself. One blow for every woman murdered in 2004. Terrible. The performance protests against the violence of men – but it also has a monastic element, a sense of self-blame and penitence, almost fanatical, and riveting.

Galindo There are many theories for why so many women are killed in Guatemala. Not all deaths originate from the same direct causes, but all murders are committed under the same premise: that it is done, it is cleaned up, and nothing happens, nothing occurs, nobody says a thing. A dead woman means nothing, a hundred dead women mean nothing, three hundred dead women mean nothing. The difference between Ciudad Juárez and Guatemala is that in Guatemala women are not only killed, but first they are subjected to horrible forms of torture, cut into little pieces and decapitated. I saw the hacked-up legs of a woman near my home one day, and nobody paid any attention to them at all.

I cannot separate myself from what happens. It scares me, it enrages me, it hurts me, it depresses me. When I do what I do, I don't try to approach my own pain as a means of seeing myself and curing myself from that vantage; in every action I try to channel my own pain, my own energy, to transform it into something more collective. [...]

Regina José Galindo and Francisco Goldman, extract from interview, trans. Ezra Fitz and Francisco Goldman, *Bomb* magazine, no. 94 (Winter 2006).

Barry Chudakov
Hasan Elahi: Surveillance as Storytelling//2011

Few people have as fully realized a Metalife as Hasan Elahi. Its necessity, a case of mistaken identity, was the mother of considerable invention. In 2002, when he stepped off a flight from the Netherlands, he was detained at the Detroit airport. FBI agents later told him they had been tipped off that he was hoarding explosives in a Florida storage unit. While subsequent lie detector tests convinced them he wasn't their man, Elahi knew after this detention he would be carefully watched.

So rather than avoid the watching, he abetted it. Instead of pushing against constant surveillance, he embraced it. He sensed that his perceived necessity could spawn a new art form: the surveillance of his life mounted as a museum without walls. Elahi not only chose willing tracking and scrutiny as a means of verifying and documenting every moment and every day of his life; he began to continuously display that 'work' in a digital gallery that functions simultaneously as database and witness.

Born in 1972 in Rangpur, Bangladesh, Elahi is a professor of interdisciplinary art. Logging more than 70,000 air miles a year exhibiting his artwork and attending conferences, Elahi has documented and 'lifecast' virtually his every waking hour since 2002. He posts copies of each debit card transaction, showing what he bought, where and when. A GPS device reports his real-time physical location on a map. Apparently the US government, while once mistakenly listing the Bangladeshi-born artist on its terrorist watch list, has not abandoned watching him. Elahi's server logs show hits from the Pentagon, the Secretary of Defence, and the Executive Office of the President, among others.

Yet Elahi's *Tracking Transcience: The Orwell Project* is more than the perfect alibi. It is a statement of identity in the modern world. In this self-induced Metalife, Elahi chose not only an exercise in artistic expression. His Metalife became a way of being in the world, a survival kit cum *Weltanschauung*. But especially, Hasan Elahi became a new kind of storyteller.

Throughout the past fifteen years, I have found myself with one foot in art and one in science, and consider my media to be databases and other electronic forms of information. I am intrigued by the way humans interact with this information, and prefer to investigate the acceptance of technology rather than technology itself.

In this new narrative Hasan Elahi is both the story and teller, hero subject and harrowing object, text and ironic commentary. By pushing surveillance to its logical extreme, by enfolding and enhancing its contours he deliberately courts what most of us either ignore or avoid. He forces us to look at the stunning level of detail constant monitoring accumulates, moment by moment, day by day, year by year, location by location.

From plastic plates of packaged sushi to airport urinals and a daily GPS update, complete with red arrow signalling his exact residence du jour hovering over a NASA Terrametrics map powered by Google, Elahi displays his life in what he calls Un/Real Time.

It is in the border between society and technology that I am interested, and my work attempts to bridge the human and virtual worlds ... At the same time, this conjunction of the physical and the virtual parallels my exploration of the intersection of geopolitical conditions and individual circumstances. Both quantitative and qualitative information is incorporated into my work, and the entire process results in translations and mistranslations between the physical and the virtual, between the body politic and the singular citizen.

This translation and mistranslation between the physical and virtual is at the core of Metalife. Elahi's narrative echoes the shared voyeurism we see, for example, in COLOR – the location-based, photo-sharing app that takes voyeurism to post-Twitter levels by letting users see all of the photos that are being taken by strangers who happen to be within a 150-foot radius of the user's smartphone. (Peter Pham, COLOR co-founder, described the effect of using the app as a sort of bug-eye experience – one where you're seeing the world through dozens of lenses at once. 'Essentially, everybody is sharing one lens', said Pham.)

Elahi's world is increasingly similar to ours. His is not a journey to which we can feign indifference: these are the airports, restaurants and toilets that constitute the transient places of our world; we travel through his checkpoints; his food is what we eat too. And so his presentation back to us, using image capture as reverberating realization, reveals him to be at the centre of a panopticon. The watched is watching back. He flaunts what English philosopher Jeremy Bentham described as 'a new mode of obtaining power of mind over mind, in a quantity hitherto without example'. Effectively Hasan Elahi is using his life to tell us of a science fiction, an alternate reality so close to our own that we might be tempted to see ourselves in it. Said Elahi, 'It's a bizarre feeling watching the government watch you.'

We know the feeling.

Barry Chudakov, 'Hasan Elahi: Surveillance as Storytelling' (30 August 2011) (www.metalife.org.uk).

Annemarie Jacir
Ramallah, 15 November 2006//2006

This afternoon I thought we were going to die.

Four hours ago my sister Emily, her curator Carolyn and I were shot at by the Israeli army. My nerves are still shaky. We've been drinking ever since. My legs are weak. I feel I can't stand on them.

Today in downtown Ramallah at around 4:15 pm, we were driving down Main Street. We were buying kanafa to eat after spending the day at 'Amari refugee camp.

A taxi driver cut me off. I rolled down the window and cursed at him. We pulled over and Emily and Mohammed jumped out to buy kanafa. Then we continued, dropping off Mohammed at his car, which he had left in the centre of town. We agreed to meet at Mohammed's place down the street.

I was alone in the front seat. Emily and Carolyn were in the back. Suddenly, there was a van directly in front of our car. He veered a bit towards our car. I slowed down, wondering how I was going to pass him. And then he emerged from his window ... pointing an M-16 across the street and spraying bullets.

The three of us hit the floor of the car. All around us ... shooting, shooting, shooting. So close. So close.

And then on the other side of the street, another van – looking exactly like the first ... men with guns spraying bullets everywhere.

Next to us, a man with his five-year old daughter ... Like us, stuck between all the shooting. He opened his door and tossed his daughter to the ground with him.

I lifted my head ... the man shooting was around six feet from me. Shooting away. Israeli secret service ... dressed up like an Arab. They do this all the time ... so they come into town and no one notices. Then I saw tens of Israeli soldiers crawling the streets all around us. Did they come out of the vans? They were in full uniform, unlike the two van 'drivers' who had dressed as plain clothes Arab men. Mustarabeen ... Israeli agents who dress like Arabs.

Shooting, shooting. I covered my head. All I could think about was Emily in the back seat and Carolyn. Emily ... my precious sister ... my beautiful sister ... Kamran in Scotland ... the man who escaped with his daughter. I braced myself as the shooting continued. Told myself calmly that if the windows of the car were hit. Which they surely were about to be. That it was nothing. To remember that all that meant was the window was broken and not necessarily that one of us had been hit.

Mohammed called ... I picked up the phone ... my voice broke. Crumbled. I hadn't realized my fear until that moment. Why couldn't I speak? Why?

I didn't recognize my own voice. I knew I sounded hysterical. I didn't want to sound like that.

Took another peak. Army everywhere. The men shooting shooting shooting shooting ... god, that sound.

Emily. Emily in the back. We made eye contact. What could we do?

We were stuck in the middle of a shoot out ... right in the middle of it ... with nowhere to go.

We couldn't even get out of the car and make a run for it.

We'd have been shot down.

I wondered if they'd kill us. I wondered if someone on the street might duck into our car for cover. But the streets were empty.

We stayed on the floor of the car for 20 minutes like that. I thought, really truly felt, I was going to die this way. And I didn't want to die like that. Totally helpless. Trapped in a car.

The more the shooting went on, the more I felt my nerves turn to jelly.

And then ...

Bam! Our car was hit. I heard glass break. I covered my head. My head was covered anyway, I think, for fear of the car windows being hit.

We were okay. Emily was okay. Carolyn was safe.

More time passed. How stupid to have my hands on my head. What would that do? Where is Emily? I think I will die today. I am going to die today.

I peeked out. I saw the Israelis grab a man off the street and shove him into the other van.

Then the undercover Israeli closest to us, in the van, decided to leave. Operation over. He pulled towards us. The criminal. I stared at his face, my head on the passenger seat ... He didn't have enough room to get by us, so he smashed into our car and scraped his way by. The whole time I couldn't take my eyes off his face. He didn't even notice us I think. Three women so close to him, stuck to the floor of the car ...

We are all okay. Nothing happened. There's a bullet in the car. It hit the back of the car. It didn't hit the gas tank. It didn't hit the gas tank. We are okay. But three young men tonight are not. And many, many more are not. This is nothing new, nothing out of the ordinary.

A man disappeared this afternoon. Two men were killed. It won't even make the news.

Emily Jacir
Independence Day//2006

Today is November 15th.

Today is our supposed 'Independence Day'.

A joke.

Was almost killed today.

This will be brief and inarticulate. I am still in shock.

I do not remember now the exact time ... around 4:25 p.m. Ramallah time. I was so happy and excited. I had finally convinced my art dealer from New York to come see me in Ramallah. I wanted her to see our Palestine, she would understand my work better, etc., etc ...

Carolyn arrived last night. We had spent the morning going to cultural centres, namely PACA and Riwaq. Then I took her to 'Amari refugee camp for the afternoon. All was cool.

My sister, Carolyn and our friend Mohammed had lunch and then we gave her a tour of the Muqata'a. After, driving down the main street of Ramallah, we stopped, and Mohammed and I hopped out of the car to buy kanafa. Of course Carolyn had to eat our kanafa!!!

We hopped back in the car. It was a beautiful afternoon, the streets were packed full of people, and we were headed to Mohammed's restaurant to chill out, eat our kanafa and let Carolyn take in the intensity of all she had seen. Mohammed hopped out of the car to pick up his own car, and we continued down the main street on our way.

We were a block away from Ziryab Coffee Shop when, all of a sudden to our immediate right, a van pulled up and stopped at a 90 degree angle. We couldn't drive forward because part of the van blocked us in. The doors opened and mustarabeen (Israeli army dressed as Arabs) hopped out with giant machine guns and started shooting. We were trapped.

After this point it is hard to remember what happened. We all ducked down, trapped ... To our left another van full of mustarabeen were shooting away. We were surrounded.

A man with his five-year-old daughter to our right throws his daughter to the ground. Then he grabs her and makes a run for it into a shop.

Damn it. I was calm. There was shooting from M-16's all around the car.

It was hot. I was hot hot hot. I couldn't focus on anything else. My scarf was suffocating me. I was burning up with heat. I took off my scarf. I focused on trying to figure out how to take off my coat.

Annemarie's phone rang – it was Mohammed (he had just gotten out 2 minutes earlier) – 'Be careful, there are mustarabeen in town!' When I heard my sister's voice, in the way she responded to him, the reality of what was going on set in.

She was trying to cover her face and head because we were sure we were about to be covered in broken glass. I have never heard my sister's voice sound like that in my entire life. Panic began to set in. But I was really hot, hot.

I rolled down the window. Annemarie locked the doors of the car. I rolled the window back up.

All I could think of was my sister's safety. God forbid anything happen to her. I grabbed her hand. She was in the front, I focused on her back (her dear, blessed back) as we huddled as low as we could on the floor of the car.

Shooting shooting shooting. My sister. My sister. That is all I cared about. Oh no! Goddamn it! Carolyn is next to me. I am responsible. I brought her to this place! Shit. I apologized to her over and over. She kept peeking to see what was going on! I begged her to keep her head down.

Our car got hit.

I make a note of it out loud. So does Carolyn.

No word from Annemarie. I call out to her fearing that she is silent because she has been hit.

She hasn't been. More shooting.

Shooting continued all around us. I kept repeating to everyone: 'Keep your heads down ... Keep your heads down ...'

Panic began to set in. We were completely exposed. I peeked up to see Israelis in uniform, now shooting in our direction.

I started trying to make a plan as to when I would open the car door and make a run for it.

I peeked again, to see some Israelis beating the shit out of a Palestinian man and throwing him into their van.

The mustarabeen next to us got back into their van. As we were in their way they smashed into our car and sped off. Meanwhile in front of us and to the right, the Israelis started to pull back.

Kids started throwing stones. They shot at us again. They started pulling back again.

I started feeling a little safe again. Now we might have a window to get out. The next thing I knew, the kids and shebab were alongside our car (they were heading towards the wounded) when they looked in and saw us in there.

They were horrified. To see that we were in the front row – right in the line of fire this whole time – huddled in the car. A friend of Annemarie's stopped running with the men, ordered us to reverse backwards, and helped us get out.

We parked and jumped out of the car and ran into a space between two buildings for shelter.

I saw a friend of mine. He asked if I was alright. I showed him the bullet hole in our car that made its way along the length of the whole car and exited out of the back.

He said we were lucky it did not hit the gas tank.

(I had not even thought of that!)

Anyway, in short, the Israelis came in – in the middle of the day – onto the main street of Ramallah – the most crowded street and attacked us on our 'Independence Day'.

We are alive and not injured. We are okay.

I do not know if the rental car insurance covers bullets from Israeli M-16s, or dents from being crashed into by mustarabeen.

And so it goes, so it goes. Another day in Palestine.

This is not a story.

A small nothing in the larger context of what happens on a daily basis here.

I am sure it won't be on any news.

Another day in Palestine.

Another Independence Day gone by.

But I am with a bottle of arak and good friends now. God damn. Damn. Damn. What could be better after a day like today? Thank the god for arak. Thank god for friends.

Annemarie and Emily Jacir, texts retitled for this publication; first published together under the title 'A Tale of Two Sisters: Witnessing an Undercover Israeli Operation in Ramallah' (2006) (electronicintifada.net)

Biographical Notes

James Agee (1909–55) was an American journalist, poet, screenwriter and film critic.

Kutlug Ataman is a Turkish artist and filmmaker based in Istanbul.

Ariella Azoulay teaches visual culture and contemporary philosophy at the Program for Culture and Interpretation, Bar-Ilan University, Israel.

Walter Benjamin (1892–1940) was a German/Jewish critical theorist and writer associated with the Frankfurt School.

Ursula Biemann is a Swiss artist, theorist and curator based in Zurich.

Adam Broomberg and Oliver Chanarin are London-based artists who teach in London and at the School of Visual Arts in New York.

Judith Butler is Professor of Rhetoric and Comparative Literature at the University of California, Berkeley.

Barry Chudakov is the Founder of Metalife Consulting, Florida, and a research fellow in the McLuhan Program in Culture and Technology at the University of Toronto.

Georges Didi-Huberman is a philosopher, art historian and Professor at the École des Hautes Études en Sciences Sociales, Paris.

Harun Farocki is a German filmmaker and artist who has taught in Germany and as a visiting professor at the University of California, Berkeley.

Omer Fast is an Israeli-born artist based in Berlin.

Joan Fontcuberta is a Spanish artist based in Barcelona.

Regina José Galindo is a Guatemalan artist based in Ciudad de Guatemala.

David Goldblatt is a South African photographer based in Johannesburg.

John Grierson (1898–1972) was a Scottish-born documentary filmmaker, critic and theorist who worked in the United States in the 1920s and in Canada from 1938 to 1945.

Philip Jones Griffiths (1936–2008) was a Welsh-born photographer whose documentary assignments included the Algerian Civil War, the Vietnam War and the Yom Kippur War.

Craigie Horsfield is a British artist based in London and New York.

Alfredo Jaar is a Chilean-born artist based in New York.

Annemarie Jacir is a Palestinian filmmaker and poet based in Amman, Jordan.

Emily Jacir is a Palestinian artist based in Ramallah and Rome.

Lisa F. Jackson is an award-winning American documentary filmmaker and teacher.

An-My Lê is a Vietnamese-born artist based in New York.

David Levi Strauss is a writer and critic based in New York.

Elizabeth McCausland (1899–1965) was an American writer, art critic and curator.

Renzo Martens is a Dutch artist based in Brussels, Amsterdam and Kinshasa.

Boris Mikhailov is a USSR-born artist based in the Ukraine and Berlin.

Daido Moriyama is a Japanese photographer based in Tokyo.

Carl Plantinga is Professor of Communication Arts and Sciences, Calvin College, Grand Rapids, Michigan.

Walid Raad (aka The Atlas Group) is a Lebanese-born artist based in New York, where he is an Associate Professor at the Cooper Union.

Jacques Rancière is Emeritus Professor of Philosophy at the University of Paris (St Denis).

Martha Rosler is an American artist, writer and teacher based in Brooklyn, New York.

Jean-Paul Sartre (1905–80) was a French existentialist philosopher, writer and critic.

Allan Sekula is an American artist, writer and teacher based in Los Angeles.

W. Eugene Smith (1918–78) was an American documentary photojournalist.

Sean Snyder is an American-born artist based in Kiev and Tokyo.

Susan Sontag (1933–2004) was an American critic, writer and filmmaker.

Hito Steyerl is a German artist, filmmaker and writer based in Berlin.

Trinh T. Minh-ha is a Vietnamese-born filmmaker and writer and Professor of Women's Studies and Rhetoric (Film) at the University of California, Berkeley.

Marta Zarzycka is Assistant Professor of Gender Studies at the University of Utrecht.

Bibliography

This section comprises selected further reading and does not repeat the bibliographic references for writings included in the anthology. For these please see the citations at the end of each text.

Armstrong, Carol, and Bart De Baere, *Craigie Horsfield: Confluence and Consequence* (Ghent: Ludion, 2010)

Austin, Thomas, and Wilma de Jong, eds, *Rethinking Documentary: New Perspectives, New Practices* (Milton Keynes: Open University Press, 2008)

Azoulay, Ariella, *Death's Showcase – The Power of Image in Contemporary Democracy* (Cambridge, Massachusetts: The MIT Press, 2001)

Bush, Kate, and Mark Sladen, eds, *In the Face of History: European Photographers in the 20th Century* (London: Barbican Art Gallery/ Black Dog Publishing, 2006)

Barnouw, Dagmar, *Critical Realism: History, Photography and the Work of Siegfried Kracauer* (Baltimore: Johns Hopkins University Press, 1994)

Barthes, Roland, *Camera Lucida: Reflections on Photography* (1980); trans. Richard Howard (New York: Hill & Wang, 1981)

Bezner, Lili Corbus, *Photography and Politics in America: From the New Deal into the Cold War* (Baltimore: John Hopkins University Press, 1999)

Biemann, Ursula, *Mission Reports: Artistic Practice in the Field – Video Works 1998–2008* (Bristol: Arnolfini, 2008)

– ed., *Stuff It: The Video Essay in the Digital Age* (Vienna: Springer Verlag, 2003)

– and Stephane Geene, *Been There and Back to Nowhere* (Berlin: B-Books, 2000)

Birnbaum, Daniel, et al., *Sean Snyder* (Cologne: Verlag der Buchhandlung Walther König, 2007)

Broomberg, Adam, and Oliver Chanarin, *Chicago* (London: SteidlMACK, 2006)

– *Ghetto* (London: Trolley, 2003)

– *Mr Mkhize's Portait & Other Stories from the New South Africa* (London: Trolley, 2004)

Bruzzi, Stella, *New Documentary* (London and New York: Routledge, 2006)

Cadava, Eduardo, *Words of Light: Theses on the Photography of History* (Princeton: Princeton University Press, 1997)

Chapman, Jane, *Issues in Contemporary Documentary* (London: Polity Press, 2009)

Coles, Robert, *Doing Documentary Work* (Oxford: Oxford University Press, 1997)

Corner, John, *The Art of Record: A Critical Introduction to Documentary* (Manchester: Manchester University Press, 1996)

Comolli, Jean-Louis, and Annette Michelson, 'Documentary Journey to the Land of the Head Shrinkers', *October*, no. 90 (Fall 1999) 36–49

Cramerotti, Alfredo, *Aesthetic Journalism: How to Inform Without Informing* (Chicago: Intellect Books, 2009)

Curtis, David, *A History of Artists' Film and Video in Britain* (London: British Film Institute, 2007)

Daney, Serge, and Paul Grant, *Postcards from the Cinema* (London: Berg Publishers, 2007)

Demos, T.J., 'Travelling Images: Hito Steyerl', *Artforum* (Summer 2008) 408–413, 473

— 'Desire in Diaspora: Emily Jacir', *Art Journal* (Winter 2003) 68–78.

— 'Poverty Pornography, Humanitarianism and Neoliberal Globalization: Notes on Some Paradoxes in Contemporary Art', *Stedelijk Bureau Newsletter*, no. 121 (2011)

Didi-Huberman, Georges, et al, *Alfredo Jaar: The Politics of Images* (Zurich: JRP Ringier, 2007)

Durden, Mark, and Craig Richardson, eds, *Face On: Photography as Social Exchange* (London: Black Dog Publishing, 2000)

Edwards, Steve, *Photography: A Very Short Introduction* (Oxford: Oxford University Press, 2006)

Elkins, James, ed., *Photography Theory* (London and New York: Routledge, 2007)

Ellis, Jack C., and Betsy McLane, *A New History of Documentary Film* (London: Continuum, 2005)

Elsaesser, Thomas, *Harun Farocki: Working on the Sight-Lines* (Amsterdam: Amsterdam University Press, 2004)

Evans, Walker: *Walker Evans: American Photographs* (New York: The Museum of Modern Art, 1938)

Ewenzor, Okwui, ed., *Archive Fever: Uses of the Document in Contemporary Art* (New York: International Center of Photography/Göttingen: Steidl, 2008)

Fast, Omer: *Omer Fast: The Casting* (Vienna: Museum Moderner Kunst Stiftung Ludwig Wien/Cologne: Verlag der Buchhandlung Walther König, 2007)

Featherstone, David, ed., *Observations: Essays on Documentary Photography* (Carmel, California: The Friends of Photography, 1984)

Fontcuberta, Joan, ed., *Photography: Crisis of History* (Barcelona: Actar, 2003)

Galindo, Regina José: *Regina José Galindo*, texts by Rosina Cazali, Fernando Castro Flórez, Eugenio Viola (Milan: Silvana Editoriale, 2011)

Godby, Michael, 'After Apartheid: 10 South African Documentary Photographers', *African Arts*, vol. 37, no. 4 (2004) 36–41, 94

Goldblatt, David: *Fifty-One Years: David Goldblatt* (Barcelona: Museu d'Art Contemporani de Barcelona, 2001)

Griffiths, Philip Jones, *Agent Orange: 'Collateral Damage' in Viet Nam* (London: Trolley, 2003)

— *Vietnam Inc.* (London: Collier Books, 1971)

Hall, Doug, and Sally Jo Fifer, eds, *Illuminating Video: An Essential Guide to Video Art* (New York: Aperture, 1990)

Hariman, Robert, and John Louis Lucaites, *No Caption Needed: Iconic Photographs, Public Culture and Liberal Democracy* (Chicago: University of Chicago Press, 2007)

Heron, Liz, and Val Williams, eds, *Illuminations: Women Writing on Photography from the 1850s to the Present* (London: I.B. Tauris, 1996)

Jaar, Alfredo: *Alfredo Jaar: It is Difficult – Ten Years*, texts by Alfredo Jaar, Patricia Phillips and Rick Pirro (Barcelona: Actar, 1998)

Jacir, Emily, et al., *Emily Jacir: Belongings – Works 1998–2003* (Bozen: Folio Verlag, 2004)

Jacir, Emily: *Emily Jacir*, texts by Emily Jacir, Roland Wäspe, Andreas Baur (St Gallen: Kunstmuseum St Gallen/Nuremberg: Verlag für Moderne Kunst, 2008)

Kracauer, Siegfried, *Theory of Film: The Redemption of Physical Reality* (Princeton: Princeton University Press, 1960)

Langton, Loup, *Photojournalism and Today's News: Creating Visual Reality* (Oxford: Wiley-Blackwell, 2008)

Lê, An-My, *Small Wars* (New York: Aperture, 2005)

Lind, Maria, and Hito Steyerl, eds, *The Greenroom: Reconsidering the Documentary and Contemporary Art #1* (Berlin: Sternberg Press, 2008)

Linfield, Susie, *The Cruel Radiance: Photography and Political Violence* (Chicago: University of Chicago Press, 2010)

Maggia, Filippo, *Daido Moriyama: The World Through My Eyes: The World Through the Eyes* (Milan and New York: Skira 2010)

MacDonald, Kevin, and Mark Cousins, *Imagining Reality* (London: Faber & Faber, 2006)

McCullin, Don, with Lewis Chester, *Unreasonable Behaviour: An Autobiography* (New York: Alfred A. Knopf, 1992)

Mikhailov, Boris: *Boris Mikhailov: A Retrospective*, texts by Urs Stahel, Ekaterina Degot, Anne von der Heiden, Michael Schischkin, Inka Schube, Helen Petrovsky, Margarita Tupitsyn (Zurich: Scalo 2003)

Michelson, Annette, 'The Estates General of the Documentary Film', *October*, vol. 91 (2000) 140–48

Morris, Errol, *Believing is Seeing: Observations on the Mysteries of Photography* (New York: Penguin 2011)

Nakas, Cassandra, and Britta Schmitz, *The Atlas Group (1989–2004): A Project by Walid Raad* (Cologne: Verlag der Buchhandlung Walter König, 2007)

New Documents, curated by John Szarkowski (New York: The Museum of Modern Art, 1967)

Nichols, Bill, *Introduction to Documentary* (Indianapolis: Indiana University Press 2010)

– *Representing Reality: Issues and Concepts in Documentary* (Oxford: John Wiley & Sons, 1991)

Panzer, Mary, *Things As They Are: Photojournalism in Context Since 1955* (London: Chris Boot/World Press Photo, 2006)

Rabinowitz, Paula, *They Must Be Represented: The Politics of Documentary* (London and New York: Verso, 1994)

Rancière, Jacques, *The Emancipated Spectator* (2008); trans. Gregory Elliott (London and New York: Verso, 2009)

Reid, Gwendolynne, *The Rhetoric of Reality Television – A Narrative Analysis of the Structure of Illusion* (Saarbrücken, Germany: VDM Verlag, 2007)

Roberts, John, *The Art of Interruption: Realism, Photography and the Everyday* (Manchester: Manchester University Press, 1998)

Rush, Michael, *Video Art* (London: Thames and Hudson, 2003)

Russell, Catherine, *Experimental Ethnography: The Work of Film in the Age of Video* (Durham, North Carolina: Duke University Press, 1999)

Schaschl, Sabine, ed., *Omer Fast: In Memory* (Berlin: The Green Box, 2010)

Schmidt, Michael, *Berlin Nach 1945* (Göttingen: Steidl, 2005)

Schmidt, Michael, *U–Ni–Ty* (Zurich: Scalo, 1996)

Sekula, Allan: *Allan Sekula: Performance Under Working Conditions*, ed. Sabine Breitwieser (Vienna:

Generali Foundation/Ostfildern-Ruit: Hajte Cantz, 2003)
– *Allan Sekula: Dismal Science: Photo Works 1972–1996* (Chicago: University Galleries, Illinois State University, 1999)
Sekula, Allan, *Fish Story* (Rotterdam and Düsseldorf: Richter Verlag, 1995)
Smith, W. Eugene: *W. Eugene Smith: His Photographs and Notes* (New York: Aperture, 1993)
– *Let Truth be Prejudice: W. Eugene Smith: His Life and Photographs* (Philadelphia: Philadelphia Museum of Art/ New York: Aperture, 1986)
Smith, W. Eugene, and Aileen M. Smith, *Minamata* (Tucson: Center for Creative Photography, 1981)
Sontag, Susan, *Regarding the Pain of Others* (New York: Farrar, Straus & Giroux, 2003)
Stallabrass, Julian, 'Bureaucracy and Crime: Photography at Guantánamo', in Edmund Clark, ed., *Guantánamo: If the Light Goes Out* (Stockport, England: Dewi Lewis Publishing, 2010)
– 'Museum Photography and Museum Prose', *New Left Review*, no. 65 (2010) 93–125
– 'What's in a Face? Blankness and Significance in Contemporary Art Photography', *October*, no. 122, (2007) 71–90
– 'Sebastião Salgado and Fine Art Photojournalism', *New Left Review*, no. 223, (1997) 131–60
Stange, Maren, *Symbols of Ideal Life: Social Documentary Photography in America, 1890–1950* (Cambridge: Cambridge University Press, 1989)
Hito Steyerl, 'In Defence of the Poor Image', *e-flux*, no. 10 (2009) (www.e-flux.com)
Szarkowski, John, *Mirrors and Windows: American Photography Since 1960* (New York: The Museum of Modern Art, 1978)
Tagg, John, *The Burden of Representation: Essays on Photographies and Histories* (London: Macmillan, 1988)
Taylor, John, *Body Horror: Photojournalism, Catastrophe and War* (Manchester: Manchester University Press, 1998)
Trinh T. Minh-ha, *Cinema Interval* (London and New York: Routledge, 1999)
– *Framer Framed* (London and New York: Routledge, 1992)
– *The Digital Film Event* (London and New York: Routledge, 2005)
Vartanian, Ivan, et al., eds, *Setting Sun: Writings by Japanese Photographers* (New York: Aperture, 2006)
Wall, Jeff, *Selected Essays and Interviews* (New York: The Museum of Modern Art, 2007)
Wayne, Mike, *Theorizing Video Practice* (London: Lawrence & Wishart, 1997)
Willumson, Glenn G., *W. Eugene Smith and the Photographic Essay* (Cambridge: Cambridge University Press, 1992)
Winston, Brian, *Claiming the Real: Documentary: Grierson and Beyond* (London: BFI Publishing, 2008)
Zarzycka, Marta, and Bettina Papenburg, eds, *Carnal Aesthetics: Transgressive Imagery and Feminist Politics* (London: I.B. Tauris, 2012)

Index

ACKNOWLEDGEMENTS

Editor's acknowledgements
I would like to thank Marian Ang, Imogen Coker and Katy Wan for their skilled work as research assistants on this book. It would have been poorer, in terms of concept and contents, without their contributions. I also owe a great debt of thanks to the Leverhulme Trust and to the Paul Mellon Centre, who granted me fellowships that allowed me to work on this book. My understanding of the subject has developed in large part through conversations with colleagues, students, artists and friends: I would particularly like to thank Adam Broomberg, Malcolm Bull, Benedict Burbridge, Oliver Chanarin, Edmund Clark, Steve Edwards, Regina José Galindo, Ashley Gilbertson, Philip Jones Griffiths, Sara Knelman, Sarah James, Paul Lowe, Renzo Martens, Antigoni Memou, Alexandra Moschovi, Mignon Nixon, Emilia Terracciano and Sarah Wilson. The editorial board and team at Whitechapel Gallery have offered much support and many useful suggestions.

Publisher's acknowledgements
Whitechapel Gallery is grateful to all those who gave their generous permission to reproduce the listed material. Every effort has been made to secure all permissions and we apologize for any inadvertent errors or ommissions. If notified, we will endeavour to correct these at the earliest opportunity. We would like to express our thanks to all who contributed to the making of this volume, especially Dore Ashton, Kutlug Ataman, Ariella Azoulay, Ursula Biemann, Adam Broomberg, Phong Bui, Judith Butler, Oliver Chanarin, Barry Chudakov, Georges Didi-Huberman, Hasan Elahi, Joan Fontcuberta, Harun Farocki, Omer Fast, Regina José Galindo, David Goldblatt, Stefan Goldby, Francisco Goldman, Alan Gilbert, Mark Haworth-Booth, Ana Finel Honigman, Alfredo Jaar, Annemarie Jacir, Emily Jacir, Lisa F. Jackson, Thomas Keenan, Ben Kharakh, An-My Lê, Thomas Y. Levin, David Levi Strauss, Louise Liwanag, Sven Lütticken, Renzo Martens, Boris Mikhailov, Sohey Moriyama, Joe Penney, Carl Plantinga, Walid Raad, Jacques Rancière, Martha Rosler, Allan Sekula, Melissa Silverstein, Sean Snyder, Hito Steyerl, Trinh T. Minh-ha, Ivan Vartanian, Marek Wieczorek, Marta Zarzycka, Christina Zelich. We also gratefully acknowledge the cooperation of Art21, Bomb Magazine, The Brooklyn Rail, Buzzine Networks, University of California Press, University of Chicago Press, College Art Association, Thomas Dane Gallery, Foto8, Christopher Grimes Gallery, Murray Guy Gallery, Harvard University Press, Houghton Mifflin Harcourt, Philip Jones Griffiths Foundation,

Lisson Gallery, The MIT Press, Anthony Reynolds Gallery, Estate of Susan Sontag, Sternberg Press, I.B. Tauris, Taylor and Francis Books, Verso Books, Violette Editions, Zone Books.

Whitechapel Gallery is supported by

ARTS COUNCIL ENGLAND